'Wh
pare
ents
main
the c
abou
the c
gentl
to be

'This
on h
forth
ance
them
child
is also relevant for parents with older children, and for relationships in general. In particular, I found her suggestion that we
should THINK before we respond to others – that is to consider
whether what we have to say is True, Helpful, Inspiring,
Necessary and Kind – to be pertinent, both within and beyond
the sphere of parenting.'

Gill Rapley, PhD, co-author of *Baby-led Weaning*
and the 'baby-led' series of parenting books

THE
GENTLE
PARENTING
BOOK

SARAH OCKWELL-SMITH

How to raise calmer, happier children
from birth to seven

piatkus

PIATKUS

First published in Great Britain in 2016 by Piatkus

3 5 7 9 10 8 6 4

Extract on page 39 is reproduced with the
kind permission of Dr Michel Odent

Authors note
The names of individuals mentioned in this book
have been changed to protect their privacy.

A CIP catalogue record for this book
is available from the British Library.

ISBN 978-0-349-40872-9

Illustrations by Rodney Paull

Typeset in Stone Serif by M Rules
Printed and bound in Great Britain by
Clays Ltd, St Ives plc

Papers used by Piatkus are from well-managed forests
and other responsible sources.

MIX
Paper from
responsible sources
FSC
www.fsc.org   FSC® C104740

Piatkus
An imprint of
Little, Brown Book Group
Carmelite House
50 Victoria Embankment
London EC4Y 0DZ

An Hachette UK Company
www.hachette.co.uk

www.improvementzone.co.uk

About the author

Sarah Ockwell-Smith is the mother of four children. She has a BSc in Psychology and worked for several years in Pharmaceutical Research and Development. Following the birth of her firstborn, Sarah re-trained as a Paediatric Homeopath, Antenatal Teacher and Birth and Postnatal Doula. She has also undertaken training in Baby Massage, Hypnotherapy and Psychotherapy. Sarah specialises in gentle parenting methods and is co-founder of the GentleParenting website (www.gentleparenting.co.uk). Sarah writes a parenting blog (www.sarahockwell-smith.com), which is read by three million parents per year, and is the author of *BabyCalm*, *ToddlerCalm* and *The Gentle Sleep Book*. She frequently writes for magazines and newspapers, and is often called upon as a parenting expert for national television and radio.

Contents

Acknowledgements   ix

Introduction: What is Gentle Parenting?   1

Chapter 1
Sailing the Seven Cs   15

Chapter 2
It Starts in the Beginning – From Bump to Birth   25

Chapter 3
The Fourth Trimester – Birth to Three Months   51

Chapter 4
Early Babyhood – Three to Six Months   79

Chapter 5
Older Babyhood – Six to Twelve Months   93

Chapter 6
Welcome to Toddlerdom – One to Four Years   125

Chapter 7
Growing Up – Four to Seven Years   180

Chapter 8
Transitioning From Mainstream to Gentle
Parenting   218

Chapter 9
What to Expect in Terms of Results   231

Chapter 10
Taking Care of Your Own Needs   241

Chapter 11
Gentle Parenting in Special Circumstances   257

A few closing words   272
The Seven Cs: a reminder   274
Resources   277
Bibliography   283
References   284
Index   295

Acknowledgements

This book is dedicated to my oldest friends in the world and my partners at Gentle Parenting Ltd: Kate and Lorraine. Who would have thought that we would all be working together, having trained in such similar fields with ten children between us, when we were eleven-year-old, giggly school girls?

As ever, I am grateful to all of the parents who have helped me with this book, in sharing their stories, answering my endless questions and guiding me on the information they would like to see included. Thank you all for your unwavering support of gentle parenting and my work.

I would also like to say a big thank you to all of the staff at Piatkus and Eve White Literary Agency for bringing this book to life, including Anne, Jillian, Eve, Jack and Kitty.

Last but by no means least, thank you to my family for providing me with the inspiration to do what I do.

What is Gentle Parenting?

Never doubt that a small group of thoughtful, committed citizens can change the world. Indeed, it is the only thing that ever has.

Margaret Mead, cultural anthropologist

Tiger parenting, French parenting, helicopter parenting, free-range parenting … the twenty-first century has seen a tremendous surge in new trends of parenting styles. How, you might ask, is there room for another one?

And therein lies the beauty of gentle parenting. Gentle parenting isn't a trend; it isn't a label for a precise way of doing things according to one person's point of view. Gentle parenting is an ethos – a way of being, you might say. It is mindful of current science and child psychology, while remaining respectful of cultural and historical practices of child-rearing. It is a holistic philosophy that considers the emotional, as well as the practical, aspects of parenthood. In a nutshell, gentle parenting is a lifestyle that encompasses both your physical and psychological behaviour, not only towards your children but to yourself, too – because parenting should be a dance between the needs of children and parents. With practice, this dance can lead to something quite beautiful, and tremendous growth for both.

Gentle parents come from all walks of life and make all sorts of choices. Some decide to birth naturally at home, some elect for a Caesarean section. Some carry their babies in slings, some use prams. Some breastfeed, some formula-feed. Some stay at home, some return to work. Some home-school their children and some take a mainstream educational route. They all have one thing in common though: their choices are all informed, educated and made out of respect and empathy for their children, as well as themselves. This is gentle parenting – nothing more, nothing less.

For too long parenting has been viewed as a battleground. Some parenting methods give all control to the parents, for fear that children will become unmanageable monsters as they grow; others give children far too much control, with parents scared to discipline when necessary, for fear of upsetting their delicate offspring. Gentle parenting is all about finding a balance – giving children just enough control, at a time when they can handle it, while putting appropriate boundaries and limits in place. It is about being ever mindful of the long-term effects of your actions, as well as your child's safety and the expectations of society.

When it comes to societal expectations, gentle parents understand that many of the beliefs that society holds about the behaviour of children, at any age, are unrealistic, and that a number of today's parenting practices are not only at odds with the needs of children in the present moment, but may also inhibit their development in the future. Gentle parents are not afraid to question received wisdom, no matter who it is coming from, or to be advocates for their children, even when their behaviour is frowned upon by the mainstream. Gentle parents have a close connection to their children. This allows them to feel safe, respected and valued. In turn, this nurturing environment helps children become confident, free-thinking adults.

What if everyone embraced the notion of gentle parenting, would it change the world? I think it might just.

Gentle parents are not perfect

Gentle parenting is not about being perfect. All parents make mistakes. The key is learning from them: understanding what happened, why it happened and how we can be and do better next time. From this perspective, making mistakes as a parent is not only understandable, but crucial. For it is only when we don't quite do our best that we can learn to do better in the future. Gentle parenting therefore is about accepting our imperfect selves, forgiving our mistakes and striving to grow as parents. As much as our children are learning, so are we. We all have bad days – days when we shout, days that make us feel ashamed. But gentle parenting is about being real – recognising when we are stressed and in need of some 'me time' in order to be a better parent. In fact, this is so important I have dedicated a whole chapter to it (see Chapter 10).

Gentle parenting requires nothing more than love, dedication and consistency. It isn't reserved for the most naturally calm or highly educated parents, for stay-at-home parents or for those with only one child. Money, qualifications and temperament are not relevant; and it doesn't matter how you were parented yourself or if you started your own parenting journey using a different approach. Chapter 8 is devoted to those parents who previously adopted other, perhaps less gentle, methods and are now looking for another way. You will also find a section dedicated to coping with criticism of your parenting and what to expect in terms of results – when you might start to see them and what to do if it gentle parenting doesn't seem to be working for you.

Why does gentle parenting matter?

We live in a world that places more value on things than on people. It is all about the acquisition of 'stuff' and the pursuit of more. We spend so much time dwelling on the past and planning for the future that we forget to live today, often missing the things that really matter. Our society is selfish, violent and short-sighted, valuing conformity over respect for individuality. And this is the world we are preparing our children for. But do we really need to raise them to buy into this ideology?

What matters more: happiness or fitting in? Can we raise children who respect their own thoughts and bodies, rather than lay the foundations for body-image and confidence issues? Can we raise a generation who care about the environment, rather than view everything as quick, easy and disposable? Ironically, in our quest to bring up children to fit with society's goals, we often bypass what is really best for them. How will anything ever change in our world if we don't question commonly held beliefs and encourage our children to do the same?

Gentle parenting is so much more than what you do with your child at any given moment in time. Raising our children gently builds a better future for us all.

Gentle parenting is about creating a future where happiness is not dependent on the house you live in, the car on the drive or the labels in your clothes; it is about a future where violence is dramatically reduced and where differing opinions and beliefs are not only respected but valued; and a future where discipline does not involve inflicting physical harm and pain, exclusion, shame and guilt on some of the most vulnerable members of society.

POPULAR CHILDCARE ADVICE OVER THE PAST CENTURY

In order to make sense of our own upbringing and the prevalent opinions of society today, I think it is important to understand how mainstream childcare advice has developed over the last century.

At the beginning of the twentieth century the focus was on high demand, low responsivity and a great degree of parental control – a style which can be summed up as authoritarian. In 1913, Sir Frederick Truby King, a physician who founded New Zealand's 'Plunket Society' (a service providing a range of health services for baby and children), published his childcare book *Feeding and Care of Baby*. Credited with dramatically improving the nutrition of children in New Zealand, Truby King is perhaps better known for his authoritarian discipline and ethos of detachment. He advocated a regimented schedule that included feeding only every four hours during the day and not at all at night. Babies, he said, should sleep in their own room from birth, should be left outside to nap in their pram during the day and should not be cuddled for more than ten minutes per day. This, he believed, allowed the baby to place all of his or her energy into growing and developing without being hindered by too much bonding with parents. Truby King said that boys should be 'toughened up' and readied for entering the military when at school, while girls should be trained to be mothers and homemakers.

In 1928, American psychologist John B. Watson published his book *Psychological Care of Infant and*

Child. He viewed children, in a sense, as made and not born. He believed love was conditioned in babies by touching and stroking their skin, and, with this in mind, warned mothers in particular to not 'over coddle' their children, lest they grow into adults who would permanently need 'coddling' and have difficulty forming relationships if their attachment to their mother was too strong. Watson summarised these ideas thus: 'Never hug and kiss them, never let them sit in your lap. If you must, kiss them once on the forehead when they say good night. Shake hands with them in the morning. Give them a pat on the head if they have made an extraordinarily good job of a difficult task.' Watson also emphasised the importance of a formal strict daily routine encompassing all areas of the child's life, including eating and drinking, toileting, sleeping and playtime. Although Watson is well known for his harsh and potentially damaging recommendations, his advice was not all bad. He was in favour of children being brought up in a calm, non-violent environment and encouraged parents to promote their independence, keeping them well occupied and engaged in order to reduce the onset of tantrums.

In 1946, American paediatrician Dr Benjamin Spock published his book *The Common Sense Book of Baby and Childcare*. Spock is well known for bringing more affection and emotion to parenting and his ground-breaking views differed significantly from the mainstream approach to parenting at the time. Spock is famous for telling mothers around the world that, 'You know more than you think you do', encouraging them to listen to and trust themselves and their babies. He advocated a more flexible, individualised, baby-led routine when almost all experts recommended parents practise strict control. At the time, Spock was heavily criticised for promoting permissive parenting and 'instant gratification' for babies and children. Despite the book selling over 50 million copies, these criticisms remained for over fifty years until Spock's death in 1998.

In the 1950s and 1960s, British paediatrician and psychoanalyst Donald Winnicott developed his concepts of 'holding' and 'the good-enough mother' which apply just as much today. Winnicott described a mother's physical and psychological 'holding' of her child as providing them with the confidence and support necessary for them to grow and develop into a healthy individual. He believed that 'the foundations of health are laid down by the ordinary mother in her ordinary loving care of her own baby', and was also a proponent of increased empathy and trust in mothers. His idea of the good-enough mother highlighted the fact that the mother's small mistakes actually facilitated the development of her child. He held that no mother was perfect and, indeed, that perfection as a mother was actually undesirable: 'It is when a mother trusts her judgement that she is at her best.'[1]

In 1951, the work of British psychologist John Bowlby was published by the World Health Organization under the title 'Maternal Care and Mental Health'. His thinking was largely based on his observations of hospitalised children separated from their parents, and on the work of René Spitz, who studied the effects of children orphaned or separated from their parents during and after the Second World War. In contrast to Watson and Truby King, Bowlby believed that love and affection are vital for a child to thrive. His theories advocated high responsivity. He is famously known for saying, 'The infant and young child should experience a warm, intimate, and continuous relationship with his mother (or permanent mother substitute) in which both find satisfaction and enjoyment and that not to do so may have significant and irreversible mental health consequences.'[2] Alongside his colleague Mary Ainsworth, Bowlby later developed his theories into a concept known as 'Attachment Theory', elements of which have been used to formulate a style of parenting known as attachment parenting.

In 1977, British psychologist Penelope Leach's bestselling book *Your Baby & Child* was published and has since sold over two million copies. Her focus was on empathy, trust and connection, promoting an authoritative parenting style, high in parental responsivity. Leach strongly advocated a child-led style of parenting, as opposed to parent-imposed routines.

Then, in 1985, American paediatrician Dr Richard Ferber brought the idea of 'cry-it-out' sleep training to the fore – a concept first put forward almost a hundred years earlier by the American paediatrician Dr L. Emmett Holt. Although Ferber examined several approaches to tackling problematic infant sleep, he is perhaps best known for what is commonly referred to as 'Ferberization' – the process of leaving a child to cry for increasing lengths of time in order that they learn to not cry out at night and sleep through without parental assistance. This approach can be seen as highly demanding of children and requiring little in the way of responsivity from parents – a classic example of the authoritarian approach to parenting.

In 1999 the bestselling book *The Contented Little Baby*, by maternity nurse Gina Ford, marked a firm return to this more authoritarian, parent-centric style. Ford encouraged a parent-imposed routine covering almost all aspects of the baby's day, including the time to eat, sleep and play. She also recommended sleep training for babies.

This theme continued into the 'noughties' with nanny Jo Frost, perhaps better known as 'Supernanny', introducing millions of families to a strict, 'no-nonsense' style of authoritarian parenting through her books and television programmes. Frost has become widely known for her use of 'the naughty step' as a tool for controlling unwanted behaviour.

So, in little over a hundred years we seem to have come full circle, despite much scientific research indicating that the responsive authori*tative* – not authori*tarian* – parenting style is the most healthy and effective. With this in mind, it is important to remember that the prevailing messages when our parents and grandparents were raised were likely authoritarian in nature. Simply put, they probably thought that their parents were doing the best by raising them in this style and thought that this was the best way to raise you, too. They may then, perhaps, wonder why you do not choose it for your own children.

What gentle parenting *isn't*

Let's get this out there right now. Gentle parenting is not permissive parenting. Among those who are new to the concept, perhaps practitioners of more mainstream methods, the most common criticism is that it is permissive. But, in fact, boundaries, limits and discipline play a crucial role in gentle parenting. If you do not discipline your child, how can you be truly respectful of them?

Part of this misconception lies in the general understanding of what it means to discipline a child. Did you know that the word discipline stems from the word 'disciple', defined in the dictionary as: 'A follower of the doctrines of a teacher or a school of thought'. It is from the Latin *discipulus*, pupil and *discere*, to learn. So discipline implies that there are two active roles – the adult as teacher and the child as learner – and both should play an equal part in the process. Children learn best by imitating us, learning at their own (developmental) pace in a place of safety and security and in a space where their natural desire to make sense of the world is not only respected, but fostered.

Yet if you take a straw poll among a group of people as to what discipline means to them, the chances are you will be met with a list that includes: 'I got the cane', 'My parents smacked me if I was out of line', 'Send the child to the naughty step', 'If he's naughty he goes to time out', 'I was sent to my room with no dinner if I was rude' …

In my opinion, none of these is an effective form of discipline. They all rely on inflicting physical or emotional pain through shame and exclusion. How does a child learn if they are not shown what to do, if they have nothing and nobody appropriate to model themselves on or if they do not understand what they did wrong and what they should have done instead?

True discipline in society is rare. Most children today are punished. They are punished for being a child, for not acting like an adult, for being too inquisitive and eager to learn and for not having a well-developed centre of self-control. Misbehaviour is usually a cry for help – a signal that all is not well in the child's world. But most of the behaviour-control methods used today penalise the child for having a problem, rather than trying to help them solve it.

The dictionary definition of punishment is 'causing or characterised by harsh or injurious treatment; severe; brutal'. When children are punished, no real learning takes place: the role of the child is passive; the goal of the adult is control and conformity. And while the vocalisation or physical manifestations of the child's problems may disappear, the issues remain, ready to rise another day, like a festering wound covered with a fresh bandage. Why not help children to solve their problems? Surely then we are better teachers?

Authoritarian, authoritative and permissive parenting approaches

In 1966, psychologist Diana Baumrind identified her Parenting Typology– a description of three distinct parenting styles: authoritarian, authoritative and permissive.[3] These can be briefly summarised as follows:

Authoritarian

- Highly demanding. Parents expect behaviour that is perhaps not age-appropriate.

- Strict boundaries and limits, often in excess.

- Boundaries and limits enforced using punishments.

- Child is given very little autonomy.

- Little regard is given to the age appropriateness of the punishment.

- Very parent-centred approach – the adult knows best.

- Parents not concerned with their own behaviour and often not good role models.

- Low levels of affection. Low levels of responsivity.

- Little respect for the child, but demands a lot of respect for the parent.

Authoritative

- Parents are demanding of the child, but their expectations are age-appropriate.

- Parents set realistic boundaries and limits.

- Boundaries and limits are always enforced respectfully.

- The child is given some freedom and age-appropriate autonomy.

- Age-appropriate discipline is key.

- A largely child-centred approach. The child is respected, as well as the parents.

- Parents understand the effects of their own emotions.

- Parents show a great amount of affection and have a good connection to the child.

- Parents are highly responsive to the child's needs.

Permissive

- Parents demand little of the child and have very low expectations of their behaviour.

- The child is often capable of better behaviour, but this is not encouraged.

- Few or no boundaries or limits.

- Any boundaries that do exist are not enforced.

- Child is often given too much freedom or allowed to do whatever they like.

- Unwanted behaviour is not disciplined and is often explained away.

- Child is in control; parents have little control.

- Parents may struggle with their own emotions.

- Highly affectionate parents.

- Parents are highly responsive to the child's needs, but can misinterpret them.

So what is the ideal parenting style? It is one where parents walk a carefully balanced line of good responsiveness and making appropriate demands of their child, ever mindful of their development. The definition of this? Authoritative parenting, or, as I like to call it: gentle parenting.

Chapter 1

Sailing the Seven Cs

You can't stop the waves, but you can learn to surf.

**Jon Kabat-Zinn, Professor of Medicine
and mindfulness expert**

Parenting is like a journey of discovery: as you watch your child exploring the world, you grow as an adult in many ways too. And, as with all the best journeys, you have a great travelling companion – your child. As you navigate new and undiscovered lands together, there are unexpected twists and turns, hurdles to jump and obstacles to avoid.

Just as the great explorers sailed the seven seas, parents must find their way around parenting and childhood, learning as much about themselves as they do about their children. This is where my own seven seas come in: the Sevens Cs of gentle parenting. These are seven points (and points they are, not rules) to enable any parent, whatever their background or parenting history, to steer a course through the world of parenting as calmly and confidently as possible, while keeping an eye on their final destination – the creation of a happy, confident and secure individual. The Seven Cs are:

- Connection

- Communication

- Control

- Containment

- Champion

- Confidence

- Consistency

The Seven Cs are appropriate at any age – whether you have a baby, a toddler, a five-year-old, ten-year-old or a teen; for the purposes of this book, however, we will be focusing on their application from birth to seven years of age. The next six chapters deal with specific age brackets, examining particular aspects of the journey at each stage and how the Seven Cs can be applied to areas of difficulty commonly experienced by parents.

But first, let's look at each of the Seven Cs in more detail.

Connection

Connection, or rather a lack of it, is often at the root of many behaviour issues in children of any age. Whether it's a nine-month-old baby experiencing separation anxiety and waking many times at night, a toddler starting day care for the first time and crying inconsolably at every drop-off, a preschooler regressing in their toileting behaviour following the arrival of a new baby, or a six-year-old competing with siblings for the attention of busy parents, all of these situations can be dramatically improved by noting the child's need for connection and responding with the thing they need the most – more of you.

Connection is important both 'in the moment' and in the long term. In the short term, a child may 'misbehave' in order to seek reconnection with the parent. For instance, a toddler may tantrum in response to not receiving enough attention from a parent who is involved in a long conversation with a friend or is talking on their phone. In this case, the parent recognising the child's need is key to resolving the behaviour. In the long term, a chronic lack of connection can lead to more serious behaviour issues. This is often the case with slightly older children who spend increasingly more time away from their parents, especially when siblings are involved and particularly if the parent uses exclusion methods of punishment, such as time out. If the child's need for connection is met with a further undoing of the bond between them and their parent, the problem is likely to be compounded not resolved. So it is vital for parents to spend time reconnecting with their children on a regular – preferably daily – basis. What might this look like?

A fifteen-minute chat while putting a child to bed every night is a great start; or ten minutes of playing together in the evening when everybody is home, topping up at the weekend with some one-to-one time; an hour at the park, baking a cake together or sharing a book while snuggled on the sofa. It needn't be anything complicated or expensive. All too often we will take our children to clubs and classes to aid their development when, ironically, what they need most of all is downtime with us.

It is also important to recognise the need to reconnect with your child during a period of unwanted behaviour. Crying babies, toddler tantrums, preschool whining and sulks from older children can leave parents understandably frazzled. But when we are exhausted, at the end of our tether and wondering why we ever had children in the first place, this is precisely the time when it is crucial to reconnect. It will not only help to reduce unwanted behaviour in the short term, but will also help your child to feel that you and they are part of the same team, leading to less likelihood of it happening in the longer term. Children should always feel loved by you, no matter what they do. You may not like their behaviour but you love them unconditionally, and, however angry and exhausted you may feel, it is essential that they know this, especially at a time when you reactions may show otherwise.

Communication

All behaviour is communication: crying, whining, throwing, hitting, biting, sulking, clinginess and more. The key is to translate what the behaviour is saying. Your child may have a physical need such as hunger, thirst, tiredness, discomfort or pain. These are usually the easiest reasons to spot and usually ones that most parents consider first. But what if their behaviour has a more emotional cause? Are they overstimulated or overwhelmed by a new situation? Or, conversely, perhaps they are understimulated or bored? Is another child invading their personal space and making them feel threatened? Or perhaps they are feeling scared or lonely? The more vocal children become, the easier it is to work with their emotional needs, but even an eloquent seven-year-old can have trouble putting the way they feel into words and they may express their discomfort via their behaviour instead.

On a related note, think carefully about your own communication. Communication is not just verbal. What are your actions and body language telling your child? What might you be conveying if you are deep in conversation with a friend and keep 'shushing' your child's attempts to tell you something important? What might you be demonstrating to your child if you snap and yell at them when they fight with their sibling?

Communication is about listening as well as talking. Showing children that we hear them and value what they say is vital to their confidence and self-esteem. The old authoritarian phrase 'Do as I say, not as I do' is a great example of what we are often communicating. And children are great imitators: what we do they will do. The way you behave, therefore, communicates to your child how they should behave. If you struggle with shouty children, the chances are that you may be shouting too much yourself. So consider carefully your body language and behaviour as well as your words.

It is also very important to remember that children are not the same as adults when it comes to their understanding of language. Their grasp of instructions, for instance, is far more basic than ours. So telling a child to 'Stop running' does not explain what you want them to do instead. Should they hop? Jump? Stand still? Of course, as adults we know that what we really mean when we say this is, 'Stop running and walk slowly instead', but we haven't communicated that to the child. Telling them to 'Walk please' would be much better.

Communicating effectively with a child can be likened to a doctor with a good bedside manner. Getting down to the child's level in terms of both in words and height, talking eye to eye and perhaps connecting physically in a gentle manner through hand contact is far less threatening and more positive than if you are towering above them. Think about how you like to be communicated to, and emulate that in your communication with your children.

Control

Babies and young children have little or no control over their day-to-day lives. What do they really get to choose for themselves? When they go to bed? What they eat? When they eat?

How they spend their time? In most cases, control is in the hands of the parent and much unwanted behaviour is, therefore, the child's desperate attempt to regain some of that control and assert their autonomy. Toileting, eating and sleeping behaviours are most commonly linked to a control problem, and allowing the child to have as much control as possible (age appropriateness and safety permitting) can dramatically change their behaviour.

This needs to go hand in hand with boundaries and limits. Giving a child more control does not mean permissive parenting. Children raised with few or no boundaries or related discipline can feel very insecure, and while it is their job to test these limits, it is ours to set and enforce them. Children need to know what is expected of them and boundaries are a great way for them to learn. Deciding on the appropriate boundaries for your family is an important part of parenting and enforcing them calmly and compassionately is crucial.

Containment

Babies and young children are not neurologically capable of regulating their emotions. This is not a fault or a problem, it is simple biology. As adults, the mature emotion-regulation centre of our brain tells us it is not socially acceptable to scream loudly in a packed cinema when we are scared. When we are frustrated, our brain tells us that it is not 'the done thing' to shout and swear in the middle of the supermarket. And when we are angry, our brains tell us that it is not appropriate to hit or bite the person who is annoying us. Unfortunately, children under seven do not have these resources; they do not have the ability to use 'self-talk' to calm themselves down. They are like a boiling pot with no lid. Everything explodes unchecked. And when you think about how many things upset them in their daily lives, largely related to their need for connection and control, compounded by their relatively poor verbal communication skills, it is no wonder that their pots so readily boil over.

So, babies and young children need a mature adult to act as a container for their big emotions (and that is what they are – not naughtiness which implies that they have control over their actions). This allows the child the space to release those emotions safely. They need an adult to say, 'It's OK, I'm big enough for the both of us; I can help you to diffuse your emotions'. A parent's role here is to act as an external regulator for the young child until they are old enough to readjust their own emotions, which can take much longer than society thinks.

Of course, as parents our own containers can get full too and sometimes we also explode and overflow. This is a sign that it is time for us to empty some of our own emotional load. Finding a listening ear, a hobby or a way to relax that allows you to create this space to hold your child's feelings is critical. We will look at this in much more detail in Chapter 10.

Champion

Do you have somebody who believes in you, who stands up for you and who looks out for your interests? Maybe your partner, a friend or a relative? Think about the last time somebody helped you out or when somebody really 'got' what you were about and defended you when others didn't. Every child needs a champion too, and their first champion should be their parent.

Even before they were born you had begun to 'champion' for your baby, making informed choices about the delivery and the environment in which your son or daughter would enter the world. And throughout babyhood many tough decisions are made with the baby's best interests at heart. Each one of these involves you championing your child. Through toddlerhood, into the school years and beyond, your child needs to know that you are on their side, that they needn't be afraid to come to you and tell you their version of the story, that you will listen to them and that, even if you are angered by their behaviour, you will be there for them, working with them to resolve the situation.

As children grow older, their need for a champion grows stronger. When they venture into the territory of friendship issues and struggles with teachers, the need to know that there is at least one person they can rely on is huge. When everyone else gives up on them, the knowledge that you still believe in them is invaluable. Your unwavering support can give them confidence and courage to face the world when what they may want to do is run and hide.

Of course, being your child's champion can be hard, particularly when they are not acting in a way that makes you feel proud, but these are the very moments when they need you the most. When you are called into preschool to discuss a biting incident, the time when they are rude to their teacher at age five or when they refuse to do their homework at the age of seven – these are the times when you need to look deeper into their behaviour and champion their cause.

Confidence

Gentle parents have confidence in their child and also in themselves. Being confident in ourselves and particularly our own decisions helps us to parent in a much more calm and considered way. This might mean that we need to remove ourselves from situations that test us, and distance ourselves from people who make us doubt ourselves. When we are truly confident in our choices we can also avoid the nagging doubt of guilt and make better decisions. Confidence is about being in connection with our hearts and our minds, as well as our children. It can also mean making peace with the way that we ourselves were raised, particularly if it differs from the way we hope to raise our children.

Confidence comes from making well-informed decisions and from being surrounded by like-minded people – parents who feel the same way as you and raise their children in a similar manner. It comes from building a village of support around yourself and your family. Confidence comes with time and experience, from living in the moment, being mindful of your child's stage of development and taking care of yourself as well. It comes not from following a prescribed way of parenting, but from feeling empowered to make your own decisions. We will look at all of these things throughout the book.

Having confidence in your child is as important as being confident yourself. In many ways we expect too much of babies and young children, but conversely we overparent them and do not give them adequate space to explore and develop. Picking up a toy that a baby has spent the last ten minutes trying to pick up themselves, finishing a jigsaw puzzle that a toddler is struggling with, telling a five-year-old the word they are struggling to read in a book or immediately stepping in to resolve an argument between two seven-year-olds – these are all instances of underestimating a child's abilities and not giving them a chance to achieve something themselves. Learning to sit with a child through their struggles without interfering is difficult for some, but showing them that you believe that they can do something and trusting them to do it is so important.

Consistency

Many parents implement six of the Cs well for a few weeks, but the busyness of everyday life, or a lack of instant results can cause them to lose heart. Transitioning to parenting gently is not easy and the effects can often be seen only infuriatingly slowly. We live in a 'quick-fix' world and we are used to instant gratification and fast turnarounds, but gentle parenting can take anything from a month to years to really make a difference. That's why taking a long-term view is vital, so as not to lose heart and begin second-guessing your parenting.

It is essential to decide on your boundaries and limits, and reinforce them every single time, and to stick to your beliefs, no matter how busy or tired you are. Far too many parents send mixed messages to their children, allowing them to do something one day and not the next. While it may be tempting to take the easy way out and permit something 'just this once', think about how confusing this might be for your child. Likewise, keeping your own feelings in check and nurturing yourself are not 'one-off' events. They have to be done on a daily basis.

Put simply: the more consistent you are in your parenting, the better the results will be.

The Seven Cs will provide a framework for you to solve any issues you may have in a gentle way. In Chapters 2–7 we will revisit them and look at their practical application at specific stages in your child's development.

Chapter 2

It Starts in the Beginning – From Bump to Birth

Faith is taking the first step even when you can't see the whole staircase.

Martin Luther King Jr, civil rights activist

For many parents-to-be, the focus during pregnancy is on practical issues. Long hours are spent getting the nursery ready, choosing prams, cots and car seats, stocking up on nappies and Babygros and thinking about finances. One of the other major preoccupations of expectant parents is the impending labour and birth, and certainly this is what most antenatal classes concentrate on. Conversations about the reality of parenting – how to raise the baby, coping with sleepless nights, feeding (both milk and weaning onto solids) and introducing discipline at an appropriate time (and an exchange of ideas as to what that discipline might look like) – are relatively rare. Yet, in my opinion, it is vitally important to ensure you are making informed choices, discussing things with each other and are doing as much (flexible) forward planning as possible.

Pregnancy is a perfect time for you to explore your own upbringing, your thoughts and feelings about childhood and your views on raising children. It is also a time to create a 'tribe' around you – a network of support, not only for the pregnancy, but for years to come. When thinking about the birth it is also important to consider all parties involved, and that means your baby's experience, too. The more time you can spend discussing and working on these issues now, the more prepared you will be and the easier you will find life after your baby has arrived. This chapter is dedicated to looking at each of these points in a little more detail.

Making peace with your own upbringing

How were you raised? Were you always treated with respect? Did you feel valued? Did you feel listened to? Did you have a good connection with your parents? Did you have a champion?

Some of us had a positive upbringing and are happy to emulate it, while others who experienced harsh discipline may wish to move away from that parenting style with their own children. A third group who experienced a more controlling upbringing, involving the use of smacking and shaming, defend it, saying, 'I was raised this way and it never did me any harm.' This always makes me deeply uncomfortable as it is commonly used to justify things like smacking, which we know, beyond doubt, has the potential to cause psychological damage. I would question whether any fully grown adult who believes that smacking does no harm has grown up unharmed themselves. The very fact that they believe it is OK to hit a child indicates a lack of empathy.

One of the most important things you can do during the pregnancy is to make peace with how you yourself were raised. If your parents are still around, chatting with them about why they made the choices that they did can be enlightening. If they did take a more authoritarian line, and they are no longer alive, then forgiving them for the choices they made based on the prevailing messages at the time is paramount.

Most important of all though, remember that each generation has the opportunity to start afresh, and this is your chance to give your son or daughter a childhood full of love and respect. In many ways, when you become a parent, you are not only raising your own children, but might also influence the way in which your grandchildren and great grandchildren are raised, too.

Creating a tribe

Throughout most of their existence human beings, like other mammals, have tended to parent in groups or tribes, with women in particular forming social circles where they raise their young with the support and guidance of other mothers. This is the way it has been for most of human history. Until now, that is. But our new trend of parenting in isolation, away from our own family or the watchful eye and the protective wing of those more experienced than us, is at odds with our needs. We are social beings; we are not meant to do this alone.

In his book *The Motherhood Constellation*, psychologist Daniel Stern wrote about the importance of creating a tribe. He believed that throughout pregnancy and early parenthood mothers focus heavily on their baby's wellbeing and their connection with them. This helps to provide the mother with a new sense of self which hinges heavily on her child. While he acknowledged that this is an important part of parenthood, Stern felt that this new world could be overwhelming for the new mother and that she needs encouragement, understanding and advice from others in order to complete the transition. He explained that this support network – the 'maternal matrix' as he called it – is formed almost unconsciously by the mother-to-be and new mother. And while Stern's focus was on new mothers, I strongly feel that the same principle also applies to new fathers and that a 'paternal matrix' is equally as important.

In the twenty-first century these matrices are increasingly virtual, being formed via social media and parenting website discussion forums. If you find the right groups and websites these can certainly be very helpful, but never underestimate the importance of a real, physical matrix, or what many refer to as a 'parenting tribe' or 'a village', regardless how much support you have online.

If you do not have family or friends with children close by, then one of the easiest ways to create a tribe or matrix around you is by attending antenatal or baby classes. Antenatal classes in particular are often much more about making new friends than learning about birth, if not more so. Ideally, if you have a partner, you will both attend all antenatal classes together. Try to find one that takes place in the evenings or at weekends when you are both more likely to attend. Significant emphasis is usually placed on mothers keeping in contact after the classes have ended, but it is just as important for fathers to maintain their tribe of supportive fathers too. When thinking about the tribe that you may like to create around you, consider the classes and places where you are more likely to meet people who are similar to you and who share your ethos. Try to keep them as local as possible.

Joining a class can be daunting enough, without the pressure of needing to make friends and stay in touch afterwards, so if nobody asks you for your contact details, don't think that this means they don't want to stay in touch – it's highly likely that they are feeling as nervous as you and are just too shy to ask. You could suggest a meet-up at the end of the course, or even ask the course leader if he or she would be prepared either to organise an informal get-together or to circulate everybody's contact details via a handout or email. The members of this new group could become some of the most important people in your life – if not for ever, then for at least a year or more – so it's worth making the initial effort.

These parents highlight why forming a tribe is so important:

I've met so many mums through my local breastfeeding group. I've found their support invaluable; being around other mums who are going through or have been through the ups and downs of breastfeeding has helped me overcome any difficulties that have arisen. I'm sure I've made some friends for life.

It was really good to be around people who understood how I felt and to be able to talk to them about the things I wouldn't normally tell anyone else.

I thought I was going mad in the first few months with our first – I admitted how overwhelmed I was feeling to my ante-natal group by email and their responses were amazing. They really helped me get some perspective – I'm not sure how I would have got through it without their support!

The group of mums I made friends with antenatally have been invaluable in surviving the first roller coaster months and beyond. I really feel I have made friends for life and I am so grateful to have them to share, vent and laugh with.

Making the birth baby-friendly

Most parents-to-be have heard of the idea of a 'birth plan', or as I prefer to call it, 'birth preferences' – after all, things rarely go to plan! – but I'm not so sure that everyone truly understands their importance.

Birth preferences are important long before the day of the birth arrives. I think perhaps their principal role is in getting you to think about your options (and for many this means realising that you do have options!) and discussing them with your partner. This communication is vital, not only to the birth outcome, but in helping you to work as a team so that the needs of every party involved are considered – namely, parents, doctors, midwives and, perhaps the most important participant of all, your baby. Their experience is all too often not considered adequately, if at all.

Once you have researched and discussed your preferences with your partner and anybody else who will be with you at the birth, you should compile them in a form that can be easily read (never more than one side of paper), make several copies (they tend to go missing) and ensure that they are actually read on the day.

Good birth preferences will be optimistic, but also realistic, outlining your choices for your ideal birth, but also what should happen if events deviate from this. You may be hoping for a natural birth, but consider too what you might want if medical intervention is needed. If you are planning a home birth, think about how you would like things to proceed in the event that you are transferred to hospital.

These are the topics I would advise adding to your birth preferences:

1. The onset of labour – and why you should allow it to happen naturally

One of the ways that you can be baby-led when it comes to the birth is to allow the baby to be born when he or she is truly ready, if all is well, by waiting for labour to start naturally. Not only will this mean that the baby is most ready for life ex utero, but also that the birth itself is likely to be easier on both baby and mother.

Most people believe that babies arrive at, or around, forty weeks of pregnancy. What they don't realise, however, is that the idea of a forty-week pregnancy is not evidence-based, and that only 4–5 per cent are born on their 'due date', with the majority arriving after. The forty-week calculation, known as 'Naegele's rule' (named after the German obstetrician who devised it in the early nineteenth century), counts a human pregnancy for 280 days from the first day of the last menstrual period (LMP) and also assumes that all women have a regular twenty-eight day menstrual cycle, with ovulation occurring on day 14. According to Naegele's rule, therefore, the average time from ovulation to birth is 266 days.

In fact, research has shown us that the average length of pregnancy is 274 days from ovulation for a first-time mother and 269 days from ovulation for subsequent children.[1] This effectively means that due dates should be considered as forty-one weeks and one day for first-time pregnancies and forty weeks and three days for second or subsequent ones. This new evidence-based calculation throws into question the current practice of inducing labour at forty-one to forty-two weeks of pregnancy. Could it be that many inductions are simply performed too soon?

Furthermore, the National Institute for Health and Care Excellence (NICE) state that 'most women will go into labour spontaneously by forty-two weeks' and refer throughout their guidelines to induction of labour as an 'offer' that should be discussed (both risks and benefits) and that can be refused. Yet for many parents induction is not presented as an offer or a choice, but rather something that 'will' happen. Often, the benefits to inducing labour (the safety of the baby) certainly do outweigh the risks, but in many cases this is simply not true and the induction may present more of a risk than waiting for labour to begin spontaneously. Risks of induction include:

- an increased chance of needing an epidural

- an increased chance of an emergency Caesarean

- a negative effect on the establishment of breastfeeding

- hyperstimulation of the uterus, causing distress to the baby due to lack of oxygen

- an increased chance of bleeding heavily post birth

- an increased likelihood of umbilical-cord prolapse (where the umbilical cord falls into the vagina pre-birth, compromising oxygen delivery to the baby).[2]

The goal of parents-to-be is to try to find a balance between risk and benefit, and the good news is that the NICE guidelines state that they should be supported by medical staff in weighing this up and reaching their decision. Healthcare professionals offering induction of labour should, they say:

- allow the woman time to discuss the information with her partner before coming to a decision

- encourage the woman to look at a variety of sources of information

- invite the woman to ask questions, and encourage her to think about her options

- support the woman in whatever decision she makes.

A good way to consider an offer of induction is to use the acronym BRAIN:

B = Benefits – what are the benefits of an induction?
R = Risks – what are the risks of an induction?
A = Alternatives – what could you do instead?
I = Intuition – what do you instinctively feel is the right thing to do?
N = Nothing – what happens if you do nothing, or wait just a few more days?

Using your 'BRAIN' can really help you to weigh up the offer of an induction with medical staff and to reach the decision that you feel most comfortable with. And this acronym doesn't just apply to induction of labour – it can be adapted for use at any point in your labour, birth and parenting where you would like to make an informed decision.

The last point to consider on this subject is whether inducing labour can ever be natural. There are several old wives' tales regarding 'natural' methods (some of which do contain a shred of truth), but whether or not they work is not the point. If you are forcing labour to start – be it with medical intervention or 'natural' methods – you are forcing a process that is not yet ready to happen. And that is anything but natural or respectful if all is otherwise well. I feel strongly that, in a healthy pregnancy, waiting for labour to start entirely of its own accord is the most gentle way.

2. Birthing environment

Do you feel most comfortable with the idea of giving birth in a hospital, at home or in a birthing centre? All three of these options are considered safe for low-risk pregnancies, with research suggesting that a home birth may present a very slightly higher chance of complications for a first-time mother.[3] However, if the mother is low-risk, then these risks of complications are still very low. For those expecting a second or subsequent baby there are no increased risks of complication when comparing home and hospital birth.

For those with low-risk pregnancies, then, it's about choosing the environment where they think they will feel most calm and relaxed and in control of the birthing process. Some will feel reassured in a medicalised setting, while others will feel more on top of things in familiar surroundings, with their home comforts and, more likely, midwives they already know.

The ideal environment for giving birth is one that is quiet, calm, warm, dimly lit without any sights, sounds or smells that could cause the labouring mother to feel anxious. Labour and birth rely on the secretion of the hormone oxytocin – the very same hormone associated with relaxation, love and sex. In order for labour to start and progress smoothly, the mother needs to secrete enough oxytocin. However, this is hampered by the secretion of the stress hormone adrenaline, cold and bright lights. So it makes sense that the best setting to birth in is a romantic, relaxing one.

When I used to teach antenatal classes I would ask parents-to-be to draw me a picture of a place that they felt would relax them deeply. Commonly, they drew pictures of the ocean, big sofas and beds, lots of cushions, candlelight, firelight and moonlight. These are the sorts of environments that we need to birth in. Instead, many parents find themselves in atmospheres that are anything but relaxing.

As well as thinking about your own preferences, you should also consider the place that you are welcoming your baby into. What would be the best possible surroundings for your baby immediately after the birth (see the 'golden hour', page 41)?

It is possible to make your environment birth- and baby-friendly no matter where you give birth. You may not be able to light a hospital room with candlelight, but you can buy very convincing battery-operated candles to take in with you, for example. You could also take your own soft towels to dry your baby. You could consider birthing in water and requesting immediate skin-to-skin with delayed dressing, weighing and cord clamping, and leaving their head free of hats in order that you can kiss and nuzzle them. Taking in objects from home, such as your own pillow or blanket, could also really help you to relax, which, in turn, is likely to help the birth go more smoothly.

3. Birth companions

Who helps you to feel relaxed? The ideal birth companion is somebody who will remain calm and who trusts in the mother's ability to give birth. Some parents-to-be opt to have a friend or relative at the birth (as well as, or sometimes instead of, a partner), while others prefer to be alone. If you do decide you want a friend or a relative to be present, they should be someone who shares your views on birth and who is fully briefed as to your wishes. Try to choose a companion who, as well as being naturally calm, is good at reading your emotions and needs.

Some people hire professional birth companions, known as doulas. A doula is most often a women who has given birth herself, though male doulas do exist, as do female doulas who have yet to give birth themselves. Translated literally, the Ancient Greek word 'doula' means 'servant' or 'female slave' and to some extent this highlights the role, which is to work for the parents-to-be in a way that they choose, in order to provide the best birthing experience possible. Doulas ensure parents-to-be are informed about their options and choices, and give them confidence. They commonly help the labouring mother (and father) to feel comfortable both emotionally and physically, and they can take care of the environment, making it as birth- and baby-friendly as possible. Research has shown that the presence of a doula at a birth can make the outcome significantly more positive, with a lowered risk of a Caesarean delivery, less need for an epidural, a shorter labour, increased breastfeeding rates and a faster postnatal recovery.[4]

4. Relaxation strategies

Staying relaxed throughout labour is key to a smoother birth. This applies to everybody around the labouring mother, as well as the mother herself, of course. Again, this highlights the importance of the birth environment, but you also need to think of other ways to stay calm. Perhaps music relaxes you, or a certain scent, for example.

For birth partners, taking a good book can be a great relaxation strategy (labour does tend to be quite long and boring, and it is much better to read a book than sit staring at the labouring mother). Make sure also that the clothes you plan to wear are comfortable and that you have lots of pre-prepared food, drinks and snacks on hand.

Relaxation methods such as mindfulness, hypnosis for birth or special breathing techniques can really help you to stay calm. One very simple breathing technique that I like to use is as follows: close your eyes and, breathing solely through the nose, breathe in for a count of seven, then exhale, through the nose again, to a count of eleven. Focus on the rising and falling of the abdomen and diaphragm and the feel of the air as you slowly inhale and exhale.

Relaxation strategies are important for birth companions and partners too, not just the mother-to-be. An anxious birth partner can quickly cause a birthing mother to become stressed.

5. Pain relief

All forms of pain relief have risks and benefits and you need to understand your options. Applying the BRAIN acronym (see page 33) here can help you to make an informed choice. There is a huge variety of pain-relief options, ranging from the pharmaceutical – epidurals, gas and air (entonox) and pethidine – to alternative forms, such as warm water, massage, aromatherapy, homoeopathy, hypnotherapy and focused breathing, movement and TENS machines.

Before any of this though, think about your expectations. Do you consider birth to be an inherently painful process? If everything is progressing as it should – in a calming environment, with free-flowing oxytocin and endorphins (the body's natural pain-relievers) and a mother who is focused on her breathing – then severe pain is not a necessary accompaniment to labour. Many women do give birth easily with no need for pain relief. Indeed, I have given birth to two eleven-pound babies without any pain relief. I do not have a strong tolerance for pain and I was not resisting pain relief out of a desire for an 'all-natural' birth. I simply didn't need anything as it didn't hurt that much.

If you do think you might like some pain relief, however, it is essential to have researched all the options beforehand and to make sure that all birthing companions are aware of your choices (which are also recorded in the birthing preferences document). I found it useful to add the following statement to my birthing preferences: 'Please do not offer me pain relief. If I need anything, I will ask for it'. The thought process here was that if I was offered pain relief, I would feel this was as a result of a negative assessment of how well I was coping without it.

6. Special circumstances

While it is important to think about your ideal birth scenario, it is also vital to be realistic and to consider what might happen if special circumstances – such as a medical need to be induced, the need for a forceps or ventouse delivery, or an emergency Caesarean section – dictate that you deviate from your plan. Here again, the BRAIN acronym (see page 33) can be incredibly useful in helping you to make informed choices. In most cases, however, it is still possible to make the experience a positive one by asking for your music to be played in the operating theatre, for example, requesting immediate skin-to-skin contact or the presence of your birth companion throughout.

7. The second and third stages

The second stage of labour is what many commonly refer to as 'the pushing stage' and the third indicates the delivery of the placenta. Often, parents-to-be don't consider these two phases enough, if at all, when working on their birth preferences, although both can impact on early experiences of parenting.

The female body is not designed to 'push' strongly for an hour or two. In fact, in a normal physiological birth, a chain of chemical and physical reactions, focused, again, on oxytocin, is meant to trigger a reflex which should be enough to expel the baby from the birth canal with little or no conscious involvement from the mother. In the 1960s, American psychologist Niles Newton named this reflex the 'fetus ejection reflex' (FER), following her work with pregnant mice.[5] However, to do its job, the FER needs an environment of peace, quiet, trust and calm. Obstetrician Dr Michel Odent writes in his essay 'Fetus Ejection Reflex and the Art of Midwifery':

The passage towards the fetus ejection reflex is inhibited by any interference with the state of privacy. It does not occur if there is a birth attendant who behaves like a 'coach', or an observer, or a helper, or a guide, or a 'support person'. It can be inhibited by vaginal exams, by eye-to-eye contact, or by the imposition of a change of environment. It does not occur if the intellect of the labouring woman is stimulated by a rational language ('Now you are at complete dilation; you must push'). It does not occur if the room is not warm enough or if there are bright lights.[6]

MY OWN BIRTH EXPERIENCES

I was lucky enough to experience the FER with my last two babies, but my first two were delivered by what's termed as 'purple pushing', medically known as the 'Valsalva Manoeuvre'. This is where the woman is told to 'take a deep breath, hold it and *push*'. I experienced a significant amount of tearing, requiring suturing, in both births, I burst a blood vessel in one eye and developed haemorrhoids. I was exhausted and so were my babies. In contrast, my last two births were both at home and in warm water. My living rooms were dimly lit. Nobody touched me, nobody spoke to me, but I felt completely supported. My eyes were closed and I focused on nothing but my breathing and the sensations of my babies moving down. Both babies were born after second stages of no more than a minute or two. I didn't push or hold my breath. In fact, I didn't consciously do anything – my body unconsciously birthed them. All I did was to 'catch' my babies under the water when they were born. I needed no stitches, I felt exhilarated, not exhausted and both babies were much calmer and more alert at birth than their older siblings. You don't need to 'push' to birth a baby, but you do need the right environment for it to happen.

Often, once the baby is born, lights will go on, phones will come out to make calls or text about the happy news, congratulations will be shared and the atmosphere will become much louder and busier. But at this stage only two phases of labour have been completed – the mother is still in labour and she will remain labouring until the placenta is birthed. With this in mind, it is vital that the ideally quiet, calm, dimly lit environment that she was in only moments before remains. The same hormones that birthed the baby are needed to birth the placenta, but in most cases oxytocin is inhibited due to the bright lights and 'fussing' that occur (which will also overstimulate the baby).

The majority of new mothers at this point will receive an injection (syntometrine) to deliver the placenta. This is known as a managed third stage and is standard procedure as it can hasten the delivery of the placenta and reduce the likelihood of the mother bleeding heavily. But what many women don't realise is that the syntometrine injection does come with some risks. Minor risks include nausea and vomiting, which can adversely affect the important immediate bonding time with the new baby. A more serious risk of a managed third stage is that it can affect the mother's success at initiating breastfeeding.

If the birth has been complicated in some way (such as a prolonged labour, delivery by forceps or ventouse or augmented with syntocinon – a drip to speed up or induce labour), then it may be beneficial for the mother to accept the injection for placental delivery. If the birth has otherwise been natural and uncomplicated, the risks may outweigh the benefits.

Research in 2009 found a link between the administration of third-stage injections and a decreased likelihood of breastfeeding forty-eight hours later.[7] Some experts have also hypothesised that the use of exogenous oxytocin (that made outside of the body) can suppress the body's release of its own oxytocin and particularly that circulating within the brain. When you think about the vital role that oxytocin plays in love and bonding, is it possible that the syntometrine injection (which contains artificial oxytocin) can be detrimental to bonding with the new baby? Again, using the BRAIN acronym can help you to make the best decision for your family here.

8. The 'golden hour'

Imagine that you have just spent nine months inside a warm, dark place where everything you touched was soft. You were surrounded by warm water and constantly held. Now imagine what birth must feel like for most babies: they are suddenly catapulted into a world of bright lights, cold air, being rubbed by a towel, weighed in cold plastic or metal scales, having a scratchy nappy put on and being clothed for the first time. And how must it feel to be handled by strangers whose scent and touch you don't recognise?

If I was a baby, I'm sure I would choose to be enveloped in the warm skin and touch of my mother whose body and scent are the only ones that I know. I would choose not to have clothing, nappies, towels and hats hampering this skin-to-skin contact. I would choose to wait before being held by other people and to be weighed only once I have grown accustomed to my new world. I would choose for the lights to be as dim as possible while my eyes adjust to the presence of light after living in the dark for nine months. I would certainly choose not to have photographs taken with bright flashes in my sensitive eyes. And I would choose for the room to be quiet, calm and peaceful with only the reassuring whispers of my parents in my delicate new ears. What would you choose?

The first hour after birth is vital for establishing breastfeeding, safely delivering the placenta physiologically (without an injection) and bonding with your new baby. If possible, the setting should be no different from that of the birth during this time. The lights should still be dim, it should be warm and quiet and the baby should, ideally, be on the new mother's chest covered by the softest towels and blankets and nothing else.

If you choose to breastfeed, it is during this hour that the baby learns to attach him or herself to the breast through a process known as the 'breast crawl'. This is a reflex that helps new babies to crawl towards the mother's breasts and begin to feed by themselves. Newborns do not need to be manhandled and attached to the breast by adult hands – indeed, this can hinder the initiation of breastfeeding and can sometimes cause difficulties with the latch. In order to allow them to capitalise on their innate skill, newborns should be placed on the mother's abdomen and left to their own devices – this way breastfeeding has the best possible chance of getting off to a good start. In addition, a concept known as 'Biological Nurturing', developed by midwife and breastfeeding consultant Suzanne Colson, stresses the importance of the mother sitting or lying back a little during this period, so that gravity does not pull the baby away from the breast, as it would if she was sitting upright or lying on her side.

In the first hour after birth, all of the above should be borne in mind. The baby will, preferably, not leave the mother's chest (even to go to the father for a cuddle) and their connection will not be interfered with in any way. In many ways this 'golden hour' is the most vital in terms of the future psychological and physiological health of the baby.

9. Cord clamping

A Cochrane review (a review of research by scientists and professionals) suggests that a third of the baby's blood volume at birth is in their umbilical cord.[8] This blood, belonging to the baby, is rich in important nutrients, stem cells and iron. It makes no sense, therefore, to cut the cord immediately after birth, leaving some of the baby's blood in the cord rather than their body. If the cord is cut too soon after birth, the baby also has a higher risk of developing jaundice, a lowered haemoglobin level and an increased risk of becoming iron deficient as they get older.[9] The authors of the Cochrane review referred to above summarise their findings as follows: 'A more liberal approach to delaying clamping of the umbilical cord in healthy term infants appears to be warranted, particularly in light of growing evidence that delayed cord clamping increases early haemoglobin concentrations and iron stores in infants'. As well as the physical benefits to the baby, delayed cord clamping can also enhance the golden hour by preventing separation of mother and baby, which can, in turn, aid a physiological delivery of the placenta and also the initiation of breastfeeding.

If you choose delayed cord clamping for your baby, the cord will be cut when the blood has very clearly drained from it. In this instance the cord, which initially appears quite rigid and takes on a purple colour with a faint pulse (indicating the presence of circulating blood), will not be cut until it is flaccid and white (indicating that the blood has entered your baby's circulatory system). On average, this takes around ten minutes from the moment of birth, but it can take up to twenty. Many parents like to cut the cord themselves, seeing it as an honour. If you would like to do this, make sure that your wish is expressed in your birth preferences, along with delayed cord clamping if that is your choice.

Some parents opt to use soft fabric cord ties or tape to tie it off as these are viewed as being much more comfortable for the baby than the large plastic cord clamp that is generally used as standard. If you wish to use a tie or tape for the cord, it is best to check with your midwife before the birth if these are available; alternatively, many parents source them themselves.

Finally, some parents prefer not to cut the cord at all – a process known as a 'lotus birth'. This symbolic gesture allows the baby to detach from the cord of their own accord – a natural separation that tends to occur somewhere between days two and five after the birth.

10. Infant feeding

Deciding how to feed their baby is a big choice for some parents and an easy one for others. Once again, using the BRAIN acronym (see page 33) can help here.

The most important point to consider when deciding how to feed your baby is that breastfeeding is the physiological norm for our species. Therefore breastfeeding is the baseline by which all other infant-feeding methods should be measured. This means we should consider the risks, to baby and mother, of feeding in a way that is not intended for our species. Parents who choose to formula-feed must understand these risks.

Potential problems with formula-feeding include an increased risk of:

For babies:

- otitis media (ear infections)

- gastroenteritis

- pneumonia

- type-1 and type-2 diabetes

- leukaemia

- obesity

- SIDS (sudden infant death syndrome)

- necrotizing enterocolitis (a disorder where the tissue in the baby's bowels becomes infected and dies)

For mothers:

- breast cancer

- ovarian cancer

- type-2 diabetes.[10]

The precise reason for these increased risks is sometimes unclear, however the general consensus is that the deviation from the norm of infant feeding can block natural protection mechanisms for the baby, as well as the mother. As an example, suppression of the hormone oestrogen that is meant to occur when a woman breastfeeds does not take place if she is formula-feeding, and the raised levels put her at a higher risk of those 'feminine' cancers with a high oestrogen-correlated causation compared to her breastfeeding counterpart. As far as the baby is concerned, breast milk is a living substance, full of immune-boosting properties and 'good' bacteria, which form a vital part of their immune system. Conversely, formula milk lacks these properties, is not a sterile product and can contain unwanted bacteria that can make a baby sick (hence the increased risk of gastroenteritis). Formula milk can also cause responses in the baby's body that are not the human norm; for instance, it decreases 'active' sleep (a lighter sleep state) and promotes a deeper state in which babies are more likely to succumb to SIDS (or cot death). Breastfed babies, in contrast, spend more time in the lighter, protective sleep state.

When deciding how to feed your baby, don't allow yourself to be swayed by the clever marketing of the multi-million-pound infant-feeding industry. The formula and bottle manufacturers want you to view breastfeeding as painful, difficult and inconvenient. And to convince you they employ experts and health professionals to promote their products via infant-feeding helplines, free samples, talks at baby shows and magazine and newspaper articles. Often, you will not even know that the expert in question is on the payroll of these industrial giants. Why would you not trust their advice?

If you do plan to breastfeed, be sure that this is mentioned in your birth preferences. Sometimes new parents can be pressurised into giving their newborns formula milk in hospital when in most cases it is not necessary. If a professional calls into question your choice to breastfeed exclusively, or at any point suggests that you should supplement with formula, remember to use the BRAIN acronym when making a decision (see page 33), and seek immediate advice from a breastfeeding counsellor or lactation consultant. Even if it transpires that your baby does need additional nutrition, research suggests that it is better to use donor human breast milk than from formula milk (you will find organisations who can provide support here in the Resources section, pages 278–9).[11] The World Health Organization's 'Global Strategy for Infant and Young Child Feeding' recommends the following order of preference:

1. milk from own mother by breastfeeding
2. milk from own mother, expressed
3. milk from a wet-nurse, or
4. milk from a milk bank, or
5. breast milk substitute (formula milk) fed from cup.

Lastly, there are also the practicalities of feeding to consider. Pre-parenthood, many believe that formula-feeding is more convenient and will help them to get more sleep. In reality this is rarely true and the opposite is more commonly the case. Ensuring that you always have sterilised equipment and access to boiled water to kill the bacteria present in formula can be quite a task. Having to make up fresh feeds in the middle of the night while your baby screams can often result in far less sleep for everybody. Research has shown that breastfeeding mothers and fathers get more and better-quality sleep than their formula-feeding counterparts and are also at a lower risk of postnatal depression and exhaustion.[12]

If you do choose to feed your baby using formula or expressed breast milk, try to remember it is perfectly possible to do so in a natural, nurturing, baby-led way, and there are tips in the next chapter to help you with this (see page 51).

Making informed choices about parenting strategies

Will you be an authoritative parent? This is certainly the style that fits most with a gentle approach to parenting. Is your partner on the same page when it comes to parenting style?

How will you both cope with a baby who wakes many times throughout the night? How will you cope with a toddler who ignores your requests? How will you cope with the exhaustion that accompanies new parenting? How will you meet your own needs as well as those of your child? These are all important questions that you should consider before your baby arrives.

Of course, you can't plan for all eventualities now, but many new parents find themselves so deeply entrenched in their situation and so exhausted that they don't have the time or the head space to analyse and compare their parenting beliefs, so doing your research and communicating well with one another from the very beginning can save an enormous amount of stress and anxiety later on.

Using the Seven Cs of gentle parenting from bump to birth

How will you implement the Seven Cs of gentle parenting throughout your pregnancy, birth and immediate postnatal period?

Connection

What helps you to connect with your baby during pregnancy? Playing games with your bump, reading, singing or talking to the baby in utero are all great – babies recognise the sounds of their parents' voices when they are born and singing during pregnancy has been shown to aid labour. Making a belly cast can also be an ideal way to spend some time focusing on and bonding with your growing baby, as can taking a few moments each day to visualise them. Think too about how you can help your baby to remain close to you after birth in order to start the connection off well. Remember the importance of the 'golden hour' and skin-to-skin contact.

Communication

The first few hours after birth are all about communication. Babies are incredibly social when they are born and are wired to communicate with us by looking at our faces and even mimicking our behaviour. Watch your baby's early communication and think about your own. Help them by keeping the post-birth environment as quiet and calm as possible. Watch for your baby's cues. Crying is communication and can be a sign that they are not happy with what is being done to them.

Control

The ultimate way to give your baby control at birth is by allowing them to be born when they are ready. If your pregnancy is otherwise healthy, consider the risks and benefits of a post-dates induction using the BRAIN acronym (see page 33). Remember that there are no natural ways to induce labour; the only natural way for labour to start is spontaneously, when the mother's body and the baby are both ready. Anything else, no matter how 'natural' the method used, is an unnatural start to labour.

Containment

The best way to contain your new baby's emotions is 'in arms' and preferably skin-to-skin. Nothing tells a newborn 'I love you' more than being held close to your skin. Even if they do not stop crying, your arms and your love will be containing their upset.

Champion

You are your baby's best advocate. It is up to you to consider their emotional and psychological needs during the birth. Remember BRAIN again. Is everything suggested absolutely in the best interests of your baby? Be your baby's champion when it comes to the birthing environment – is it warm enough for them? Too bright? Too noisy? Too busy, with too many people? And never be afraid to request changes if you feel that something is not in your baby's best interests.

Confidence

One of the best ways to aid your confidence as an expectant and very new parent is to build your tribe and to surround yourself with people and information that enlighten and empower you. If something or someone is making you question your abilities or beliefs, don't be afraid to put some distance between it or them and yourself.

Consistency

One of the best ways that you can stay consistent during the pregnancy, birth and immediate postnatal period is by writing down, referring to and using your birthing preferences. This is particularly important in the case of special circumstances or where the birthing may deviate from what you had imagined, making it is easy to get sidetracked.

Chapter 3

The Fourth Trimester – Birth to Three Months

A person's a person, no matter how small.

Horton Hears a Who! by Dr Seuss

Human newborns are perhaps the most ill-equipped mammals for life outside the womb, as they are completely reliant on their parents to fulfil all of their needs for many months. A newborn's brain and body, while developing and growing rapidly, takes time to adjust 'earth-side', and during this transition babies need their parents to keep them safe, physically and emotionally. The easiest way for parents to meet this need, and to reduce as much as possible the time that their baby cries, is to view their first twelve weeks of life as a 'fourth trimester' (the pregnancy having been divided into three). And this fourth trimester should mimic life 'in utero' as much as possible.

To fully understand the enormous transition a newborn has made from being in utero to life after birth, it is helpful to compare these two worlds. The summary below illustrates the vast change a newborn experiences in only a matter of hours.

Environment during pregnancy	Environment after birth
Darkness twenty-four hours per day	Natural light for at least ten hours per day and artificial light at night
Sounds of mother's body and very muffled external sounds	A complete contrast between total silence (often at night) and loud, unexpected and changeable sounds
Constant comfortable, warm temperature (averaging 37°C)	Fluctuating temperatures, often too cold or too hot
Constant nutrition via the umbilical cord; no concept of hunger or thirst	Frequently hungry and thirsty
Very confined space	Lots of space around them
Aquatic environment	Air
Constantly 'held' by the mother's uterus and in permanent physical contact with her	Held for only a few hours a day; many hours spent lying alone not in physical contact with mother
Naked	Clothed
All surroundings are warm and soft	Many surroundings are hard and cold
Ability to smell inhibited in water	Many new smells every day

This information reveals how stark the contrast is between a baby's 'womb world' and our own. Can you imagine what a shock it must be to be born and to lose everything you have ever known in an instant? In utero, the baby's world was constant, nothing changed, but, after birth, each day is different, ever changing. And perhaps the most important transition of all is that from constant physical contact with the mother to very little over a twenty-four-hour period. This is the adjustment that newborns find hardest and often the one that new parents struggle with the most – the realisation that most newborns are only happy 'in arms'.

In our society we try everything to put our babies down as much as we can, to encourage independence and to avoid 'spoiling' them. But a newborn needs to be held almost as much as they need milk. It is a physical as well as a psychological need. They do not need to be encouraged to fall asleep alone, in the mistaken belief that this will teach them to self-soothe. The ability to self-soothe is an extremely complex psychological process that takes years to acquire; it is dependent on brain development that a child does not have until they are of school age and beyond. So, in their early years, our children need us to externally regulate their emotions by soothing them until they can do this themselves. And for newborns, this means keeping them in close physical contact as much as possible.

Newborn calming techniques

Keeping the concept of the fourth trimester very much in mind, there are a number of techniques that usually work well to calm fractious newborns. Remember, however, that each baby is different. Some of these techniques will work well for you and your baby and others less so. Often babies need a combination of several different techniques in order to feel safe and calm.

Movement

While in the womb, a baby would have experienced almost constant movement (even if the mother was still): Braxton Hicks (practice contractions) would squeeze the baby regularly towards the end of pregnancy; breathing would rock them slightly; walking would move them in a gentle sway, while going up and down stairs would result in a more vigorous rock. Contrast this with the stillness most newborns experience lying in cribs, prams or on play mats and it becomes clear why they are generally happier when they are rocked. In addition to rocking, newborn babies often love being held by their parents while they dance, sway from side to side or bounce on a birthing ball; or being carried while the parents are walking or taken for a car ride. Don't be afraid to move with your newborn, as long as their head and neck are well supported.

Skin-to-skin contact

Being in direct, skin-to-skin contact with a parent has a magical effect on a newborn baby. It helps to stabilise the baby's body temperature, heart rate and stress hormones. It also stimulates the release of oxytocin (the hormone of love and bonding) in both baby and parent, aiding bonding in both.

Skin-to-skin contact is a great way for fathers to bond with their newborn too, as is taking a shared bath and practising some baby massage. Attending a baby-massage class is a great way to meet new friends, but you don't need to learn specific techniques to be able to enjoy touching your newborn lovingly and gently. Just use a mild, edible vegetable oil, such as organic sunflower oil, on your warmed hands (removing jewellery), and carefully and slowly rub the oil into your baby's skin. Pay special attention to their response and carry on for as long as they enjoy the massage, avoiding their umbilical cord stump if they still have one, and be sure to stop and cuddle them as soon as they become unhappy.

Co-sleeping and bedsharing

Many people are confused about the difference between co-sleeping and bedsharing. Co-sleeping means sharing a sleeping environment with your baby (i.e. sleeping in the same room), whereas bedsharing means sharing a sleeping surface (i.e. your bed) with your baby.

Co-sleeping is advised for all babies for at least the first six months of life as it reduces the risk of Sudden Infant Death Syndrome (SIDS). This is due, it is thought, primarily to three things: the parents' proximity means they are more easily aroused (waking sooner if they sense that something is wrong); the noises and movements made by parents can help to prevent babies from spending too much time in the very deep sleep state with which SIDS is associated; and the carbon dioxide exhaled by the parents helps to prompt the baby to breathe.

Bedsharing, however, is only appropriate when following very specific safety guidelines and for only a specific type of parent (see below). The decision to bedshare should always be an informed one that has been fully discussed and planned with all members of the household. The following is a list of guidelines to help minimise any risks when sharing a bed with your baby:

- If the baby is formula-fed it may not be safe to bedshare with them, so the mother should ideally be breastfeeding. Breastfeeding mothers tend to be more alert to their baby at night and position them at breast height in a cradle position (see image on page 57), whereas formula-feeding mothers can be less alert and do not commonly adopt this sleeping position. Similarly, breastfed babies sleep more lightly than their formula-fed counterparts. Lastly, formula-feeding increases the risk of SIDS, therefore it is best to not do anything which may increase this further.

- Both parents should be non-smokers and the mother should not have smoked during her pregnancy either.

- Neither parent should have consumed any alcohol at all during the day or evening.

- Neither parent should have used recreational or prescription drugs, including post-birth painkillers.

- Neither parent should consider themselves to be 'excessively tired', such that they have problems rousing in the night.

- The baby should never be in the middle of the bed. Only the mother possesses a special ability to easily arouse for her infant and not roll onto them, so she should always sleep between her partner and the baby.

- Always ensure that the sleeping surface is firm – never fall asleep with a baby on a sofa, bean bag or water bed and avoid memory-foam mattresses too, due to their softness and also the chemicals used in their manufacture.

- To prevent the baby from rolling onto the floor from a height, sleep on a mattress on the floor or a futon-style bed, if possible.

- Keep all pillows well away from the baby. They should always sleep at the same level as the mother's breasts, not her head. Also, keep duvets and blankets well away from the baby to prevent the risk of smothering (many mothers sleep in onesies or dressing gowns to keep themselves warm).

- Ensure the baby does not overheat; dress them in appropriate clothing.

- The mother should lie on her side and form a protective frame around baby with her body.

- Consider a separate sleeping surface (a special open-sided co-sleeper crib – see below) if the baby is small for its age or was premature.

- Consider a separate sleeping surface if the mother is significantly overweight or classified as obese.

A good alternative to bedsharing is a special co-sleeper crib which sits right beside the parents' bed. In this arrangement the baby has their own space, but they sleep very close to the mother with no cot bars inhibiting contact or access.

Done safely, bedsharing is an amazing way for everyone to get more sleep, as babies are generally much calmer and sleep more easily if they sleep with you in your bed. It is estimated that 60 to 70 per cent of parents will share a bed with their baby at some point and many of these instances will be unplanned. For this reason understanding safe bedsharing is important, even if you do not intend to do it, as one day you may well find yourself drifting off to sleep with your baby.

Many parents worry that if they allow their baby into their

bed once or twice that they will always have to do so, and that their child will not then learn to be independent, but research has shown that this is not the case.[1] Meeting your newborn's needs and nurturing them is the best way to ensure that your child will be confident and independent as they grow. Allowing your baby to be dependent on you when they are young is not a bad habit – it is in the best interests of the whole family.

Swaddling

Towards the very end of the pregnancy, babies are tightly curled inside the uterus, with little or no space to move. Once they are born, however, they can move their arms and legs, albeit in an often uncoordinated manner, and experience the space of the world around them. This new-found freedom and space can often upset babies, perhaps because they miss the snug hold of the uterus. The obvious solution is to envelop your baby in your arms but, for times when you need to put them down, swaddling is an option.

Swaddling newborn babies has been popular for thousands of years; however, if you choose to do this, there are important safety guidelines to follow in order to avoid putting your baby at an increased risk of SIDS. Also, if you are breastfeeding, you should ensure that feeding is well established before you begin swaddling your baby, and take care not to miss their early hunger cues:

- Never swaddle over your baby's head or near their face.

- Never swaddle your baby if they are ill or have a fever.

- Make sure your baby does not overheat; swaddle with a breathable/thin fabric.

- Only swaddle your baby until they can roll over, or until fourteen weeks of age, whichever is sooner.

- Always place your baby to sleep on their back.

- Do not swaddle tightly across your baby's chest.

- Do not swaddle tightly around your baby's hips and legs; their legs should be free to move.

- Start to swaddle as soon as possible after feeding is established; but do not begin to swaddle a three-month-old baby if they have not been swaddled before.

EASY 5-STEP SWADDLING TECHNIQUE

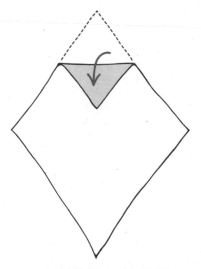

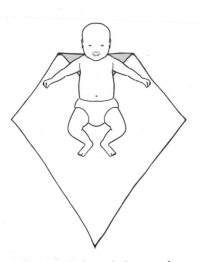

Fold over the top of the swaddle sheet to make a triangle

Place your baby with the top of the fold level with his neck

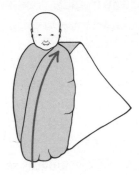

Tuck your baby's right arm at his side, take hold of the top left-hand corner and bring it down and over your baby. Tuck the sheet under his left-hand side

Bring the bottom of the sheet up to the baby's left-hand shoulder, hold the baby's arm to his side and tuck the fabric underneath his arm, torso and bottom

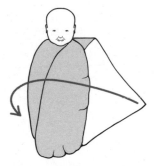

Now, bring the last remaining flap of material to your left and wrap it all the way around your baby, using his own weight to keep the wrap secure

Ensure the fabric is wrapped loosely over the baby's chest and hips – you are looking for tightness over the arms and tummy only

Carrying

Carrying your baby in a soft carrier or fabric sling, something many refer to as 'babywearing', can be a very easy way of giving your baby the almost constant physical contact that they crave, while leaving your hands free to fulfil your own needs. Babies who are carried spend more time in a state known as 'quiet alertness', and in this state of calm contentment newborns learn the most. Research has also found that increased carrying throughout the day results in significantly less crying at six-weeks old – a time when crying is usually at its peak.[2]

If you wish to carry your baby, it is vital that you use a good carrier or sling. It should be comfortable for both baby and wearer, supporting the baby's spine, while not placing any pressure on their growing hips. Look for one that allows newborns to be carried facing inwards, with their legs drawn up into an 'M' shape (as in the image below left) and the natural 'C' shape of their spine to be supported (below right). This requires a wide seat in order to support the baby's hips in a physiologically correct position and not place any unnecessary strain on them. A wide seat is also significantly more comfortable for both baby and wearer. The most

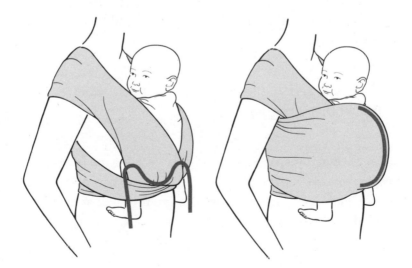

natural way for a newborn to be held in a sling mirrors how they would be held if they were resting on your chest. Facing a baby outwards in a carrier does not hold them in a physiologically correct position and can create strain and discomfort for both them and you. Facing outwards also makes it harder for the baby to 'switch off' from the world if they are tired.

Important safety points to consider when carrying a baby in a sling:

- Ensure that your baby's airway is open at all times; their chin should not be resting on their chest at any time. Carrying your baby in an upright position is usually the easiest way to hold them with their chin off of their chest.

- Make sure your baby is in view at all times and check them regularly. Their head should be close enough to yours that they are easy to monitor.

- Check your baby's temperature and ensure that they do not overheat in the carrier.

- Make sure that your carrier has passed all safety tests, and check it for any damage before use.

- Use a carrier that supports your baby's head, neck and spine at all times.

- Ensure your carrier holds your baby snugly to you and does not allow them to slip down into the fabric which could inhibit their breathing.

Many people view slings and carriers as a means of transport, only to be used when out and about, but they can prove invaluable at home too, particularly in the evenings when babies tend to need as much close contact and reassurance as possible.

Position

Some parents choose to sleep their baby on their side or tummy, but this should be avoided as it puts the baby at a significantly increased risk of SIDS. In 1990 guidelines to put babies on their 'back to sleep' were issued, following which there was a decrease in SIDS deaths of more than half in 1992, compared with 1989.[3] Research has also found that babies placed on their stomachs to sleep were up to six times more likely to die from SIDS than those placed on their back.[4]

Having said that, when babies are in utero they are never laid flat on their backs, and helping them to spend time in a position that feels more natural to them during waking hours can make them feel calmer. Many babies benefit from 'tummy time'; placing the baby on your tummy while you lay back in bed and talk with them, or the two of you lying on the floor on your tummies facing each other are lovely bonding activities that also help to strengthen their core, head and neck muscles. Babies also love to be held in a more horizontal position. The 'tiger-in-the-tree' position below, taken from baby yoga, often has a magical effect, stopping a baby crying in an instant.

Noise

In utero, babies are used to muffled voices and the sounds of the mother's internal body workings. Being born into a world that can be both silent and, conversely, very noisy can be disconcerting for them. Nights are perhaps the most quiet, and babies can be unsettled by the lack of noise that they heard in utero. Here, white noise at an appropriate volume – just loud enough so they can hear it over their crying, but not too loud – can help, whether this is the sound of a radio tuned into static or a white-noise app or CD. Many parents will instinctively sing or whisper to their newborns and research has shown that these lullabies help to calm them and regulate their nervous systems.[5]

Feeding

Feeding, particularly breastfeeding, isn't just about the nutrition – it's also about comfort and the fact that they never felt hunger or thirst when they were in utero. Allowing your newborn to feed whenever they need to in the early days will also help to get feeding established more quickly, as well as helping to keep them as calm as possible. Plus, suckling also helps a baby's skull bones to return to their normal position after birth, so frequent feeding can also help them physically.

BABY-LED FORMULA-FEEDING

Feeding is a time for bonding, emotional and physical comfort and connection and it is perfectly possible to formula-feed your baby in a natural, nurturing baby-led way. The following suggestions can help you to do this in a more psychologically and physiologically correct way.

Ignore the clock

Often formula-feeding is linked heavily with keeping to a schedule. This really doesn't have to be the case though, as it is easy to demand-feed. It is harder to respond as quickly when you are formula-feeding, as you have to make up the feed and warm it to the correct temperature, which takes time. However, with a little bit of advanced planning and close observation, so that you learn your baby's hunger cues (particularly the early ones such as squirming and rooting), it should be possible to respond fairly quickly and certainly before they begin to cry too much (which is a late hunger cue). A clock, formula tin or book cannot tell you when your baby will be hungry. Only your baby can tell you that.

Watch the baby not the bottle

Only your baby knows when they have had enough milk. The formula packaging may be able to give you a rough idea of the amount of milk they may drink, but it is only a guide. Your baby may be particularly hungry at one feed and less so at another. Be aware of your baby's satiety signals (hands softening and falling open, body softening and relaxing, falling asleep and hiccupping or burping with milk trickling out of their mouth) and watch for when you feel they have had enough milk. Don't be tempted to try to get them to take more than they want in order that they finish a bottle.

Get some skin-to-skin

Breastfeeding provides wonderful skin-to-skin contact which is a brilliant baby calmer and bonder, but there is no reason why you cannot do this when formula-feeding. Undo some buttons on your shirt, or lift it up and hold your baby close to your chest with their face on your bare skin. This isn't just for mothers, partners can do this too.

Let your baby take the bottle

When breastfeeding, it is the baby that decides to latch on to the breast to begin feeding, whereas formula-feeding is usually begun by a parent inserting a bottle into the baby's mouth. Instead, try holding the teat close to your baby's cheek and waiting for them to turn and latch onto it, pulling it into their mouths themselves. Similarly, when you feel your baby trying to push the teat out of their mouth, take it out immediately and wait for them to latch on again to restart.

Be mindful

While your baby feeds, take time to just 'be'. Be still, hug them, talk to them, stroke their legs and their arms, smell their head, feel the weight of them in your arms and just take time out from your everyday life to enjoy the moment. Soon your baby will be on the move and these sweet, early feeds will be forgotten. Don't be tempted to multitask and check texts or emails or make a phone call when you are feeding your baby: treat it as a time that is as much about bonding and connection as it is about physical nourishment.

Hold your baby in a more upright position

Many people tend to formula-feed their baby with the baby lying in a horizontal position in their lap or in their arms. In contrast, after the immediate newborn period when babies are breastfed, they are held in a more upright, almost seated, position which some believe can reduce the incidence of ear infections. A good rule of thumb is to hold your baby just upright enough that the bottle is being held parallel to the floor.

Respect your baby's pauses

When babies breastfeed they tend to feed for a while and then stop, take a rest, look around and so on, then they feed again and pause again. Encourage your baby to do the same with a bottle: after you have sated their immediate hunger, encourage them to stop and 'chat' with you, exchange smiles, have a cuddle and so on. Gently winding them by rubbing their back or shifting position every five or ten minutes or so can encourage this, as can changing the side your baby is lying in (i.e. switching from supporting with your left arm to your right).

Use a slow-flow teat

A slow-flow teat will allow the baby more control over the flow of milk.

Water

Pre-birth, babies live in an aquatic environment, surrounded by warm water heated to 37°C. So imagine how strange it must feel for them post-birth to be surrounded by air that is a comparatively chilly, at 18–20°C. Bathing together with newborns, so that they are in warm, deep water, while being held in the arms of a parent, can really help them with this transition and often works like magic when they are crying and nothing else will do the trick.

How your baby develops in the first three months

At birth a newborn's brain is around a quarter of the size it will be as an adult and is fairly primal in its abilities and actions, although their spinal cord and brain stem – the parts responsible for homoeostasis (breathing, temperature regulation, circulatory control and so on) – are well developed as they are of primary importance for their survival. The newborn's limbic system and cerebral cortex – the parts of the brain responsible for emotions and thought processes – are incredibly immature. Does this mean, then, that a newborn can't learn? In a sense it does.

While a newborn can become accustomed to things by a process known as habituation, for instance the sound of a dog barking, this does not indicate that any deep understanding has taken place. They have not learned that the dog is not scary or a threat to their life; they have simply become used to the noise and are no longer startled by it. Their brains are certainly not capable of learning to 'self-soothe' or manipulate.

Newborns largely function on reflexes, controlled by the rudimentary lower parts of the brain. These include the Moro (or startle) reflex, the breast crawl (see page 42), the 'walking' reflex (newborns will 'walk' if held upright on a surface), the grasping reflex (when babies cling onto your finger) and the 'doll's head' reflex (where their eyes will continue looking ahead if their head is turned to the side). These reflexes all help the baby to survive, along with the primitive actions that ensure homoeostasis. So it is important that the baby cries if they are not in physical contact with their parents, as this reflexive cry ensures that they will be held and kept safe. Also, at birth, a baby's vision is not the same as an adult's. They can see just far enough to focus on a face when they are being held (around 20–25cm from them) and this will remain their primary focus for the first three months.

Routines vs schedules

Routine refers to doing the same things at roughly the same time each day, whereas schedules are artificially imposed by parents with little regard for the baby's needs. During the first three months of your newborn's life it is best to be 'baby-led'. This means following your baby's cues regarding hunger and tiredness as much as possible. While it may seem tempting to try to get your baby onto a schedule in order to get some predictability back into your life, this could inhibit breastfeeding and lead to lots of tears and upset for your baby.

When they are born, babies have no concept of night or day and this remains the case throughout their first three months. As adults we may do the majority of our eating during daylight hours, but newborns will need just as much feeding at night as they do in the day, often more so, as there is less to distract them at night. This demand-feeding (which means allowing them to stop feeding if they are full, as well as feeding if they are hungry) is important, not only to increase milk supply in a breastfeeding mother, but also to help the baby to pace their feeding and begin the journey towards healthy eating habits. Allowing a baby to feed on demand is a significant part of the process through which they begin to recognise their satiety levels. Research has shown that babies who are demand-fed are less likely to be obese as adults, and further research also indicates that feeding on demand, rather than to a schedule, leads to better cognitive brain development.[6]

How to spot your baby's hunger and tiredness cues

If you are feeding your newborn baby according to their cues, it is important to recognise their early hunger and tiredness signals. These can – and generally do – differ for all babies, however the following are fairly universal. With both sets of cues it is far better to respond to them before they escalate into cries, crying being a late indicator of both hunger and tiredness.

Early hunger cues include:

- opening and closing the mouth

- turning the head to the side and 'rooting'

- stirring from sleeping

- squirming and stretching

- moving the hand to the mouth.

Early sleep cues include:

- gaze aversion

- touching the head and/or ear

- hiccuping

- jerky body movements, particularly the arms

- grunting or making an 'Ooh' sound

- yawning – although this is a fairly late sign.

Colic and crying

Despite around a quarter of newborns being diagnosed with 'colic', it is actually not a medical disorder. Colic is a label given to crying a lot for no known cause. In many cases this crying can be explained by a lack of understanding of the fourth-trimester period, an undiagnosed allergy or intolerance (such as cow's milk protein allergy) or feeding problems (for example, an undiagnosed tongue tie or poor latch or the residual effects of the birth causing discomfort to the baby).

The 'Wessel Criteria' (named after the paediatrician who conducted a study into unexplained crying) are used to diagnose colic in a baby who cries for more than three hours a day, for more than three days per week, for over three weeks.

If you have a very unhappy baby, it is always better to start by looking for the cause of the crying and addressing any relevant issues, rather than trying to mask the problem with medication. The flow chart on the following page can help you to identify, and hopefully eliminate, any concerns regarding crying and colic.

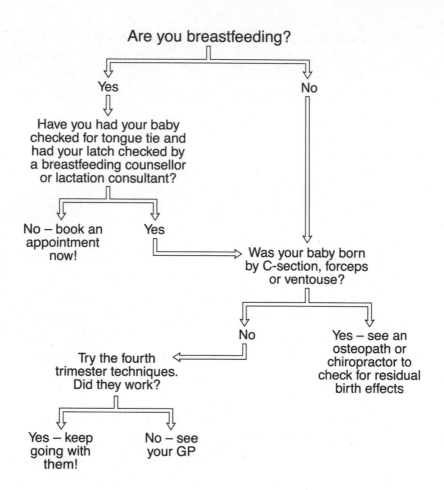

Are you breastfeeding?

Yes → Have you had your baby checked for tongue tie and had your latch checked by a breastfeeding counsellor or lactation consultant?

No → Was your baby born by C-section, forceps or ventouse?

No – book an appointment now!

Yes

Was your baby born by C-section, forceps or ventouse?

No → Try the fourth trimester techniques. Did they work?

Yes – see an osteopath or chiropractor to check for residual birth effects

Yes – keep going with them!

No – see your GP

When you can't stop the crying

Gentle parenting doesn't mean having children who never cry, or being able to stop their tears instantly. It means staying calm, empathic and responsive and being with your baby while they cry, if your best efforts have not stopped their tears.

Too many parents feel they have failed if they cannot stop their baby crying, yet that couldn't be further from the truth because those who are able to stay present and respectful of their baby through unstoppable tears are some of the gentlest there are. Although your goal as a parent in the present moment may be to stop the crying, a far greater goal is to be strong enough to take on board your child's frustrations and help them through them, whether they are ten days or ten years old.

Sleep in the newborn period

What should you expect of your newborn's sleep? The answer here is fairly simple: not a lot! As we have seen, a newborn has no concept of day and night and won't until the very end of their third month of life. The circadian rhythms, or innate body clocks, that govern our sleep as adults do not begin to function well until after twelve weeks of age. This means that a newborn does not respond to the presence or absence of light in the way that an adult or older baby or child does. In the early weeks it is fair to expect frequent waking and the need to feed throughout both the day and night (often more at night).

You cannot speed up the development of your baby's circadian rhythm, but keeping the daytimes very light and exposing your baby to natural sunlight by getting out for a morning walk, and keeping lighting at night very dim, may help once it is developing.

On the subject of lighting, it is important to not use regular nightlights or light bulbs in the evening. Most baby and child nightlights and light bulbs emit white and blue light wavelengths which cause the brain to think it is daytime and inhibit the production of the sleep hormone melatonin. It is better to have no light at all once it gets dark, but if you need light to see when feeding and changing your baby's nappy overnight, then use a low-wattage red light bulb in a lamp. Red light does not inhibit the secretion of melatonin and so will not inhibit your baby's sleep.

The following is a message I received from the mother of a newborn baby, concerning sleep, and my advice to her:

Q: *My eleven-week-old has never slept for more than three hours at a time at night. He has been reluctant to take a bottle but we're persevering with this. Do you have any other tips?*

A: Your son sounds like an amazing sleeper if he's sleeping for chunks of three hours at a time. That's pretty unusual for an eleven-week-old. He's still in the realms of the fourth trimester and adjusting to life outside of the womb. His body clock is still so immature that he barely knows the difference between night and day yet. For this reason your best option right now is waiting, knowing that this is normal for his age and things will change as he gets older. In time, his body will come to realise that he should sleep more at night and less in the day and his sleep will naturally lengthen.

If you are breastfeeding and want to give expressed milk or formula for whatever reason, then you may have more success with a special open-top cup than a bottle. However, if you are trying to give bottles to try to make him sleep longer, it is unlikely to have a positive effect. If you give expressed milk at night you'll be missing out on all of the sleep-inducing chemicals contained in the milk you make at night. If you're giving formula, research has shown that it really doesn't make much of a difference and at your son's age formula-feeding parents don't get more sleep than those who breastfed. Not all baby waking is due to hunger; your son will be waking for your reassurance and physical contact, too.

The partner's role

In the early weeks, a baby's needs are predominantly fulfilled by his or her mother. But this doesn't mean that partners don't have a role to play – because they very much do. The partner's top three responsibilities during this period are as follows:

1. Protecting the space

View yourself as a bouncer, guarding the door to a very special club, turning people away whose presence you feel may not be in the best interests of your new family, who may bring stress or anxiety or who may be too noisy or disruptive. Holding visitors at bay for a few weeks can give you all time to rest and recuperate and get to know each other.

2. Supporting and nurturing the mother

This is particularly the case if the mother is breastfeeding. By being supportive and encouraging, but also empathic, you can greatly enhance the likelihood that breastfeeding will be a success.

Have contact details of local support organisations on hand, getting in touch with them if necessary, and make sure the mother is well fed and watered, encouraging her to rest as much as possible.

3. Bonding without feeding

This is very much linked to the above point. While it can be incredibly hard for partners to watch as a new breastfeeding mother struggles with feeding and think that the struggle could all be fixed with 'just one bottle', this can signal the start of a slippery slope. Just one bottle can make a big difference to your baby's gut flora and can also lead to another and then another, which can adversely affect breastfeeding initiation. Again, the best thing you can do here is to contact a support organisation. Similarly, the old myth of 'giving the baby a bottle to bond' is incorrect. Babies bond with parents in many ways that don't include feeding. This could include taking a bath with your baby each night, taking them for a walk in a carrier to give the mother a chance to nap, massaging them, reading them stories or singing to them.

Using the Seven Cs of gentle parenting during the first three months

How will you implement the Seven Cs of gentle parenting throughout your baby's first three months?

Connection

The first three months are all about getting to know your baby and helping them to transition to life 'earth-side'. Your growing attachment to them, and theirs to you, is one of the best predictors of them becoming confident and independent as they get older. Remember that during pregnancy your baby was held all of the time, they didn't know what it felt like to be 'put down' or to be alone. Your presence and physical contact are what will help to calm them the most during these first months. Skin-to-skin contact is the icing on the cake. Don't forget that carrying your baby in a good sling can aid connection and give you two free hands for those times that you really do need to get things done.

Communication

A baby cries to communicate, and the key in these early months is to interpret their cries in order to better meet their needs. Remember, however, that crying isn't your baby's only form of communication – they have many physical cues that can indicate hunger and tiredness well before their tears escalate. Watching out for and interpreting these early signs can be very empowering.

Control

Control here is all about being baby-led: feeding on demand and allowing your baby to sleep when they are ready and following your baby's cues for hunger and tiredness, rather than enforcing somebody else's routine, can make your early months as a new parent so much more enjoyable and less stressful, as well as setting up good habits for the future.

Containment

In the first three months, containment is all about containing your baby's tears. Stay responsive to them and hold them when they cry, even if you have no idea why they are crying and they don't stop regardless of what you try. One of the best ways to contain a colicky baby's tears, if you have tried everything else, is to look after yourself as much as possible by acknowledging that your main and, indeed, most important job now is to be a parent. Enlist help from your newly formed tribe here. Cleaning the house can wait, as can writing the 'thank-you' notes for any presents you've received and welcoming guests to your home to meet the new arrival.

Champion

You and your partner are your child's only champions. Never feel afraid to say something if, for example, visitors want to hold your baby and you feel that they would prefer not to be passed around. If you are not confident enough to speak up about this, then carrying your baby in a sling is a great way to prevent it.

Confidence

Confidence is perhaps the hardest thing for new parents. You instantly become inundated with unsolicited advice, and what you read in one book will contradict what you read in another, which will, in turn, contradict what you read in a magazine article. Health professionals commonly give conflicting advice too, especially when it comes to establishing feeding. This is a good time to remember the BRAIN acronym (see page 33), particularly the 'instinct' element of it. If something that is recommended to you feels wrong, then don't do it. We have instincts for a reason. Remember also that while you are learning, your baby is too and you will grow together. To your baby you are already the best parents there are.

Consistency

Consistency is a tricky one in the early weeks too, as in many situations you will need to be very flexible in your approach, and what works one day may not work the next, particularly when it comes to settling your baby. What you do need to be consistent with at this stage, however, is sticking with the other six Cs!

Chapter 4

Early Babyhood – Three to Six Months

What we instil in our children will be the foundation upon which they build their future.

Dr Steve Maraboli , author and scientist

Three to six months is a wonderful age: your hard work during the fourth trimester is repaid with cheeky smiles, heart-warming giggles and big belly laughs; your baby is much more aware of the world now and becomes great company; colic and crying dramatically lessen; and, hopefully, you are feeling more confident in your parenting abilities. This is often the stage when parents venture out to baby groups and classes, and when having a baby can begin to feel far more sociable.

Towards the end of this period your baby will start to acquire the physical development necessary for introducing solid food. This is also the time when many mothers begin to think about their return to work, and childcare preparations can be top of the list of preoccupations at this age. This chapter will cover readiness for weaning and selecting gentle-parenting-friendly childcare, as well as looking at age-appropriate ways of entertaining your baby. We will also examine what happens during teething, and how best to help your baby cope, and the changes to your baby's brain and sleeping patterns during this time frame.

Entertaining your growing baby

The baby-entertainment industry is a booming one (an internet search using the term 'baby classes' brings up almost 200,000 results) and parents often feel that attending classes is a must in order not only to entertain their baby, but to encourage their development. In fact, neither is true.

Babies are pre-programmed to be social. Right from the moment of birth they prefer to look at a human face than any other object. So, in reality, you are all that your baby needs to develop amazing social skills. Everything he or she needs to know about social interaction happens naturally in your every-day exchanges. A shared smile, a mutual gaze, an instinctive game of peekaboo, cuddling and caressing and copying each other's facial expressions are the roots of socialisation. This two-way exchange of touch, sound and visual communication is termed 'reciprocal socialisation' and describes the dialogue or 'dance' between parent and child, which increases the adult's socialisation skills just as much as the child's. Research has proven that this time spent with parents, rather than other children, is critical to the development of the baby's socialisa-tion skills and interactions with other children when they are older.[1]

This is not to say that the plethora of baby classes available have no benefits, however, the majority of them are for the parent, rather than the child. Many parents gain hugely from attending different baby groups, which can form part of their new tribe (a valuable support network), as well as giving you some much-needed time to socialise with other adults.

For other parents, however, the idea of baby groups or classes is not an appealing one. And if this is the case for you, rest assured that if you don't attend them, your baby will not be missing out.

Remember, to your baby, everything is new. A trip to the shops in a baby carrier may be mundane for you, but to your baby the world is full of rich sights and sounds that constantly stimulate their senses. As the physician and educator Maria Montessori said: 'Our care of the child should be governed, not by the desire to make him learn things, but by the endeavour always to keep burning within him that light which is called intelligence.'[2] Fostering your baby's natural inquisitiveness doesn't mean teaching them all sorts of new skills; it simply means allowing them to freely explore the world at their own pace.

So, how do you aid your baby's natural inquisitiveness? Parents do this, naturally and unconsciously, every day in the following ways.

Play

Playing with our babies begins even before they are born, when we do things like rubbing a pregnant tummy or gently prodding a protruding limb and feeling the baby respond. Play carries on spontaneously from the moment of birth. Mimicking facial expressions and playing peekaboo are behaviours that we all do without realising. Play teaches our babies so much, including turn-taking, which becomes an important social skill as they grow.

Speech and language

Research shows us that babies begin to acquire language even before they are born.[3] They are wired for speech from the very beginning and the most important factor in their language acquisition is parental interaction. Through normal everyday interactions we teach our babies to speak; we teach them about musicality and rhythm and the art of conversation and turn-taking. We do none of this consciously – it all just happens, and we don't need flash cards, classes or DVD courses to help us. This ordinary interaction with our babies and our use of 'Motherese' – or 'baby talk' – are the foundations for language acquisition. In Motherese we naturally raise the pitch of our voice, lengthen our vowels and exaggerate our consonants, as well as tailoring our language to make it age-appropriate, with short sentences, short words and simple content. Motherese also relies heavily on eye contact, and research has shown that babies have a natural preference for it and that it helps them to acquire language skills.[4]

Everyday objects as playthings

Everyday objects are as fascinating to babies as any expensive 'developmental' toy. In the 1980s the childcare expert Elinor Goldschmied introduced the idea of 'heuristic play'. The term 'heuristic' is taken from the Greek word which means 'to discover' and refers to the child's discovery of the world around them through the exploration of objects from the 'real world'. Goldschmied believed that babies will 'suck, grasp, touch and feel objects, rehearsing behaviours which foster their earliest learning'[5] (See the box on treasure baskets on page 83, which explores this idea further.)

Stimulation from the environment

When a baby is 'in arms', their core, head and neck become strong and they learn about the environment around them, all from the security of human contact. Each time you take your baby out, whether it is a trip into town or a walk in your local park, your baby is exposed to many new sounds, sights and smells. Do ensure though that your baby is allowed to develop and learn at his or her own speed and can 'switch off' the stimulation if they become overwhelmed. In the case of walking outside with your baby in a carrier, facing the baby into your chest allows them to experience the world around them, but to close their eyes and nuzzle into you when it all gets too much.

It is important to understand the difference between the type of environment where babies will be the most naturally inquisitive and learn best (namely, a natural environment in contact with their parent), and one that will overstimulate them with no 'escape' – for example, placing them in a chair in front of a television, with their body held rigidly in a position that their muscles and joints are not yet ready for and where they are unable to turn away from the loud, bright TV set.

TREASURE BASKETS

The most common form of heuristic play is the 'treasure basket'. This need not be a traditional basket – it could be a box or a bag, so long as access is easy for the baby – and it should contain items found in the everyday world and from nature. Often these objects are those that we as adults wouldn't give a second glance, but to a baby they truly are treasures. Treasure baskets are most suited to babies who can sit unaided, although they are also wonderful for babies who sit with support from you, perhaps on your lap.

You can buy ready-made treasure baskets, but there really is no need as it is fun sourcing your own contents – and considerably cheaper. The basket should contain a mix of items that will stimulate your child's senses, so consider their smell, feel and sound. Keep safety in mind at all times, ensuring that any objects included do not present a choking or inhalation hazard for the baby, and that they have no sharp edges that may cause injury. As with all playthings, do not leave your baby unattended while playing with their treasure basket.

Common treasure basket contents include:

- a natural sea sponge
- a pastry brush
- a spatula
- a whisk
- a nail brush
- a paintbrush
- a large feather
- a large shell
- a pine cone
- a bell

- some silky fabric
- some shiny fabric
- some scrunchy fabric
- dried pasta pieces in an empty plastic container taped closed (to be shaken)
- a bunch of keys
- an old empty purse or wallet
- a small lidded box.

Is your baby really teething already?

The average age for cutting the first tooth is around six months, with many babies still remaining toothless until after their first birthday. Some, however, are born with teeth, so there is a wide range of possibilities.

For most babies, constant drooling, putting their hands in their mouth, disrupted sleep and a grouchy demeanour are signs of being three to six months old and not a sign of teething – they are normal developmental behaviours for this age, teeth or no teeth. Between the ages of three and six months, babies begin to produce more salivary amylase (an enzyme contained in the saliva which converts starch to sugars) in preparation for weaning onto solids. They commonly become very dribbly at this age (and many will need to wear a bib of some sort to protect them from dribble rash), but again, this is not a sign of teething. The mouth is also a very sensory place and a three- to six-month-old baby will begin to explore all objects (including their own hands) by putting them straight in their mouth. This doesn't indicate pain or a readiness for solids: by chomping away on whatever is put in their mouth, all they are doing is learning about the object's properties with help from their gums.

Frequent night waking is also very normal at this age, as is whining. Again, these behaviours are due to developmental changes and will pass naturally. Neither is a sign of teething or readiness to wean onto solids.

So what are the real signs of teething?

Research has indicated that the following are true symptoms of teething:

- crying
- fever
- diarrhoea
- itching

- loss of appetite
- runny nose
- rash
- ear rubbing.[6]

Further research has also indicated that many of the symptoms parents attribute to teething, such as night waking and dribbling, are actually not predictive of it either.[7] One of the most concerning issues surrounding the false diagnosis of teething is the overuse of medication by many parents. Research has found that use of paracetamol in infancy increases the child's risk of eczema and asthma in later life.[8] Similarly, many paediatric pain-relieving medicines contain artificial additives that can cause hyperactivity and sleep disruption. The main culprits are E102, E110, E122 and E124. Infant analgesics may be readily available 'off the shelf', but they are still pharmaceuticals and, as such, they carry risks like any other. Infant pain relievers should be used with caution, and only when the potential benefits outweigh the risks. There are many natural and alternative teething remedies on the market, including homoeopathic and herbal ones, and although clinical evidence as to their efficacy is lacking, many parents do find them a great help.

Signs of readiness for introducing solids

At the start of the twenty-first century it was standard practice to wean babies onto solid foods between sixteen and twenty weeks of age. Scientific understanding has come on in leaps and bounds since then and we now know that it is better to wait until the baby is around six months of age and is ready to ingest and digest foods other than milk. Despite this, research suggests that around 40 per cent of babies are weaned onto solids too soon.[9]

During their first three or four months of life, a baby's diet is such that it doesn't require salivary amylase (the enzyme that enables their body to convert starch to sugar in order to convert food to energy). Production of this enzyme begins and slowly increases over their first months, reaching comparable levels with an adult's at around five to six months. It is only at this point that babies can convert the nutrients found in starchy foods (such as cereals, fruit and vegetables) into energy. If babies are weaned onto solids before this, their nutrient absorption will be significantly poorer and can lead to them developing digestive disturbances such as diarrhoea, constipation and stomach cramps. In addition, early weaning has been linked to a higher risk of obesity, coeliac disease, diabetes and eczema.[10]

A common belief is that introducing solids into your baby's diet is guaranteed to improve their sleep. While in some cases this can be true, research has found that introducing solids before the baby has developed sufficiently may cause sleep to worsen.[11]

In addition to digestive readiness, there are certain physical developments required for weaning onto solids, which include the following:

- The baby should be able to stay in a sitting position, with support if necessary, and be able to hold their head steady.

- The baby should be able to coordinate their eyes, hands and mouth, i.e. they should be able to look at food, hold it and put it in their mouths by themselves

- The baby should be able to swallow their food. Babies who are not ready will often push their food back out (the tongue-thrust reflex; most babies should have lost this at six months).

Chapter 5 looks at the different weaning options for when you are ready to introduce solids into your baby's diet.

What's happening to your three-to-six-month-old's brain?

This age period is critical for the development of the senses, in particular vision and hearing. During this time the brain is incredibly busy increasing synaptic density, notably in the auditory cortex, which means making new neural connections, especially in the parts of the brain related to hearing. In addition, the part of the brain responsible for vision shows a great deal of metabolic activity as your baby's sight improves dramatically. Hippocampal volume – the regions of the brain responsible for spatial awareness and memory – also increases at this age which, together with the baby's growing visual capabilities, allows them to recognise people, especially their parents.

The frontal lobe is relatively inactive in comparison (remember, this is the part of the brain where complex thought processes occur, such as hypothetical, rational and analytical thought). So your three-to-six-month-old still has nowhere near the thinking capabilities of an adult, especially when it comes to regulating their own emotions or complex thought, such as the ability to manipulate others' behaviour.

What to expect of a three-to-six-month-old's sleep

Between the ages of three and six months the baby's circadian rhythms really begin to establish, and this means that you can expect them to sleep more at night than they do during the day. Night waking is still very common, however, and the majority of babies – particularly those who are breastfeeding – will still require several night feeds. At this stage, babies will sleep for an average of fourteen hours in a twenty-four-hour period, and will likely have an average of three daytime naps. Their sleep cycle is still much shorter than that of an adult and they may wake every forty-five minutes to an hour as a result. In fact, research suggests that by the end of this time period, only 16 per cent of babies are regularly sleeping through the night.[12]

From a SIDS perspective it is important that you are still co-sleeping with your baby – that is, they should be sharing a room with you until the end of this time period.

The four-month sleep regression

Just when you have emerged from the fog of the fourth trimester and your baby's physiology has developed enough for them to begin to know the difference between night and day, a common sleep regression takes place and they can start to wake hourly, if not more frequently. This can feel like a huge setback, particularly if your baby was beginning to settle into some kind of predictable pattern in their feeding and sleep.

Some parents worry that they have done something to create this 'problem'. But, in reality, this phase is normal and common. Developmentally, much happens between four and five months of age. Babies become much more aware of the world around them, yet their bodies are somewhat behind their brains, leaving them in an almost perpetual state of frustration. In addition, their transformation can be extremely confusing and unsettling for them. It makes sense, therefore, to keep everything else in your baby's life as constant as possible, so as not to introduce any more change into their lives. It might feel as though this stage will last for ever, and that your baby will never sleep again, but it will pass relatively quickly – usually in around four to six weeks. Until then, just offer as much comfort as you can.

Using the Seven Cs of gentle parenting from three to six months

How will you implement the Seven Cs of gentle parenting from three to six months?

Connection

This age is about forming a secure attachment with your baby so that he or she will be confident to go out into the world in time. Remember that at this time your baby does not need external stimulation or classes or groups to socialise; the time spent with you, doing everyday things, is what matters the most. Your baby's brain is developing rapidly, but is still very primitive. He or she is incapable of forming bad habits or manipulating you, so don't be afraid to hug him or her as much as possible: the oxytocin is good for you both – it literally grows brains!

Communication

By now you may be getting more experienced at understanding your baby's different cues and signals. Their body movements or particular cries communicate their needs and help you to understand a little more, hopefully reducing their crying. Remember, though, that crying is still their primary method of communication and sometimes, no matter how hard you try, you still won't understand what they need. And that's OK. The reciprocity between you – that 'dance' of responding to each other – is what will help to build their social skills as they age.

Control

Being baby-led at this age means still feeding on demand – and that includes introducing solids when your baby is ready, not when you are told to by friends, family or professionals. Night feeds are still very important at this age, and responding to your baby's needs at night now can help them to be more independent at night when they are older.

Containment

So much happens for your baby during this period. Their development is so fast and intense that it must feel overwhelming, and along with this often come clingy, whingey behaviour and regressions in sleep. This is not an age to encourage independence, either at night or in the day; it is a time to show understanding and empathy and to be the 'constant' for your baby in an ever-changing world.

Champion

Championing your baby at this age lies largely in defending him or her to others who ask 'Is he good?', or, 'Does she sleep well for you?' After four children I have found that the best response to these questions is to simply tell people what they want to hear: 'Yes, he's very good', or, 'Yes, she sleeps very well'. That way you can avoid much of the unsolicited, unwelcome advice about early weaning or sleep training that would follow if you answered with the truth!

Confidence

I often find that parents start this stage with fairly good confidence levels. The colic and crying of the fourth trimester have gone, their babies are happy and smiling and starting to sleep a little better and they finally feel like they know what they are doing. Then along comes the four- or five-month sleep regression and confidence plummets. Remember, quite simply, that no one is at fault here. This change in behaviour and sleep is normal and to be expected. It is not a result of your parenting and it will pass – as it does, hopefully your confidence will return.

Consistency

This is the age when parents often start to introduce a bedtime routine – perhaps a bath, massage, story and feed in a darkened room – in an effort to improve sleep. Bedtime routines can and do make a big difference to sleep, but it takes time for them to become effective. Introducing a good bedtime routine now will pay dividends over the coming months, just not yet. Keep at it though; consistency is key when it comes to baby sleep.

Older Babyhood – Six to Twelve Months

Accept the children the way we accept trees – with gratitude, because they are a blessing, but do not have expectations or desires. You don't expect trees to change, you love them as they are.

Isabel Allende, author

Your baby is growing so quickly now and turning into a fascinating, funny and entertaining little person. So many enjoyable things happen at this age: introducing your baby to solids, first words, crawling, cruising and sometimes walking, too. It can also be a bittersweet time though, as for many mothers it signifies the end of their maternity leave and a return to work, meaning that they must leave their child in the care of others for a large proportion of the day.

Towards the end of this period many parents are shocked to

find that their baby's sleep regresses again – often, to near-newborn levels, and that their happy, easy baby becomes clingy and miserable unless they are in what feels like permanent physical contact with them. Separation anxiety is a normal and healthy phase of development, but it can be hard to manage, especially if it coincides with the mother's return to work. These are two issues that will be covered in this chapter, along with the introduction of solids into your baby's diet.

Weaning onto solids

At this stage your baby is very likely to be ready to start solid foods. This can be an incredibly fun time as you learn more about your baby's likes and dislikes, but remember that they are just learning about food and it will take time for them to make the transition from a liquid diet to one focused heavily on solid food. The best tip I can give you here is to not rush. Try to enjoy the experience with your baby as much as possible and be led by their pace and interest.

What style of weaning suits you and your baby best?

However you choose to wean your baby, baby-led is always best. Traditional weaning, involving purées, can be very time consuming and expensive, particularly if you invest in special machines to help purée the food, storage pots, vegetable steamers and the like. This type of weaning involves spoon-feeding your baby puréed forms of largely vegetables, fruits and cereals initially, before moving on to more lumpy purées and accompanying finger foods. However, the premise behind it is flawed. The idea that babies are incapable of eating finger foods at the start of weaning stems from the introduction of solids into the baby's diet before they are physiologically ready for them. The foods therefore need to be as liquid as possible in order for the adult to spoon them into the baby's mouth. This style of weaning is, nevertheless, still the most popular today.

The idea of puréed baby food is a relatively novel one. In the past, mothers would have pre-chewed food before passing it, partially digested, on to their baby. While this may not seem appealing, the idea that babies are capable of handling chunks or 'finger food' from the outset holds true today. So the modern 'baby-led weaning' movement, pioneered by Gill Rapley, in many ways is not modern at all, as this is largely how babies would have eaten for most of our existence. The premise of baby-led weaning is that it is the baby themselves who decides when to begin to wean, as well as controlling the food that goes into their mouth.

On average, babies will manage to grasp food, move it into their mouth and chew it at around six months of age. These first few months, however, are all about the exploration of food, the sensations of smell, taste and touch, rather than the ingestion and digestion of it. If you introduce solids into your baby's diet in a purely baby-led way it can take several months, often until they approach their first birthday, for them to actually eat a reasonable amount. For this reason, milk remains the most vital part of their diet.

From a gentle-parenting perspective there is no right or wrong way to wean – the most important consideration is that the weaning is led by the baby, rather than the parent. This means letting your baby decide when it is time to wean, allowing them to lead the pace of the weaning, giving them an opportunity to choose which foods they do and don't eat, accepting their preferences and giving them the choice of how best to ingest the food – from their own hands or a spoon they hold themselves.

Do babies need teeth to eat solids?

Whether your baby has teeth, or not, needn't dictate how they are weaned. Babies do not need teeth to eat solid finger foods; they can grind up, suck and mush food – even meat – very well using just their gums.

What equipment do you need to introduce your baby to solids?

Following baby-led weaning requires far less equipment than you might think. These are the only must-haves in my opinion:

- a high chair or booster seat

- bibs

- muslins or wipes.

If you prefer to follow more traditional purée weaning, you will need:

- something to purée the food with

- pots to store the food in

- baby feeding spoons

- bowls to serve the purée in.

How should you go about weaning?

When the time comes to start introducing solids, you should continue to offer milk feeds as normal. Remember at this point, no matter which method you choose, the food will not be replacing any of your baby's milk feeds, and milk will remain the main source of your baby's nutrition for several more months.

Your baby should be seated upright, with support if necessary, and should never be left alone with food. Pick a time to start when your baby is alert and happy. It may help to do this at a different time of day to their usual milk feeds. If you are offering finger foods, offer chunks that are large enough for your baby to hold easily and not so small that they may choke on them. Remember to be baby-led – ideally, you will always leave your baby to pick the food up by himself. It can be hard to sit back and not interfere, especially if all of the food goes on the floor and nothing makes it into the baby's mouth, but don't be tempted to pick up the food and try to put it in their mouth for them.

You could offer your baby food when you yourself are eating, as family mealtimes can be a good way to encourage them to be a little more adventurous. Try to offer your baby the same food you are eating as a family, providing it is unprocessed, with no added salt and is not considered dangerous for a baby to consume. Continue to offer foods that your baby previously hasn't liked or has not shown any interest in, but don't put pressure on them to try them. The best approach to food is to be neutral. Keep any emotion out of eating in order to foster a good relationship with food.

Lastly, always offer your baby water to drink alongside solid food, but don't be concerned if they do not drink it, especially if they are breastfed.

What if your baby doesn't take to solids?

Some babies can take several months to take to solid food, especially if they are breastfed. It is common for babies to eat very little, or possibly nothing for several weeks, or even months. My youngest child, for example, was not really interested in eating solids until she was ten months old. So again, be baby-led: don't rush or force your baby to eat. Remember that this is all about learning and the experience, rather than the actual food intake, as your baby begins to discover the touch, taste, smell and sight of food, master control of the physical feeding process and get to know their own satiety signals. Even if no food is eaten, your baby has still achieved so much.

Also, your baby may well squidge, mash or throw their food rather than eat it (baby-led weaning is messy; there's no getting away from it), so as well as oodles of patience you will probably also need to be armed with some good long-sleeved bibs and a very large mat for the floor.

Some good first foods

The following make good first foods, prepared and offered to your baby in any of the forms below:

- carrots (puréed or cooked and cut into batons)

- broccoli (puréed or cooked and served as florets)

- banana (mashed or cut into chunks)

- avocado (mashed or cut into chunks)

- pear (puréed or deseeded, peeled and quartered)

- melon (deseeded and served as chunks with skin removed)

- apple (puréed or lightly cooked, deseeded and quartered)

- large cheese cubes

- cooked green beans

- sweet potatoes (mashed or baked and cut into wedges)

- cucumber sticks

- large chunks of meat such as chicken

- cooked pasta shapes

- toast strips

- porridge (made into fingers)

- butternut squash (puréed or cooked and cut into large cubes or strips)

- mango (mashed or cut into strips).

Are there any foods to avoid?

The following should be avoided from a health-and-safety perspective:

- Processed foods: especially with added salt or sugar.

- Honey: this contains a bacterium called *Clostridium botulinum*, the spores of which can grow and develop in a baby's digestive system, and can cause botulism, which can be fatal. As such, it should not be introduced until after your baby's first year.

- Nuts: the jury is still out on this one – peanuts should be avoided until at least six months in case of any allergy, which is more likely if you or your child suffer from hay fever, asthma or eczema, or there is a history of nut allergy in your family (in this case always speak to your child's doctor before introducing nuts into their diet). But allergies aside, nuts can be a choking hazard for babies, so it's generally better to introduce them later when their eating skills are a little more developed.

- Regular cow's milk: this does not contain sufficient nutrients for it to replace breast milk or infant formula until after the first year, so should not be offered as a main drink until your baby is one. The same is true of almond, rice, soya and goat's milk.

- Baby rice: aside from the rather unappealing consistency, colour and lack of taste, baby rice is highly processed and high in sugar and should, ideally, be completely avoided. It has virtually no nutrients and, perhaps most alarmingly, it can contain the poison arsenic. Arsenic is often naturally present in the soil of rice fields, and if flooding occurs, as is common, it can leach into the rice itself. There is currently no legislation regarding acceptable levels of arsenic in foods, although there is for water, but as babies are significantly smaller than adults, the potential amount of arsenic in rice can be much more problematic. Until such time as safe levels and corresponding legislation are established, it may be wiser to avoid baby rice altogether.

How to feed solids 'on the go'

With a little preparation it is easy to feed your baby solids when you are out and about. A banana is possibly the best 'fast food' for when you are away from home, but you could also carry some chopped-up fruit or vegetables. When eating out, if you choose wisely, you can offer your baby food from your own plate, providing it is healthy and safe. For this reason, baby-led weaning is a much easier option for when you are on the go, as there is no concern about packing food to take with you or heating purées.

What if your baby is in day care?

This is a common concern for many parents. If you have chosen to feed your baby in a more baby-led manner, don't be afraid to request that your childcare provider follows your weaning methods, even if it differs from what they normally do. Remember you are paying them for a service, so you are entitled to ask for the service you really want. This is perhaps the best way to advocate for your baby and be their champion when it comes to weaning.

When should you wean from the breast?

The term 'weaning' is confusing here, as technically it means taking something away from your baby. When introducing solids into your baby's diet, however, you are adding something in and not taking away their primary source of nutrients, namely milk. Introducing solids into a baby's diet does not indicate, therefore, that they should be weaned from the breast.

So, when *should* you wean from the breast? The answer here is complex and incredibly simple, and can be summed up in five words: 'when you both want to'. And by 'both', I mean that the decision to wean from the breast will be a mutual one shared by you and your baby. Most babies will self-wean from the breast at some point between two and five years of age. Some wean earlier completely of their own accord, but often babies who wean from the breast earlier than this do so due to the mother being pregnant with another child, a temporary nursing strike, using a dummy, starting day care or parent-instigated weaning. You will know when your baby is ready as they will refuse feeds when they are offered, and no longer ask for them.

Is a child ever too old to be breastfed?

The prevailing belief in our society today is that breastfeeding should stop at around six months of age, which often coincides with the time that a baby cuts their first tooth and starts to eat solid food. After this age many feel that breastfeeding is not necessary from a nutrition perspective. Another commonly held belief is that carrying on with breastfeeding past this point is somehow detrimental to the child, stifling their independence, keeping them a baby or creating the potential for bullying from their peers. Indeed, our tolerance of breastfeeding in modern Western society is exceptionally low, with the media in the UK frequently featuring stories about mothers who have been asked to cover up or leave establishments for fear that they are offending other customers. And given that this distaste is usually directed towards women who are breastfeeding much younger babies, it follows that tolerance of breastfeeding toddlers is sub-zero. In other places, however, such as India, West African countries and the Philippines, it is seen as completely normal to breastfeed to age three and beyond.

I think it is important to understand that many mothers who breastfeed an older baby or child do not tend to set an age at which they intend to stop. Time passes quickly and you don't notice your baby growing, until all of a sudden you realise that they are now two or three or four and the breastfeeding, which is very much a part of everyday life, is ongoing. And breastfeeding is not just about the nutrition; it is a wonderful comfort to a child that they don't outgrow after their first birthday. It's also interesting to note that many 'natural-term breastfeeders' (the term commonly used to refer to parents who breastfeed until their child self-weans) comment on how it sees their children through numerous illnesses and teething easily.

Are there any benefits to breastfeeding an older baby or child?

Breastfeeding past infancy carries significant health benefits for children, as breast milk is a great source of nutrition. Between the ages of one and two just two cups (or 448ml) of breast milk a day provides the child with 29 per cent of their daily energy require-ments, 43 per cent of their daily protein requirements, 36 per cent of their daily calcium requirements, 75 per cent of their daily vitamin A requirements, 94 per cent of their daily vitamin B12 requirements and 60 per cent of their daily vitamin C requirements.[1]

Natural-term breastfeeding also carries benefits for mothers, with the increased length of breastfeeding protecting against varying forms of cancer[2] and osteoporosis[3].

Lastly, far from experiencing psychological problems, such as becoming clingy and dependent, those children who are given continued comfort through long-term breastfeeding tend to grow up secure and confident.[4] They are often more intelligent, too.[5]

When should you wean from bottles?

As with breastfeeding, bottle-fed babies derive a great deal of com-fort from the process of feeding, and parents often struggle to know when to wean their babies from their bottle and to intro-duce cups instead. Many doctors advise removing bottles as soon as possible, with the average age falling somewhere between nine and eighteen months, although according to research conducted in the USA in 2011, a quarter of toddlers still regularly have bot-tles at the age of two, with around 5 per cent still using them at the age of five.[6]

Scientists have found that toddlers who have a bottle at the age of two are more likely to be obese by the time they are six years old.[7] Similarly, prolonged usage of bottles increases the risk of tooth decay and orthodontic problems.[8] With this in mind, the ages of six to twelve months are an ideal time to introduce a cup to your baby, with a view to slowly decreasing their use of bottles and ultimately phasing them out altogether before the child turns two. A good place to start with introducing a cup is during the day when your baby is eating solids, and also for sips of water throughout the day. When they are happily using a cup at these times you can offer their milk in a cup before their day-time naps. Lastly, once your baby is solely using a cup during the day, you can offer their bedtime milk in a cup too. In the interim, stopping them falling asleep on the bottle at night can help to break the bottle-and-sleep association and make the introduction of a cup at night much easier.

Weaning off of a dummy or pacifier

Some parents, particularly those who are formula-feeding, find using dummies, or pacifiers, a real help in the early months. Once the baby is approaching six months, however, I find they can create far more issues than they solve, especially when it comes to sleep. If a baby is reliant on a dummy for sleep, there can be frequent night waking when the dummy falls out. So if your baby is still using a dummy, now would be a good time to wean them off of it.

My preferred method of weaning from a dummy involves, firstly, making sure your baby never has one when they are calm. This means removing it once it has helped to soothe them and they are no longer crying. When they are asleep I like to start with removing the dummy a little sooner every day or so, starting with daytime naps: on the first day of the gentle dummy-weaning process, remove it after your baby has been asleep for ten minutes; a few days later remove it after only five; then progress to two, then one. The next step is to remove the dummy a few seconds after they fall asleep, until you are removing it while they are still drowsy and awake. At this point, try to remove the dummy completely during the day. Then, when you have successfully removed it for daytime naps, follow exactly the same procedure at night. The whole process can take anything from two to six weeks and, done slowly and gently, needn't cause your baby to cry or become upset.

Separation anxiety

You may notice that your baby starts to become more clingy at this stage, crying if you leave the room for only a few seconds or needing to be held by you all the time. This is known as separation anxiety and it is a normal stage of psychological development for babies that usually starts at some point between eight and eighteen months old. Many parents wonder if they have done something wrong and somehow created an unconfident baby when separation anxiety kicks in, but it is, in fact, a healthy sign. Far from suggesting that you have created a needy child, it indicates that you have done a great job raising your baby.

To appreciate why separation anxiety is a good thing we need to start with what your baby thinks and feels at birth. Newborn babies have no idea that they are a separate entity from their parents, and they only begin to understand this at around six months of age, usually peaking between nine and twelve months. The development of separation anxiety shows, therefore, that your baby has formed a secure attachment to you: they realise that you and they are separate beings, but that you are vitally important in terms of helping them to feel safe and protected.

Last century, the psychologists John Bowlby and Mary Ainsworth formulated the idea of Attachment Theory. Their work led us to the understanding that the beginnings of true independence and confidence in children stem from a secure attachment to their parents in infancy or, as Bowlby called it, a 'secure base'. One of the best measures of secure attachment is to observe a baby who is comfortable in the presence of their parent and very upset when their parent leaves. Yet in our culture this is regarded as undesirable and 'clingy' behaviour and many experts and professionals are eager to force independence as soon as possible, in the mistaken belief that it is something that can be taught. But it can't. True independence is not learned through rewards, punishments and forced separation; it stems from a loving, secure relationship with caregivers at a young age. This is what your baby learns during this period of separation anxiety and why it is so important to stay responsive at this time. So, it is absolutely not a time for sleep training, for example, which only teaches the baby that you don't come back when they need you.

Top tips for coping with separation anxiety

- Empathising with your baby's feelings is hugely important. Try to understand that this is a normal phase of development (albeit a scary one) for them to pass through and that they are not trying to manipulate you in any way. If you parent with empathy during separation anxiety, not only will your child be more empathic and confident themselves when they are grown, parenting will be easier and more rewarding for you too.

- Ignore advice from those who tell you that babies need to learn to be alone.

- Consider the timing of the end of your maternity leave, if possible. Many mothers book their return to work at around eight to ten months, but this is perhaps one of the worst times because of separation anxiety. Is it possible to push your return to work back by a month or two? Alternatively, think about settling your baby into childcare well before separation anxiety hits in order that they can form a close attachment with their new caregiver.

- Try to foster your baby's secure attachments with other people. A secure attachment can be with grandparents, aunts, uncles, babysitters, nannies, childminders or nursery key workers, as well as parents. You just need to build these before separation anxiety has started.

- Help your child to feel as close to you as possible by giving them an item of your clothing to hug. You could try a muslin spritzed with your perfume or an old T-shirt that you have worn often. Some parents even record their voices, talking to their little one or singing a lullaby. Only around 60 per cent of babies will take to a comfort object though.

- Try to keep life as constant as possible for your baby around the time of separation anxiety. It may not be the greatest time to go on holiday, for instance.

- Be kind to yourself while your baby is experiencing separation anxiety. This is the real key. You can't do much to speed up this stage, but what you can do is work on the way you respond. And in order to respond with compassion for your baby you need to nurture yourself: sleep when you can; enlist help from people your baby already has a secure attachment with, even if it is just for them to sit cuddling your baby for an hour while you soak in the bath; keep telling yourself that it is a good sign; and repeat the mantra 'This too will pass' often.

The following is an email I received from the mother of a baby experiencing separation anxiety, and my advice to her:

Q: *I'm a single parent with a very active seven-month-old. He had colic and needed to be constantly held to sleep. Now he's still quite clingy. The problem for me is dealing with my emotions. I want to be there for him and give him the attention he needs, but sometimes it only takes for me to turn my back and he cries like he's been abandoned or something! I feel an enormous amount of guilt that essentially I can't be two people and give him attention while looking after him, making his dinner or running his bath, for example. He naps in the day but only on me. He will sleep at night but by then I'm tired too, so there's no opportunity for me to catch up on things while he sleeps. How can I rationalise that guilt?*

A: Seven-month-old babies are meant to be clingy. Your son's clinginess is a sign that you're doing great as a mother. He is doing everything he should be doing and obviously has a very secure attachment with you, which means that he is likely to grow into a confident and independent adult. You are quite right that you cannot give him the attention he needs all of the time though and this is important. The way that your son learns to be independent is by short, well-timed separation from you. So those times when you're in the shower and can't pick him up or cooking his dinner and can't respond immediately are actually the times that help him learn to separate from you. It's important that these times happen naturally and are not enforced by you, however. Although he will cry when this happens, in time these little periods where he doesn't get his needs met instantly will help him to know that it's OK to wait, that you will be there for him, just perhaps not immediately and that actually he's OK without you. This is what psychologists refer to as 'the good-enough mother'. It is the good-enough mother's role to allow her child to be attached when they need it and allow them to detach as they get older and it is through these small, well-timed 'failures' that the child transitions. In fact, if you were a 'perfect mother' and your son never experienced this, you could argue it wouldn't be healthy. Your needs matter too and sometimes your son will have to cry while you meet these basic needs – showering, eating and so on. And that's OK. You are only human and you are only one person. You don't need to do anything more than you are doing already; it's more than enough.

Returning to work and choosing childcare

For many mothers, maternity leave comes to an end at this time, although childcare choices need to be made months in advance, often during pregnancy. The concern with this forward-planning is that it does not allow you to choose with the unique needs of your baby's personality in mind, and means, instead, that most parents have to approach their childcare decision generically.

When planning childcare for your child, it is vital that you take into account the impact of attachment. Too many parents are blinded by modern buildings, new equipment and glowing government inspector reviews, when what matter most are the nurturance, warmth of care, understanding of and respect for children and the attachment between caregivers and child. In some cases this could mean the oldest of buildings, minimal equipment and a relatively low official rating.

It has long been suggested that one-on-one care in a home setting is psychologically more healthy, most closely reflecting, as it does, the child's home environment. On a personal level, my preference would always be for home-based childcare for under-threes. I would not consider putting my own children into a nursery setting until after their third birthday. This is not to say, however, that there are not some incredibly good nurseries and, conversely, some bad nannies, au pairs and childminders, and a good nursery will always be preferable to a poor childminder or nanny.

When it comes to returning to work, there are a number of possibilities to bear in mind.

Is it possible to postpone your return to work until your child is older?

In a utopian world this would be the best choice. There is no doubt that the very best place for a child, in their first three years of life, is at home with their parent (providing of course that the care given by the parent is nurturing). Some parents make great sacrifices to ensure that they can do this with their families. I know several who have downgraded their house, sold their car, curtailed their social life and cancelled all holidays for the foreseeable future in order to spend this critical time raising their child. Of course, this isn't always possible. Some families already live close to the breadline and cannot cut back any more than they already have.

Flexible working or working from home

Many mothers start up their own home-based business in order to stay at home with their children. Others take on paid jobs where they are able to work from home. Another option is to work in shifts if you have a partner and split the childcare between the two of you. This is the option I took with my own family. I couldn't afford to not work so I retrained as an antenatal teacher and complementary therapist in order that I could see clients and run classes two evenings a week after my husband arrived home from work. I also ran workshops on weekends in order to boost my income as much as possible. I started work after my children were in bed during the week and their Saturdays were spent with Dad, while I was out at work. This arrangement worked really well for us, although it was pretty exhausting when the children were very young. When you factor in the cost of childcare I didn't earn much less than I would have taken home had I worked full-time outside of the home.

If you work at home during the day, there might still be times when you will require some childcare, depending on the type of work that you do and the temperament of your child.

Childcare in your own home

Ideally, your child would be cared for in their own home by a relative, but sadly, for most, this is not an option, as families live further and further away from each other and our metaphorical 'villages' are shrinking. Childcare in your own home from a nanny is very expensive – by far the most expensive option there is – but the benefits here are huge. The child is raised in familiar surroundings and receives one-to-one care from someone with whom they will, hopefully, form a strong attachment.

The downsides here, aside from cost, mostly lay in finding the right nanny. It is really important to find one whose childcare beliefs mirror your own, but some can be inflexible in their approach and believe what they have been taught in training to be 'the right way'. Ask them what they understand about attachment theory, how they feel about giving your baby lots of hugs and perhaps carrying them in a sling rather than using a buggy. How do they approach sleep and sleep training and what are their views are on discipline and behaviour? If anything rings warning bells, move straight on to the next candidate, regardless of what college the nanny attended or how wonderful her references are. When you do hire someone, remember that you are paying her wages and don't be afraid to ask her to raise your child exactly the way you would like her to. The other downside here mostly lays in the concern over what happens when the nanny is sick or on holiday, meaning you would need a back-up plan.

Childcare in a relative's home

Being looked after in a relative's home, whether that is with an aunt or uncle or a grandparent, can be a wonderful choice for childcare. It is also possible to pay the relative, and to receive help with costs, if they become a registered childminder. This sort of care requires a very good, strong and open relationship. It is important that the relative in question is flexible in their beliefs in child-raising and open to the way you would like to bring up your child. In turn, you will need to be a little flexible too, especially if you are not paying them. Here, the obvious pro is the love the relative will already have for your child and the attachment that pre-exists your return to work, making for the smoothest transition possible for everyone involved. The downsides largely focus on matching childcare beliefs and what you would do if the relative was sick or on holiday.

Childcare in somebody else's home

This could be the traditional childminder approach or it could also include the idea of a 'nanny share' in another family's home – a good way of reducing the cost of a nanny by sharing her with another family. In both cases, other children will also be present, but the child-carer ratio will be very low. The big pro here is that a comfortable home environment has been shown to be the least stressful for a child to be in; home-based childcare has been found to produce higher levels of emotional wellbeing in the child, with more sensitive caregivers and less noise than care in an out-of-home setting, such as a day-care nursery.[9] The downsides are the availability and reliability of the childminder or nanny and covering illness and holidays.

Childcare in a day–care nursery setting

Perhaps the least desirable option when it comes to a gentle-parenting ethos is that of an 'out-of-home' setting, such as a day-care nursery. As before, this is not to say that all nurseries are 'bad'; there are some wonderful ones with a very forward-thinking ethos and a strong emphasis on attachment and more natural care.

On the positive side, nursery is the only childcare option that doesn't need a back-up plan if staff are sick or on holiday. Of course, you will still need one if your child is sick, however. On the downside, research has found that the more time under-three-year-olds spend in out-of-home day care, the more likely they are to behave 'problematically' by the age of eleven.[10] Further analysis shows an increased cortisol (stress hormone) level in children younger than three who are in day care, which scientists attribute to 'their stressful interactions in a group set-ting'.[11] Another element to bear in mind with busy day-care settings is their need for fairly strict routines when it comes to organising sleep and mealtimes, due to the number of children in their care. Scientists have studied what they believe to be a more stressful eating experience for the child, particularly if they are rewarded or overly encouraged to eat certain things at certain times, which can lead to an unhealthy relationship with food as the child grows.[12]

Researchers have also found that the earlier a child enters centre-based childcare, the slower their pace of social development.[13] They found that those who spent more than thirty hours a week in a nursery setting had the weakest social skills (lowered levels of co-operation, sharing and engagement in classroom tasks) as they got older. They also displayed greater aggression than their peers who remained at home with a parent. Day-care attendance has also been associated with more frequent respiratory-tract infections and allergic symptoms, including asthma, when compared to children looked after in a home setting.[14]

The following points are important if you are considering out-of-home childcare:

- **What is the adult-child ratio?** The lower the better.

- **Do they operate a key-worker scheme?** A key worker is a specific member of staff who is mostly responsible for your child and who you can communicate with, allowing your child the best chance of forming a secure attachment with their carer.

- **Do they have flexible schedules and routines**, particularly when it comes to sleep? Are they happy to carry your child in a sling, for instance, or walk them in a buggy, or are they expected to sleep in a cot or on a mat? Are nap times set or do they follow the child's cues? And, with regard to eating, are they happy to offer different foods based on preferences and weaning style? Is there always access to food if your child is hungry or do they have set mealtimes only?

- **What is their behaviour policy?** Do they implement a time-out, naughty-step or reward scheme? Would they be happy to do something different and more gentle-parenting friendly with your child?

- **How much time do they spend outside, year round?** Do they have access to green space daily?

- **Do they have quiet areas for when your child gets overstimulated?** This is particularly important for sensitive children who might need some 'downtime' away from other children and activities.

- **Do all of the staff seem nurturing?** Are there any who you feel a little uncomfortable with?

- **Are all of the children in the setting happy and content?** Do they all seem calm and engaged?

- **What is your child's reaction to the environment and the staff?** Choose a setting based on your child's happiness and comfort – their reactions can be very telling.

- **What is their settling-in policy?** Do they allow you to make several visits prior to leaving the child for the day, or do they restrict you to only one or two settling-in sessions?

- **Lastly, but perhaps most importantly, what is your gut feeling?** Look past the décor, the building, the equipment, the testimonials and the OFSTED reports. What does your instinct tell you? Is this the right place for your child?

Settling your child into childcare

When the time comes for you to return to work and your baby to start childcare, it is realistic to expect some tears, whether your child's or your own, or, as is often the case, both. While everyone hopes for a smooth, tear-free start, it can be a fairly difficult transition in the early days for both mother and baby. You should realise that these feelings are very real and valid on both sides and acknowledge rather than dismiss them. Only when you have done this is it possible to move on to achieve the ultimate goal of a truly happy child and parent while using childcare.

Don't be afraid to raise any concerns you might have in advance, however small or silly (to you) they may feel. In many cases these small niggles can become big stumbling blocks if not dealt with early on. Be sure to raise concerns that are most pertinent to you and your parenting style – how you would like your baby to get to sleep for naps or the sort of approach you to take to eating. In most cases some forward planning and honest discussion to make sure the child-carer is on exactly the same page as you can resolve your concerns before they become issues.

Use the following tips to help your baby settle into childcare as quickly as possible:

- **Form a bond with your child's caregiver in advance.** Ideally, you will have had at least three or four settling-in sessions where you can stay with your child to allow them a chance to bond with their caregiver in advance of the start date.

- **Use visual cues to help your child.** Babies and young children do not process and store information in the same way that we do as adults. You could take some photographs of your child with their caregiver to discuss with them at home in order to build familiarity, or perhaps make a small scrapbook with pictures of the caregiver and their environment that you can use regularly at home too.

- **Condition the use of a transitional objects, comforter or 'lovey'** to help them feel as if they have a small part of you with them. If your baby already has a comforter, such as a blanket or cuddly toy, this should always stay with them while they are in childcare; otherwise, try to condition one a good month before childcare starts. (You can do this by involving the object in question in hugs, cuddles and feeds with you, placing it between you every time you hold the baby close. This can take a good month to establish and, unfortunately, will only work in about 60 per cent of cases, but can be a great comfort if it does.)

- **Help your baby by having familiar things around them.** This might be a certain piece of music that they listen to at home with you, or go to sleep to; their own cup, plate or bottle from home; a favourite storybook; or a scent that you use, perhaps as perfume or room scent at home.

- **Don't be afraid to look for alternatives.** If your child is not settling into the childcare or you don't feel comfortable once it starts, remember your instinct is there for a reason. Do listen to it.

Brain development at six to twelve months

This is a busy time indeed when it comes to your baby's brain development. Synapses (connections) are forming rapidly now (the more of the world your baby experiences, in a sensory way, the more synapses will form) and if they are reinforced, these connections will become a permanent feature of your child's brain into adulthood. So the environment that your baby experiences now – including the sights, sounds, smells and touch – will play a lasting role in their brain 'architecture', and filling this time with lots of conversation, speech and story reading will aid your baby's communication and language skills.

By the end of this time period, the baby's cerebellum is three times the size it was at birth. The increasing size and connectivity of the brain are reflected in the greatly improved motor skills the baby will demonstrate by the end of this time frame: sitting up, crawling, rolling both ways, pulling up, cruising and sometimes walking.

Between eight and twelve months the baby's frontal lobe begins to become more active. This area of the brain is responsible for more complex thought, which can be indicated in the development of 'object permanence' and separation anxiety in babies of this age. (Object permanence is the understanding that something exists when it is not in sight of the baby – for instance, they grasp that a pet cat exists even when it is in the garden and not in view.) Babies begin to acquire this skill around the beginning of this time period and it will be fairly well established by the end.

Sleep at six to twelve months

At the beginning of this age range, only 16 per cent of babies are reliably 'sleeping through' the night and 13 per cent are still waking at least three times every night.[15] Babies sleep for an average of ten hours at night at this age and between one and three hours during the day. Usually, daytime sleep is split between two naps, although towards the end of this period many babies are transitioning towards just one nap per day. Night feeds are still normal and common.

The following is a message I received from the mother of an eight-month-old baby about sleep, and my response to her:

Q: *My little boy is just over eight months old, exclusively breast-fed and wakes several times a night, where I feed him back to sleep. His daytime naps are awful: he has two naps – max an hour, which is rare, mostly half an hour each. Some days only one nap! I read he should be napping for three hours per day. Would this affect his night sleep? Is there anything I can do?*

A: The information you have read should be taken with a pinch of salt – most of the sleep charts showing you how long a baby should nap for are just educated guesswork from different experts. Nobody had really studied how long the average baby naps for until recently, when researchers found that at your son's age the average for naps was two and a half hours per day. It is important to point out, however, that this is the average, which means there will be babies at his age who don't nap at all, some who are happy with only one hour and some who need three, four or even more. This is the problem with these awful pre-scriptive charts – they overlook individuals and scare parents unnecessarily. If your son is otherwise happy and healthy, I would forget these charts and their recommendations.

Moving your baby to their own room or cot

Some parents consider moving their baby into their own room at this age, while others who are bedsharing think about moving the baby into their own cot. Many, however, continue to share a bed for several more months. There is no right answer here. Some babies appear to be happier at this age in their own sleep environment, where they are not disturbed by the noise and activity from their parents; others still need the close proximity of their parents at night and the best sleep will be gained by keeping them close for many more months.

While six months is the recommended minimum to keep your baby in your bedroom with you in order to reduce SIDS risks, keeping your baby in with you for just a little longer can also help them to cope with separation anxiety, and you may find everybody gets more sleep if your baby is close by while they work their way through this phase. If you do want to move your baby out of your bed or into their own room, I would recommend doing so well before separation anxiety sets in, or waiting until after it has passed. My personal advice is to try not to make the transition out of the family bed or room between eight and eighteen months. Similarly, if you are expecting another baby, make sure you make the move either several months before or after the new baby arrives in order that your first-born does not associate the move with their new sibling.

Lastly, if the mother is returning to work it can often help to ease the transition by keeping the baby close at night. Night-time is an important time to reconnect and the close proximity can help to alleviate any anxiety the baby is experiencing through not being with their mother during the day.

The need for night feeds

It is a common misconception that babies no longer need night feeds once they reach six months of age. It assumes that the baby's nutritional needs are being fully met by their daytime milk intake and that they are eating a good amount of solids. But we know that for babies who are leading their own weaning, the introduction of solid foods is initially slow and more than likely not enough to replace the need for night feeds of milk. It also assumes that six-month-old babies take on board all of the milk that they need during the day, but again this is commonly not true. Six-month-olds are incredibly busy exploring their world and often don't have time to feed. Daytime feeds can begin to reduce dramatically at this age and although professionals may advise you to 'feed them more in the day so they don't need to feed at night', this is often easier said than done. Catching a crawling baby who is more interested in playing than feeding is tricky, and making them feed when they would rather be exploring is nigh on impossible. Feeding in a quiet environment and using a nursing necklace to entertain busy hands (whether you are breast- or formula-feeding) can help, but it is realistic to expect night feeds to continue for a good few months yet. Personally, I feel that they remain an important part of nutrition and comfort throughout the whole of the first year.

Reverse cycling and feeding to reconnect

If a mother has returned to work, it is common for the baby to wake more at night to feed (this is especially true for breastfed babies). This is often referred to as 'reverse cycling' and means that the baby will take on board their daily milk feeds at night.

In addition to the nutrition from night-time milk, it is common for all babies whose mothers are in childcare, whether breast or formula-fed, to want to feed more at night because of the comfort and closeness to their mother that it provides. In many ways embracing this time of reconnection is perhaps the best approach for the next few months. Allowing your baby the time to reconnect with you at night via feeding can help them to grow more secure over the coming months and is likely to decrease their separation anxiety and the incidence of wakefulness at night as they grow into a toddler.

Using the Seven Cs of gentle parenting from six to twelve months

How will you implement the Seven Cs of gentle parenting from six to twelve months?

Connection

Connection is essential when it comes to helping your baby through separation anxiety. This is not an age to encourage independence, rather it is a time to allow them to be dependent on you and to reassure them as much as possible that you will be there when they need you. Simply put, they need to know that Mummy or Daddy is always there for them. Returning to work can add an extra obstacle to navigate here. Ensuring that your child has a secure attachment with their childcarer is key, and understanding that they will need to reconnect at night, which can often lead to more night waking, is crucial too.

Communication

This is such a fun age, with the appearance of first words, story enjoyment and more and more exaggerated non-verbal cues. Try to really spend time understanding your baby's communication, particularly through their body language. The frontal lobe of the brain is hard at work now and the more you talk and read to your baby, the more you will aid their language development.

Control

Perhaps the best way you can let your baby have control at this age is through the process of introducing solids into their diet. Being as baby-led as possible is not only a great deal of fun, it is also the best way for your baby to develop a good relationship with food, one which will last for the rest of their life. Be conscious of their individual likes and dislikes and don't force these to change. Remember that at this age the introduction of solids is far more about the sensory experience than the nutrition. Allowing your baby a little control when it comes to choosing day care is vital, too: perhaps the best way to be guided by what childcare to use is your baby's response to it. If, after you have made your choice, your baby is not happy, allow them to have some control by changing the provider.

Containment

Containment during this period is very closely related to connection. Understand how difficult separation anxiety can be for your baby. As hard as it is for you to take care of your baby through this often whiny and trying phase, just try to imagine what it is like for them to experience such a large amount of emotional trauma all at once. Being there for your baby and helping to comfort them by holding them in your arms whenever possible can be really demanding work for you, but will pay dividends for your baby.

Champion

At this age your baby is still not able to vocalise their own needs, so it is up to you to advocate for them. This is particularly pertinent when it comes to childcare. Is the carer not quite on board with your ethos? If not, speak up, whether you are paying for the care or not. Are you using a nursery where they are not keen on feeding your child in a more baby-led way? Or perhaps they are reluctant to rock your baby to sleep or use a carrier for naps. Again, speak up! If you are not happy with the service you are receiving, you owe it to your baby to say so.

Confidence

Confidence is relevant to parent and baby at this stage. Your baby is beginning to build the foundations of future confidence and independence when they are away from you, but they are not quite there yet. From your point of view, this can be a tricky stage to stay confident in your parenting choices and abilities, particularly if you are using childcare and your previously happy baby appears to be sad and difficult in the care of anybody but you. It can also be hard to stay focused if your baby begins to wake at night almost as much as they did as a newborn. This is an age when parents tend to question themselves and their choices rather harshly. Again, it is important to remember that gentle parenting means being in it for the long haul. It's not about short-term solutions or results. Also, remind yourself that separation anxiety is a good thing, although it may not feel like it. It is a sign that you're doing a great job as a parent.

Consistency

Staying consistent and trusting in your choices is the order of the day during this time frame. A baby-led parenting style takes time to show results. In the short term many parents question their choices, especially when it comes to introducing solids, if their seven-, eight- or nine-month-old is still doing little more than squelching food between their fingers. But keep doing what you are doing. Your little one will get it in time and things will begin to slot together like the pieces of a puzzle. And the same goes for sleep. Stay consistent and have faith in your parenting choices.

Chapter 6

Welcome to Toddlerdom – One to Four Years

The small hopes and plans and pleasures of children should be tenderly respected by grown-up people, and never rudely thwarted or ridiculed.

Louisa May Alcott, novelist

The toddler and preschool years can bring enormous joy and fun, but frustration and stress by the bucketload, too. Your little person is going through a huge change, as they move away from babyhood and complete dependence on you, towards childhood and growing autonomy. At this age the desire to be big and in control, coupled with the need to still be little and reliant on you, provides children with a difficult dichotomy that causes confusion and tension for the whole family.

At the same time, the fact that your child is becoming increasingly verbal can mean that you expect them to behave in ways that are well beyond their years. While it is great to have high expectations of toddlers and preschoolers, it also does them a great disservice. If you take nothing else away from this chapter, please take away the fact that at this age your child's brain is so different from yours that he or she may as well be a different species. Young children do not think like adults and this is reflected in their behaviour: they are not naughty, difficult, stubborn or manipulative; they are just young and still learning and developing.

Tantrums and big feelings

Why do young children tantrum so much? Quite simply because they lack the ability to regulate their emotions in the way that most adults can. If we are disappointed, scared, angry, frustrated, upset, anxious or jealous, we know it is not socially acceptable to react by screaming, throwing something, hitting someone, stamping our feet or throwing ourselves to the ground. And not only are we aware of these rules, we also have the ability to use 'self-talk' – that is, we can talk ourselves through our emotions and come up with more appropriate ways of dealing with them. So if we are scared, we can rationalise what is happening; if we are angry, we can tell ourselves to calm down and take some deep breaths; and if we are jealous (particularly of the time and attention given to others by our loved ones), we can communicate with them and tell them how we are feeling. Now imagine not being able to do any of these things, yet still experiencing those overwhelming feelings.

They also have to deal with huge amounts of frustration, disappointment and perhaps most importantly, a lack of control, every single day. Can you envisage having so little say in your own life that you never get to decide what to wear, what to eat, where to go or what to do? You would have pretty big feelings, wouldn't you? And what about if your wishes were ignored or, even worse, trivialised ('No, darling, don't be silly – you can't have the red cup, the blue cup will do just fine')?

And that isn't the only reason why life is tough for a young child. Think about how many times an average two-year-old hears the word 'no' on a daily basis. Yet they are driven to explore the world and to learn about it through experimenting with everything around them: so when they splash water, play with mud, throw food on the floor, draw on the walls, empty the contents of a bookshelf onto the floor or knock an expensive ornament off of a table, they are not being naughty and there is no malice behind their actions. They are learning. And although this behaviour is deeply annoying, and often embarrassing to us as adults, it is important to understand that it is normal.

This is the life of a young child. And huge, raw emotions build and build until, ultimately, they explode. Enter the tantrum.

Toddlers and preschoolers have no way of dealing with their big feelings other than 'flipping out' when they become overwhelming – much like a pot of hot water that will boil over if left unattended. This is the young child's brain. But it is not your job as a parent to help your child to 'keep a lid on' their feelings; it is important that they are allowed to express these big emotions, albeit in a safe and acceptable way.

The way we treat a child when they are young has a lasting effect on the structure of their brain, forming the architectural plans for their future personality: if we treat them with empathy and compassion, listen to them, honour their feelings and help them to feel validated, accepted and unconditionally loved, then we are setting the foundations for an emotionally intelligent, caring adult. If we do not treat them with compassion, but instead yell at them or ignore them, in essence we are telling them that they must cope with their big emotions alone, that their feelings are unacceptable to us and that we do not care for them enough to help them find a way through. The worry here is that it doesn't make the big feelings and harmful emotions disappear, and can cause the child to internalise them instead. We damage their sense of self-worth and, over time, this can lead to such things as depression, anxiety, self-harm and eating disorders. Alternatively, they may externalise these feelings and become violent.

The following is a message I received from a mother regarding her toddler daughter's behaviour, and my response to her:

Q: *Naughty – should it be used at all to describe my nineteen-month-old's behaviour? I don't like it. I've been trying to stay away from it, but my husband thinks that in some instances it's necessary to teach her. I don't see it as naughty. I see it as testing boundaries – it's things like throwing her plate of food on the floor. He would never call her naughty but how about her behaviour?*

A: I would not call either your daughter or her behaviour naughty. What does naughty mean, anyway? Surely it means that the child is a) doing something deliberately that they know they should not do, b) doing something that they know makes you sad/angry and c) doing something that they know will carry consequences, but not caring and doing it anyway. A nineteen-month-old is not capable of the thought processes behind any of these actions for several more years. At this age she is simply being a toddler. She is discovering the world: throwing her plate on the floor teaches her about gravity, exploring her own capabilities and, yes, learning about boundaries. Importantly, she is also trying to assert some control over her life: were you trying to keep her at the table for longer than she wanted? Were you trying to make her eat something she didn't want, or at a time when she didn't want to eat? We override our toddlers' wishes so much when they are young – we are actually very disrespectful towards them – so what else can she do to try to get some control over the above situations but throw her plate on the floor, or maybe refuse to eat or spit out her food. Trying not to put her in situations where she feels so out of control is very important. It is also important to focus on your daughter and doing what's best for her, which is very often at odds with society's strange and completely unrealistic expectations of young children. This behaviour is absolutely not naughty, it is normal toddler behaviour and calling it naughty is incredibly derogatory and possibly damaging to your daughter.

How to parent gently through a tantrum

Gently parenting a child having a tantrum doesn't mean being permissive by giving in and letting your child get their own way at all times. Nor does it mean that you are teaching them to repeat the behaviour. And it also doesn't mean that the child never cries. Parenting gently through a tantrum means keeping in mind your child's feelings, protecting them and others and, hopefully, using it as a learning experience.

The key is staying calm. Shouting at the child is doing nothing more than reverting to toddler behaviour yourself and will never result in the desired outcome in the long run. Before you respond at all, stop, take a deep breath, let your shoulders drop. Do this a couple of times. Tell yourself, 'My child is having a hard time and not giving me a hard time. As the adult, it is up to me to help them.' Most importantly, ignore anybody and everybody else around you. At this moment in time there are only two people that really matter: you and your child. Once you are calm and focused on your child, move through the following steps (they form an acronym of the word SENSE to help you to remember them):

- **Safety** When your child has a tantrum the most important thing to think about initially is safety – both theirs and that of those around them. Your first step is to make sure that your child is not in any immediate danger and is not likely to hurt anybody around them. Moving to a quiet place together, away from fragile objects, is a wise step.

- **Empathy** After you have dealt with the immediate safety issues, the next thing is to empathise with your child. Can you work out what has triggered the big feelings? How is your child feeling right now? Can you imagine what it would feel like to be in your child's shoes at this moment in time? The main point here is to let your child know that you understand how they feel and that you are on their side.

- **Name** After you have identified the big emotions that your child is feeling, help them to understand their emotions by naming them. In time, this will help your child to progress towards verbally communicating their needs as they develop a little more. Say something like, 'I can see that you are angry that the little boy took your toy from you', 'You are really sad that it is time for us to leave the park and go home', or, 'I can see that you were scared when the girl ran over and grabbed your hand', as appropriate.

- **Support** Your child needs you to help them to externally regulate their emotions. They cannot stop feeling what they are feeling by themselves. The emotion will be internalised and the tantrum will stop, but the big feelings won't go away. Most mainstream parenting methods, such as the naughty step and time out, assume that young children have the brain development necessary for emotional self-regulation and reflection, but science tells us that they do not. At best, these methods work as a form of conditioning and 'learned helplessness' (i.e. the behaviour is eventually extinguished because the child learns that there is no point in crying – all that will happen is that they are left on the step alone, without their needs met). As the adult in the situation, it is your job to help your child to calm down. Think back to the idea of that pot boiling over with nobody available to turn the gas off. Your role here is to turn off the gas and mop up the 'mess' when the water stops boiling. Some children will appreciate a big hug, while others need their space initially and a hug will only make their tantrum worse. Tell your child: 'I can see you are having lots of big feelings. I'm here for you when you need me. Please let me know if you'd like a hug.' And be there to support with listening ears and open arms when your child is ready.

- **Exchange** This point is about offering alternatives that are more tolerable to you and to society as a whole. Offer your child a more agreeable choice, exchanging the unacceptable for the acceptable. You could say, 'I can see that you want to play with water, and we can, but in the sink instead of pouring water on the floor', or, 'We don't hit people, it hurts; but you can hit this special cushion instead' and so on.

Using the SENSE tips won't work instant magic; your child will still have tantrums, and sometimes they may last for a very long time. However, if you are consistently use this approach, it will have a positive effect in the long term. Eventually, with a little practice, you will find tantrums easier to deal with and, in time, they will shorten and become less frequent.

Why young children don't like sharing

One of the top concerns of parents who have children in this age range is teaching them to share. Society in general is very keen that children should share with others, viewing this as a mark of respect and obedience to social rules. Children who don't share are often labelled as naughty or rude. Added to this is a common fear that unless we teach our children to share as early as possible, they will grow up to be selfish, with little regard for others. The irony here, however, is that in our quest to raise children who are happy to share and can appreciate the feelings of others, we often treat them in a way that is anything but empathic. With just a little understanding of the development of empathy and what psychologists call 'Theory of Mind', we can see that what is expected of young children in terms of sharing is quite frankly ridiculous.

Empathy and Theory of Mind

Empathy is being able to recognise and identify with the feelings and emotions that are experienced by another – the ability to 'put yourself in somebody else's shoes', you might say. Empathic individuals are more likely to display sociable, altruistic behaviours and are happy to share.

Empathy is not a skill we are born with. It is something that develops, through a mix of experience and mostly brain development in the first four years of life and beyond. As such, it does not truly begin to emerge until the child is in their third year of life, with maturation to a level comparable to that of an adult not manifesting until the child begins school and beyond. Far from being a problem, therefore, the lack of empathy in one-to-four-year-old children is perfectly normal.

Psychologically speaking, the development of empathy rests on something known as 'Theory of Mind' (or ToM for short), and is cognitive, meaning that it is reliant on the child's brain development and maturation. It begins when a child realises that not everybody thinks and feels the same as them – for example, understanding that their actions can make somebody feel sad, even though they feel happy. Until a child's ToM is sufficiently advanced, it is impossible for them to understand the consequences of their actions and therefore pointless trying to explain to them that what they have done has affected others negatively. In the instance of a child refusing to share a toy, something which many might consider 'naughty' behaviour, it is the child's immature neuropsychology that is to blame. Even if another child is upset and in tears over their refusal to share, they cannot empathise with their feelings or understand the consequences of their actions.

With ToM and the child's immature brain development in mind, it becomes obvious that there is no point in reprimanding the child, least of all with techniques such as time out, naughty steps or calm-down corners. Similarly, giving stickers to toddlers who *have* 'shared well' is pointless, as the toddler does not have the brain capacity and cognitive abilities necessary to theorise on their actions, hypothesise about future actions or understand how what they have done has affected others.

UNDERSTANDING THE VIEWS OF OTHERS

Last century the Swiss developmental psychologist and philosopher Jean Piaget introduced us to the concept of egocentrism, which describes the child's inability to understand the thoughts and feelings of other people. It is important to distinguish this from being egotistical, which is an undesirable adult personality trait. Egocentrism is a developmentally normal psychological stage that all children pass through. Piaget believed that all children under the age of seven are severely egocentric, and it is only between the ages of seven and twelve that they slowly move away from a position of egocentrism to one of sociocentrism, i.e. considering the feelings of others).

In the late 1970s, psychologists Premack and Woodruff developed Piaget's idea of egocentrism further, into the idea of ToM. Several famous experiments followed the work of Premack and Woodruff, including the 'Sally Ann' test, which focused on the theory of 'false belief' as a way of testing for ToM.[1] The Sally Ann experiment involved introducing children to two dolls: Sally and Ann. They were shown Sally 'leaving' the room and, while she was away, Ann removing a marble from Sally's handbag and hiding it in her own box. Sally then returned and the children were asked: 'Sally wants her marble, where will she look for it?' The correct answer – the one that an adult would give, showing an understanding of Sally's beliefs – is obviously 'in her handbag' (as Sally doesn't know that Ann has moved the marble). Eighty-five per cent of children under four, however, will answer this question with what the researchers term as 'false belief', saying that Sally will look for the marble in Ann's box. This simple experiment shows clearly that young children cannot think 'in another person's shoes', due to their undeveloped ToM, or empathy (although further research has shown that the age at which a child develops ToM varies greatly from child to child).[2]

Crucial changes in ToM happen at around four years of age, when children begin to be able to interpret more accurately the beliefs and views of other people. It is only at this stage that we can expect their behaviour to be more empathic and sociable. Therefore we should not expect a child to be able to share until they have reached school age, and readjusting expectations of children under this age is really important.

Mind-mindedness parenting

Perhaps the best way to ensure that a child grows up to have a well-developed ToM, and thus a good sense of empathy, is to be more empathic and respectful towards them. Simply put, we should act towards our children the way we want them to act towards others. This means we need to take time to understand how they feel and the limitations of their brain development and base our parenting and handling of situations on this understanding.

The concept of mind-mindedness illustrates this idea well. Mind-mindedness describes a parent's ability to be empathic towards their child and to understand, and accept, that they have important feelings of their own. Research has shown that mothers who are more mind-minded raise children with a better established ToM and a greater level of empathy.[3] This is an important consideration when reflecting on the mainstream practice of punishing a child for not sharing. Any punishment of a child displays a lack of empathy from the adult and often no understanding of normal child development. The mainstream way of encouraging a young child to share, therefore, can actually inhibit the development of the very processes needed for this behaviour to emerge naturally. The more we punish our children for not being empathic the more counterproductive our efforts are.

The problem with punishing or ignoring bad behaviour

'Time out' and the 'naughty step' are popular modern parenting methods, recommended by everyone from TV parenting experts to health professionals. The idea is simple: if your child is doing something you don't like, then ignoring the reasons behind the behaviour and punishing the child by removing them to a step or corner for a few minutes will ultimately extinguish the behaviour. These techniques presume that children only 'act up' to get our attention, so if we ignore the behaviour, they will stop acting that way. They also presume that punishment makes children consider their wrongdoings and resolve to be 'better' next time. Both of these presumptions are incorrect.

In most cases, young children behave in a certain way simply because they cannot stop themselves from doing so. Children experiencing big emotions are in great need of our attention. A child whose behaviour is regressing is most likely crying out for more time and attention from their parent. But the type of attention they need is positive in nature: one-to-one time and hugs, conversation and recognition. They need somebody to listen to them, to help them to calm their big feelings and to make them feel safe and secure. The 'attention' they get from 'time out' or sitting on a 'naughty step' is anything but that. All it does is teach them to internalise their emotions and, in time, to stop communicating their fears, worries and concerns to us. They need 'time in' not time out.

On a similar note, the assumption that punishing a child by withdrawing your attention or by removing them from something they enjoy will result in them thinking about what they have done wrong (and resolving to change their behaviour in the future) is also incorrect. Under the age of three or four years the neocortex (the sophisticated frontal section of the brain) is exceptionally immature. This segment of the brain is responsible for critical, analytical and hypothetical thought. It is not biologically possible for a young child to calm themselves down and really 'think about' what they have done. They don't consider the implications of their actions or motivate themselves to 'do better' next time because they can't. So, punishment involving the withdrawal of the child from an activity or the presence of their parents may cause a change, in time, but this is because the child has been conditioned to not let the parent know how they are feeling. This might seem like a good thing, at least for the parents, who now have a quieter, more compliant child, but for the child it is potentially highly damaging. It can lead to them either internalising their emotions or externalising them later, both of which can be very harmful.

One of the best ways to ensure a close and open relationship with your child as they grow is to listen to them and show them empathy and respect in their early years. You don't have a 'naughty child' – you have a child who is unable to control their impulses (because of their immature brain structure), who cannot calm themselves and who has not yet grasped the idea of empathy.

The problem with rewarding good behaviour

While many people understand why punishing bad behaviour can be counterproductive, it is sometimes harder to appreciate why rewarding good behaviour can also be damaging.

On the surface, rewards such as stickers and treats seem innocuous enough. The child is happy because they get a sticker, a sweet or a fun day out and the parents are happy because they get to restore peace to their household. Reward charts and the like may well be preferable to yelling or smacking a child, but they are far from ideal. Not only do they lack any convincing evidence of efficacy, they can also cause more problematic behaviour in the future. For most parents, the idea that their well-meant sticker chart can create problems in the tween and teen years is tough to swallow.

Several psychologists, including Warneken and Tomasello, have studied the effects of rewarding children for a desired behaviour and concluded that a child's motivation to repeat a task is actually lowered if they received a reward for the task initially.[4] This means that if you constantly reward your child for something, you are effectively reducing the chances of them repeating that behaviour, unless they are coerced with more rewards. The use of sticker charts stems from techniques of behaviour modification that have been popular for over half a century – the same concept that forms the basis for modern-day dog training. But while there is no denying that rewards may be helpful in training a new puppy, they are arguably inappropriate for training children.

Rewards can produce remarkably quick results and can seem, therefore, like a good solution for a multitude of behaviour problems. This is why they are so popular with the parenting experts on TV, who need to show quick and impressive results in order to draw in an audience. What you don't see on these shows, however, is what happens six months later when the cameras have long since stopped rolling and the behaviour of the child has likely regressed to worse than it ever was. If something seems quick and easy, the chances are it is superficial, ineffective in the long term and not without risk.

Rewards work by increasing the extrinsic (external) motivation of children. Researchers have shown that if you remove the offered reward, then children are even less likely to respond in the way that you want them to, than they would have been before the reward was used.[5] If you want to create a real behaviour change in your child, then this behaviour needs to be *intrinsically* motivated. Long-term positive change only happens when the child is internally motivated to behave in a certain way. Simply put: you want them to do something purely because they want to do it.

So rewards do not teach children 'right from wrong' – they merely result in compliance. And what starts off as a sticker or a lollipop at this age can quickly progress to increasing amounts of money and expensive treats as your child gets older and demands a higher price for their compliance. The alternative, once again, focuses on connection and respect. You need your child to want to do something because they want to help you and because they respect you; because they feel good being helpful and because they know that you would do similar for them. If you constantly yell at or punish your child, they are unlikely to be intrinsically motivated to behave well. Why should they treat you with respect if you don't respect them? But if you are compassionate towards your child, listening to and responding to their needs, they will be more likely to want to behave in the way that makes you feel good – because it makes them feel good, too.

To praise or not to praise?

Praise is a confusing issue. While it seems innocent enough, it can be more damaging than punishing or rewarding for a certain behaviour.

How many times have you said, 'Well done', 'Good boy' or 'Good girl' to your child? Have you ever said it while not being fully present or focusing solely on them? A good way to imagine how this feels for a child is to think in terms of an annual appraisal at work. In the run-up to this you have been working as hard as you can on a project, giving it your all. You have sacrificed personal time and have put in over and above your contracted hours. You are really proud of the results that you have achieved and even prouder that you stuck it out and didn't give up when the going was tough and you questioned your abilities. Now imagine that your boss simply nods and says, 'Well done, good girl', while looking at a computer screen. How would you feel? Valued? Respected? Noticed? Next, imagine the same appraisal, only this time your boss says, 'I must admit I was really proud of all of the work you put into that project. Your extra time and effort didn't go unnoticed: I saw that you took work home with you and that you came in early. I also noticed that you stuck it out when things got tough.' How would that make you feel?

So what does it mean to a child when we say, 'Good boy'? Do they know what 'good' means? Do they know what they did to make you happy? And what about when we say, 'Well done'? Well done for what? What if they haven't actually achieved something, but have persevered for hours, 'failing' each time at the task in hand, be that tying a shoelace, putting a shape in a shape sorter or building a tower of blocks. Is their effort not worth anything? Most praise from parents is incredibly shallow and superficial. It focuses on outcome and not effort, and doesn't tell the child anything about what they have done, what they should do or how they have made others feel.

Praise needs to be specific. Instead of 'Well done', say, 'I noticed that you've been building that tower for ages; it took you a long time to finally be able to make the blocks stay up, didn't it?' Praise needs to show your child that you're interested in what they do, so instead of saying, 'That's a lovely picture, darling', say 'Tell me about the picture you've just painted; what made you paint the cat orange?' And praise needs to be effort- not outcome-focused: 'Tying shoelaces is difficult, isn't it – but you're working so hard to learn how to do it, and you'll get there in time', rather than, 'Well done, you did it', once the outcome has been achieved.

Three things in particular that you should not praise a child for are their appearance, characteristics that they cannot change and their eating. Here's why:

- Praising a child for their appearance raises issues with body image at a very young age. If they feel their worth is based only on their looks, this has the potential to affect them negatively as they grow, making them believe that they must remain thin or beautiful in order to be loved by others.

- Praising a child for something they cannot change, such as their intelligence or sporting talent can actually undermine their self-esteem. Praising them for something they have control over and, importantly, can change, on the other hand, gives them motivation to do better and be better.

- Praising a child for their eating habits, particularly 'good' eating can lead them to develop a very unhealthy relationship with food as they grow, causing them to feel good only when they eat lots of food or override their own likes and preferences and satiety cues.

Think, too, about the amount you praise your child. What might happen if you overpraise them? Research has shown that praising can inhibit the child's intrinsic motivation.[6] Ultimately, you want them to do things because they want to, but if you constantly praise their actions, you run the risk of them only doing things to please you and earn your praise. In a sense, responding to praise is a form of compliance, in much the same way as peer pressure. Older children often do things in order to fit in with their peers and gain their approval. And younger children can fall into this trap and be more likely to bow to peer pressure if they grow up needing constant praise and assurance for everything they do.

Is distraction a good idea?

Many parents choose distraction as a good method of coping with difficult behaviour. If you can distract your child with something, then the tantrum often lessens, or can perhaps be avoided in the first place. But is distraction respectful and empathic towards the child? Imagine yourself in the following scenario. You are in a park with your friend, having a picnic. You have just had a big argument with your partner and are feeling really angry. You've tried to 'hold it together' all morning, but now you just can't push the thoughts to the back of your mind any more. All of a sudden you scream, 'Arghh', and start crying. Your friend grabs a cake and says, 'Look, look it's a cupcake and it's got pink icing. You love pink icing, it's your favourite. Eat the cake!' They make no mention of your little public display of anger, or your tears. How would that make you feel? Would it make you feel validated? Would you know that your feelings matter to your friend? Would you feel as if he or she was on your side? Would it help you to deal with your emotions? I'm not so sure. In many cases, distraction as a means of behaviour control is incredibly disrespectful to the child. In a sense, it tells them, 'I can't cope with your feelings right now, so let's pretend you aren't having them.'

But is distraction always bad? Not necessarily – it depends on what is causing the behaviour and how your child is feeling. If they are at a playgroup and want to play with the red car, but another child beats them to it, then saying, 'Look, honey, this blue car looks good, let's play with that', is OK, so long as you also recognise and respond to any feelings of anger and disappointment they may display.

Gentle discipline

What does gentle parenting look like when it comes to dealing with the challenging behaviour of young children?

- The first place to start is always to understand what normal child behaviour is. The chances are that your child is behaving perfectly normally for their age and knowing that this is the case makes it a lot easier to deal with. Keep reminding yourself that your child is going through a tricky stage and that their behaviour is their way of expressing their big emotions. They are not trying to manipulate, punish or wind you up.

- Next up comes empathy. Try to see things from your child's point of view. How might they be feeling? How were they feeling before the tantrum? During? After?

- Be aware of the triggers for your child's behaviour, so that you can try to avoid situations that initiate it.

- A tantrum is scary for your child, so instead of ignoring them during a tantrum, try to comfort them.

- Try to communicate at your child's level: bend down, so you are at eye level with them and use simple words and short sentences. Don't forget a hug is communication, too – you are saying, 'It's OK, I'm here for you, I love you.' But if they don't want to hug you, don't be offended or worried – just be there for them when they are ready.

- Describe the behaviour you want from your child, instead of what you don't want. Say, 'We use gentle hands', rather than, 'Don't hit people'. As we've seen, your toddler's brain processing works differently from yours, and if you keep repeating 'Don't do this' (naming the undesirable behaviour), you may as well be telling your child to do it. Similarly, 'Don't hit people' doesn't tell your child what you want them to do instead.

- Remember your child's need for autonomy versus their need to be dependent on you, and the daily struggle they face with this. Giving them a little more control over their life can hugely improve their behaviour. Sandwiches being cut into squares instead of the triangles they wanted may seem a ridiculous thing to you to get upset about, but to your child at that moment in time it is the most important thing in their world, so try not to trivialise their feelings.

- Naming emotions: if your child tantrums when another child takes a toy from them, try to help them recognise their emotions by giving names to them. For instance: 'I can see you are angry', or, 'That really made you sad when he took your toy, didn't it?' Helping them to do this will, in time, allow them to understand what they are feeling, and later, when they are more vocal, they will be able to express this to you. It also helps to validate their emotions: it's OK to be sad, mad or angry.

- Modelling the behaviour you want from your child is the best way to teach them to express their feelings in a more socially acceptable way. If you want them to be calm and respectful, you should act that way with them: being shouty and bossy will very quickly make them shouty and bossy! This is a particularly tough point to remember when your child is mid-tantrum and you feel your anger levels and the volume of your voice rising. In many ways, parenting is all about bettering ourselves and nurturing our own new behaviours. We must learn to extinguish those parts of ourselves that are not such positive personality traits. This is often what makes parenting so hard, as you begin to realise flaws in yourself that you never knew existed.

- When you are helping your child to manage their behaviour and feelings, you should never care what other people think. Don't be tempted to chastise or punish your child when they misbehave in public just because a disapproving old lady is tutting at you. Her opinion is not relevant. Part of becoming a parent is learning to develop a thick skin when it comes to the opinions of others.

The following is a message I received from the mother of a toddler, concerning her daughter's public tantrums, and my response:

Q: *My two-year-old has suddenly started having huge tantrums when we're out in public. Most of them are unprovoked outbursts. During the outburst I am unable to comfort her as she attacks me. It is very upsetting for us both. I'm sure this is normal, but I'm at a loss as to what to do. She is also quite an introvert and shies away from others, even though we are very well socialised.*

A: I wonder if this is being triggered by being out in public and around others. If she is introverted, she could feel over-whelmed by the people/sights/sounds and feel anxious because of this. Similarly, she could feel uncomfortable with her personal space being invaded. It's hard when you are an extrovert parent with an introverted child, but sometimes stay-ing home a little more is what helps the most. If you are extroverted, understand that she *needs* to 'shy away' from people, and this is not something you can change, but should accept.

Biting, pushing, shoving, hitting and throwing

Show me a young child who never bites, pushes, shoves, hits or throws and I'll show you a pig that flies. These behaviours are just part of the territory that comes with being little. They don't mean that the child is 'naughty' or 'bad' and, in most cases, are not a reflection of 'bad parenting' either. For the majority of chil-dren, such behaviour is simply down to biology, and usually due to one or more of the following:

- Frustration (that they can't have something or do something, or perhaps because they are being made to do something they don't want to do)

- Feeling unhappy, sad or insecure (perhaps after the arrival of a new sibling, a house move or starting preschool)

- Brain immaturity causing a lack of impulse control, the inability to regulate their big emotions or to understand the consequences of their behaviour and an absence of developed empathy

- Inability to cope with an invasion of their personal space

- Insufficient exercise, physical or messy play

- Tiredness or overstimulation

- A need for adult attention and connection

- Simple enjoyment of the physical sensations – this is particularly true of biting

- Overly strict, authoritarian and controlling parenting

- Modelling the behaviour of their parent or that of another adult or child close to them.

The easiest way to deal with hitting, biting, shoving and throwing is to look for the cause of the behaviour and, once you've identified triggers, to try to avoid these as much as possible. Importantly, consider any emotional cues. By reconnecting with your child and spending more time playing, roughhousing and enjoying fun 'special time', these unwanted behaviours usually lessen dramatically. Giving your child more control over their daily activities, choices and self-care also helps hugely.

Come up with a strategy to help 'in the moment'. The first step, and indeed the key here, is you: your reactions and your behaviour when your child is behaving violently are perhaps the most important predictors of whether you will be able to extinguish the behaviour. Remember, you are modelling to your child the behaviour you want to see from them, which means you need to be calm, kind and respectful at all times. If you yell, spank, put the child in time out or on the naughty step, you run the risk of perpetuating this cycle of behaviour for years to come. The idea is to put a big space between your child's action and your reaction.

Once you have taken time to calm yourself, it is time to respond to your child with your full attention. Put the phone down, abandon your conversation or shopping temporarily and focus on your child and nothing else. At this point, you also need to keep them, yourself and anybody else in the situation safe, by moving away from roads and dangerous objects. Next, calmly and simply tell your child what they have done wrong and why. You could say, 'Gentle hands – your hands weren't gentle and now little Johnny's crying', or, 'Owww, be gentle, please', or, 'Stop – cars stay on the floor, so we don't break something.' Next, help your child to understand and name their feelings: 'I can see you didn't like it when he hugged you and it's OK to be angry, but you mustn't hit people'; 'Did it feel good to bite me? Are your teeth hurting?'; or, 'Are you bored with being in here?' After this, help your child to find an alternative, more acceptable solution. You could say: 'You can come and hit this cushion if you want to?'; 'How about I give you an apple to bite into?'; or, 'Shall we go in the garden so you can throw your ball around?'

It is important to realise, however, that responding gently won't elicit a magic response or prevent your child from acting in the same way the very next day. Until their brain matures you can expect lots more similar behaviour, but, with consistent responses (and I cannot emphasise how important that consistency is), your child will learn and, in time, the behaviour will cease. This could take weeks, months or even years. There are really only three things that eliminate these totally normal behaviours for once and for all: time, patience and understanding. And the last two you'll need by the bucketload.

Boundaries and limits

Many people consider gentle parenting as 'too child-centric'. Gentle parents can often be accused of 'mollycoddling' their children or of being 'too scared to discipline in case they make their child cry'. What the dissenters are demonstrating, however, is a misunderstanding of infant psychology and the parenting philosophy they are attacking. Having said that though, compassionate, respectful parenting that is mindful of the normal development of the child brain does demand discipline. Setting boundaries and limits for our children helps them to feel secure and to provide them with a safe environment in which to explore the world. Knowing what is expected of them helps them to form ideas of what sort of behaviour is appropriate in society and what isn't. If we didn't set boundaries and limits, we would actually be showing a lack of regard for their development, but the point here is that this discipline should be age-appropriate and respectful.

Sometimes, often in fact, reinforcing boundaries will cause your child to be upset. But those who parent with compassion and respect are not afraid of making their child cry through their attempts at reinforcing limits. Gentle parents are strong enough to sit with the resulting strong emotions that will surface in the child as a result of enforcing the boundary.

Those who parent with compassion also know how important it is to say 'No' or 'Stop', but they do consider why they are saying it and whether it's really necessary. And those who parent with compassion and respect understand the need for discipline and limits as much as they respect and value the need for attachment and love, because a child really does need both in order to thrive.

Why you shouldn't be afraid to make your child cry

It is absolutely possible to allow your child to cry and still show respect, empathy and understanding. Causing your child to cry is a normal, and indeed necessary, part of parenting. The key is in how you respond when they do cry.

Imagine feeling very upset. Now imagine that whatever is causing these feelings is so great that you just cannot stop crying and you are sobbing uncontrollably – big, heaving sobs that wrench your whole body and shake you to your core – and you are unable to stop your tears or soothe yourself. Now, pick one of the following two scenarios:

- **Scenario One**: your partner or friend sees you crying and asks if you are OK. You are too upset to respond. He or she then says, 'It's OK, you're OK, you're going to be fine', puts an arm around you, gives you a big hug and then walks out of the room closing the door. Or perhaps he or she doesn't leave the room, but goes to sit on a chair nearby, not touching, talking or looking at you. Would this help you or would you continue to feel sad, isolated or alone?

- **Scenario Two**: your partner or friend sees you crying and asks if you are OK. You are too upset to respond. He or she then asks if you would like a hug. You nod. Imagine feeling their arms embracing you and your sense of relief as you melt into them. They say, 'I'm right here for you; I'm not going anywhere'. Their arms tell you that they care enough and are strong enough to remain present through your tears. They don't belittle you by telling you it's OK. You continue to cry – the emotions are so big and all-consuming that you can't stop – but knowing that somebody who cares for you is strong enough to contain your tears makes you feel loved, and the knowledge that you are not alone helps immeasurably.

Scenario Two is what happens when your child is crying, perhaps because of you, and you respond gently. Gentle parents make their children cry often, but it is your response that matters.

When the tears don't stop

As a parent, remember that your aim should not always be to stop your child's crying. You should aim to be present and empathic during your child's tears and to act as an external regulator at a time when your child is too immature to regulate their own emotions. Your worth as a parent should not be measured by a superhuman ability to always stop their crying. Your role is to be big enough, mature enough and calm enough yourself to contain your child's tears and still remain present to comfort them when they do eventually stop.

When we can't meet our child's needs (or don't understand them)

There are many reasons why we don't meet our children's needs. With young children this is often because we simply don't understand why they are upset. Sometimes the child themselves doesn't know why. This little 'failure' on our part each day is actually an important part of their development and, ultimately, what will lead them to separating from us when the time comes.

Being 'good enough' really is enough. If your child cries and you have no idea why, you simply do everything possible to soothe them and to try to understand their needs, and not take it personally if they don't stop crying. In fact, in my opinion, it's more than 'good enough' to sit with a crying child. It takes strength and patience to remain present at these times. As a parent, you should never be afraid of your child's tears. So long as you remain empathic, understanding of their needs and responsive, it's OK for them to cry.

When children lie and when we lie to children

For many parents, knowing how to deal with their child when they lie is a top concern. But before you consider how to respond when this happens, you have to look at why they lie in the first place. Certainly, at this age the top reason children lie is to please their parents. When you ask your child, 'Did put your toys away?' or, 'Did you put your shoes on?', they know that the answer that will please you is: 'Yes'. Likewise, when you ask, 'Did you draw on the wall?' or, 'Did you empty the breakfast cereal onto the floor?', they know that answering 'Yes' is likely to upset you or make you angry. They don't want to make you angry or sad, so instead they answer 'No'. From this perspective, it is clear that our response is crucial if we want to encourage our children to tell the truth.

Without realising, we encourage our young children to lie almost every day. Picture this scenario: you are at the park and your child pushes another child off of the piece of play equipment that they want to use. Would you tell your child to say 'Sorry' to the other child? Most parents would. Teaching our children to say 'Sorry' instils in them good manners, surely? What if they are not sorry though? What are we teaching them to do then? We know that young children do not have a sufficiently developed sense of empathy to truly appreciate how another person feels, nor do they have a sufficiently developed neocortex to be able to understand the consequences of their actions. Both are needed in order for the child to be truly sorry for pushing the other child. So, they are not sorry – they cannot be – and when we make them say 'Sorry' we are doing nothing more than teaching them to lie.

Are there any times when we, as parents, lie to our children? Often, on a daily basis. We say 'Just a minute', when we really mean five, ten or more. We tell them we are watching them, when really we may be on the phone. We say 'Maybe tomorrow' when we often have no intention of doing what has been asked of us. And what about Father Christmas, the Easter Bunny and the Tooth Fairy? These are all lies, albeit ones that have our children's feelings at heart. But if we want our children to be honest, it is important, firstly, that we stop lying to them and, secondly, that we don't encourage them to lie. For this reason, many gentle parents choose to not lie about Father Christmas, the Easter Bunny and the Tooth Fairy to their children.

Once again the concept of connection is crucial here. If we want our children to tell the truth, they have to be able to trust us enough to know that, whatever the truth, we won't love them any less or act in a way that suggests this.

Encouraging body autonomy

This may seem a very young age to foster your child's body autonomy – that is control over their own body – but it is never too soon to start. As parents we want to make sure that our children do not let anybody touch them if they don't want to be touched, wherever that touch may be. We want them to grow up feeling able to say 'No' if anybody does something to them that they don't like. How you behave with your child at this age is key to how they feel about their body when they are in their teens.

Many parents undermine their child's body autonomy at this age without even realising it. As a child, were you ever made to 'give Granny a kiss' or 'give Granddad a hug' when you really didn't want to? I certainly was. But what are we teaching a child in this scenario about their bodies and their consent? Do we teach them that their consent matters? As embarrassing as it may be when your child refuses to kiss Great Aunt Ethel goodbye, it is important to your child's sense of body autonomy that you allow them to decide who they make bodily contact with.

On a related note, many parents struggle with knowing what to call their child's 'private parts', often settling on cutesy pet names. From the perspective of body autonomy and consent, it is very important that your child knows the anatomically correct names for these parts as early as possible. This is important for two reasons: firstly, if anything should happen, they need to be able to vocalise exactly which part of their body was touched without any confusion over pet names; and, secondly, calling a body part the correct anatomical name removes any potential embarrassment or shame in the future for the child. So young boys should know the terms penis and testicles and little girls should know the terms vulva and vagina (and the difference between the two – the vulva being the external genitalia and vagina being the internal), and they shouldn't ever feel embarrassed to use them. Neither should they be afraid to touch themselves. Telling a child 'Don't touch, it's dirty' can cause them to develop a very uncomfortable relationship with their own body as they grow up. There is nothing sexual or inappropriate about a young child touching themselves. It feels good – there is nothing more to it – and they do it often. They just need to be gently encouraged to do it when they are alone at home and not in the middle of the supermarket!

The importance of play

Play can be wonderful for helping your child to feel in control of their world. It is also an effective way for them to release big emotions.

Try never to direct your child's play, as frustrating as it is when they are painting a tree pink or when they put the puzzle piece in the wrong way round for the twentieth time. It is important that they do things themselves, their way. Try to spend as much quality time with your child as possible, playing together. Ideally, you should allow your child to lead the play as much as possible. Roughhousing or just generally 'horsing around' is also a great way to reconnect. Very often a child's unwanted behaviour is their way of expressing that you aren't giving them enough attention, particularly if a new sibling has arrived recently, you have just returned to work or they have not long ago started pre-school or nursery.

The problem with toys

Many parents despair of their child's inability to play alone for any length of time, or the speed at which they get bored with toys. The biggest problem with most toys today is that their play appeal is limited. A shape sorter is just a shape sorter: put the shapes into the holes and the toy no longer offers interest. An entertainment centre loses appeal after the buttons have been pushed, the beads moved along and the xylophone chimed. Most toys have a specific purpose that doesn't allow the child to explore. When the child bores of the set purpose, the toy no longer holds appeal for them.

As children grow up, the overprovision of toys can stifle their imaginations. The overwhelming choice of playthings offered to most children today is perhaps one of the worst curses of modern childhood. I often hear parents mutter, 'You should be grateful you have so many toys. In my day, I didn't have half the amount you have.' But these parents are the lucky ones: their childhoods were likely filled with the amazing games of make-believe that their own children lack. Studies conducted by German researchers Elke Schubert and Rainer Strick found that removing toys from children results in them becoming more creative and more social.[7] In their experiment, entitled 'Der Spielzeugfreie

Kindergarten' ('The Nursery Without Toys'), all toys were removed from children for a period of three months, the only items left being chairs and blankets. Initially, the children were bored; however, they quickly readjusted and were soon building dens and enjoying the new set-up. By the end of the experimental period, not only were the children playing imaginatively and creatively, they were also more confident and social with each other, with better interpersonal relationships and less friction and fighting between themselves. This led the researchers to conclude that children can be 'suffocated' by the presence of toys and also find it harder to concentrate when surrounded by them.

While the idea of having a completely 'toy-free' home may fill you with horror, there are some points from Schubert and Strick's research that can be implemented with ease. Firstly, thin out the toy supply – removing those items that are barely or rarely played with. Next, consider rotating toys. At the end of the experiment, toys were reintroduced to the nursery and the children were happy to see them return (the saying 'absence makes the heart grow fonder' applies to toys too!), so rotating your child's toy supply and putting some away in a cupboard for a month or two, so they remain fresh is a great idea. Lastly, never underestimate the play value in everyday objects. In the experiment, it was simple chairs and blankets, but there are many other options. Here are some examples:

- Cardboard boxes – so many possibilities: anything from spaceships to houses

- Old handbags and purses – great to fill with treasures

- Cornflour and water – makes a wonderfully intriguing, gloopy blend

- Mud, mud glorious mud: mud pies, mud modelling, mud kitchens and more

- Water – freeze toys in ice, 'paint' with it on pavements, make boats to float

- Den building – inside with blankets and sheets, outside with sticks and branches

- Bubble wrap – put it on the floor and jump and roll on it (make sure you supervise this one!)

- Plastic cups – great for stacking, pouring and scooping

- Old phones and remote controls – pressing buttons and pretending to control things

- Old baby wipes boxes and tissue boxes – great for 'posting' things and sorting.

Starting preschool

For many children, this age heralds the start of preschool. For some, this transition can go really well but others may struggle. Attending preschool only has benefits for a child if they enjoy it. If leaving their parent is difficult for them and they seem unhappy and withdrawn at preschool, then it would be much better for everyone involved if their needs were respected and they didn't go. Sometimes problems are experienced when the child is just too young to leave their parent and simply waiting and delaying the start is the most obvious solution.

Children are attending preschool at an increasingly young age and sometimes the advantages are much more for adults than the children themselves. An ideal starting time is somewhere around three years of age, but obviously this depends on the individual child: some are ready at two while others are not ready until four. As a parent, your role is to stay responsive to your child's needs. If they are not ready, don't be forced into putting them in too soon by comments such as, 'But he needs to socialise; it will be good for him to have some space away from you.' We know that this is not true. A young child's primary socialisation happens with their parents, and it is not necessary for them to spend time in a preschool environment in order to develop social skills. Similarly, it is not possible to force independence if a child is not yet ready for it.

When the time comes to start preschool, ensure that you choose one with a good key worker and settling-in scheme. Ideally, you will have at least two or three settling-in sessions where you can stay with your child. This will give them a chance to bond with their key worker in advance of the start date, which will make the transition to staying at preschool on their own much easier.

Here are a few tips to help you:

- **Use visual cues.** Young children do not process and store information in the same way as adults. During the settling-in sessions take some photographs of your child having fun with their key worker to discuss at home in order to build familiarity. You could also form a small scrapbook with pictures of the preschool and other staff that you can use at home regularly.

- **Use a transitional object.** If your child already has a comforter, a cuddly toy for instance, this should always go with them to preschool and should never be taken away by staff there. This object will help them to feel as if they have a little piece of you with them. If your child doesn't have one, then try to introduce something a good month before they start preschool. Tell your child that if they are missing you, then they should hug the comforter and think of you.

- **Make sure that you never leave your child crying**. Even if staff encourage you to leave, stay for as long as is necessary and only go once your child is calm. If you do not reach this point, then go home together for the day and try again the next day. It may take you several days, or even weeks, until you are able to leave your child happily. Forcing them to stay, however, will not help and could make any separation anxiety worse. When they are calm, make your goodbye as positive as possible. Talk about what they will do, but don't tell them that they will be fine without you or that they will have fun. This undermines their feelings. It is better to say, 'I know today you are going to do painting and go to the park and then I will come back to pick you up after story time'.

- **Don't be afraid to find an alternative setting if your child is failing to settle**. Likewise, if they are struggling with leaving you, consider postponing their start by a few months.

Welcoming a new sibling

For many children, this age signals the arrival of a new baby brother or sister. Historically, the usual spacing between children was somewhere around three to four years, fertility and breastfeeding dictating a natural spacing between pregnancies. Nowadays, with fewer babies being breastfed or for far less time, the average spacing is closer to two and a half years. Research has suggested that waiting at least two years between pregnancies can improve the cognitive abilities of the older child.[8] Allowing the first-born time with parents alone naturally increases parental interaction, particularly when it comes to reading to and playing with the child. Further research has suggested that babies should not be born fewer than twenty-seven months apart, to allow each child individual time and attention with the mother.[9] This spacing allows for a strong attachment and the best chance for the child to reach his or her potential. In terms of health, the best outcomes for both mother and baby occur with spacing of at least eighteen months between pregnancies.[10]

Allowing a child sufficient time to be with his or her parents before a sibling arrives is perhaps the best way to create a smooth transition to becoming a big brother or sister. And from the point of view of the new arrival, a gap that allows them as much one-to-one time with their parents as possible is the best way to ensure their future psychological health. Preparing your child well in advance of the birth can also help. A lovely way to do this is to share books about pregnancy, birth, babies and welcoming a new sibling. Involving your child in antenatal appointments and shopping for the new baby is a good idea – selecting items of clothing or toys for the new baby can make them feel much more involved.

Try to make sure that your child's life stays as normal and as predictable as possible when the new baby arrives. It can often unsettle new big brothers or sisters if their daily routine is disrupted, which commonly happens with Dad at home from work, lots of visitors and perhaps time off from nursery or preschool.

Involving the new big brother or sister in the new baby's care can be really helpful. Try to assign them a special task, such as always fetching the baby's nappies and alerting you when they need a change. The responsibility can help them to feel needed. Buying a 'newborn' doll and nappies and encouraging them to change and feed their doll while you feed and change their new sibling can also help. Perhaps the best purchase, however, is that of a good sling or carrier for the new baby. This means that the newborn will have his or her needs met by being 'held' as much as possible, while you will have two free hands to play with the new big brother or sister. This time with your first-born is crucial to how they handle the transition. The sad truth is that the time when you most want to be resting and bonding with your new arrival is when your first-born needs you the most.

Imagine the following scenario: you arrive home and your partner introduces you to their new girlfriend or boyfriend. They tell you that they still love you just as much as they ever did, but now they have somebody new to love who is going to move in with you. They say, 'It's OK. I have enough love for both of you.' How would you feel? Insecure? Jealous? Sad? Angry? Probably all of the above. This is just how many new big brothers and sisters feel. All they have known for their entire life is their relationship with you and now somebody new has entered. It doesn't matter how much you tell them that you still love them just as much as before or how fun it will be in the years to come – everything they have ever known has changed, and, as a result, their behaviour can often regress.

Night waking and refusal to go to bed, a regression in potty training, eating refusal, reluctance to go to preschool, tantrums and more are all normal and common reactions to the arrival of a new sibling. And these may well last for months after the baby has arrived. What your child needs now is your empathy, respect and connection, perhaps more than ever before. They need as much one-to-one time with you as possible, without the baby involved, and they need you to show them that you still love them – through your actions, as well as your words.

Always avoid saying, 'You're a big boy now', or 'You're not the baby any more'. These two phrases can be incredibly damaging for a child who has just seen the arrival of a new baby brother or sister. They highlight that only a baby gets attention from Mum and Dad and that being 'big' perhaps isn't as great as people make it out to be. Although they may want to be 'grown up', being a baby at this point is much more appealing, which is often why behaviour regresses and a first-born may start to speak in a baby voice, want to breastfeed or use a bottle or a dummy again. Your emphasis, and indeed most of your time and attention, need to be spent on your first-born and not your new baby, which is why a sling can help so much in the early weeks.

The following is a message I received from a mother concerning the transition to two children, and my response to her:

Q: *How do you 'gentle-parent' two children (or more?!). I have a twenty-two-month-old and an eight-week-old. At various points in a day one or other are not getting their needs met as I am meeting the needs of the other. Gentle parenting my first-born was a full-on 100 per cent task, but you can't give two children 100 per cent. One is always 'missing out'.*

A: You need help, if not with the children, then at least around the house, so that you can concentrate on mothering and as little else as possible. Accept any and all help given and if it isn't offered, then ask for it, whether from a charity or paid for from an organisation specialising in postnatal care. Next, consider the immediate needs of each child. At eight weeks your baby needs little more than contact with you, feeding and communication, all of which can be done with him or her in a sling. It can often feel as if you are neglecting your second-born as you spend so little time actively with them, compared to when it was just you and your first-born, but rest assured that their needs are being met.

In many ways nights are the perfect time to connect with your baby: night feeding and hugs can give you that one-to-one time you may not get in the day. But it is your toddler who needs most of your attention in the day, and I would make sure that you reserve at least thirty minutes daily of one-to-one time for just you and them (baby should then be with your partner/friend/family, ideally in another room). Make sure your toddler knows that this time will happen every single day – give it a special name – and allow them to dictate what happens in this time, leaving your phone somewhere else and focusing solely on them.

Lastly, you won't be able to do all of this unless you look after yourself. Things like eating well, taking vitamins, going to bed early, practising mindfulness, etc., are really important because it is exhausting and it will be for quite a few more years yet.

Television viewing

Research has shown that an average child between two and five years of age spends thirty-two hours per week watching television.[11] That's an average of four and a half hours a day. Television viewing in young children does not come without risk. For one thing, it is no surprise that increased television viewing replaces time spent playing, especially creatively, and time spent outdoors.[12] In addition, it reduces quality time spent with parents and siblings.[13] Research has also shown that television viewing in early childhood can negatively affect sleep, weight, behaviour and academic achievement.[14] These effects are not necessarily negated by watching child-specific television programmes, however age-appropriate they are deemed to be.

At this age, television does not present a good learning opportunity; children need to learn through experience in the real world. The American Academy of Pediatrics (AAP) recommends that children over the age of two watch no more than one to two hours of television daily, while those under two should watch none at all.

From a sleep perspective, children should not be exposed to

television, or any other screen, for the two hours leading up to bedtime.[15] As well as being highly stimulating, making it hard for the child to unwind, the blue light emitted by the television – and all electronic screens – is a major cause for concern, as it is known to inhibit the release of melatonin, the hormone of sleep. It also causes cortisol levels to rise, as the eyes sense the presence of light and presume it is daytime. Even if a child is tired, their brains will keep their bodies awake, confused by the artificial light. In order for their sleep hormones to rise, their brains need to perceive it to be night. This process is aided by lowered levels of white and blue light source, which means that even 'bedtime-hour' children's programmes are problematic. For this reason, a child should never have a television in their own bedroom, whatever their age.

How to cope with picky eating

Picky eating often tops the list of concerns of many parents of one-to-four-year-olds. And they are right to be concerned, as the first few years of life play a tremendous role in the child's future eating habits, albeit not quite in the way that most people think.[16] Researchers have found that young children are predisposed to favour foods that are sweet and salty, rather than bitter in taste. From an evolutionary perspective these preferences keep children safe – for example, foods found in nature that may poison them are usually bitter, and they will therefore avoid them. Children are also hard-wired to be food 'neophobic', that is they are biologically programmed to refuse most foods at first taste. It is only after repeated exposure to food that their preferences can and do change, again keeping them safe and preventing them from eating foods that may potentially be harmful.

But it is these natural, protective habits that many parents struggle with, even though scientists suggest that, when allowed to, children actually do a fairly good job of regulating their food intake, and that it is advisable to allow them control over their eating habits. According to researcher Leanne Birch from the Department of Nutritional Sciences and the Center for Childhood Obesity Research at Pennsylvania State University:

> Although children are predisposed to be responsive to the energy content of foods in controlling their intake, they are also responsive to parents' control attempts. We have seen that these parental control attempts can refocus the child away from responsiveness to internal cues of hunger and satiety and towards external factors such as the presence of palatable foods.[17]

In other words, well-intentioned parents can cause a child to override and ignore their satiety signals, which can place them at risk of poor eating habits as they grow.

Another point to consider is that it is not normal for humans to eat three 'square meals' a day. As a species we are meant to graze and eat little and often. This is what young children tend to do. Their eating habits are normal and it is adults, who eat according to the clock, who are not. So allowing your toddler to graze, rather than forcing them to eat breakfast, lunch and dinner, is vital if they are to learn to understand their hunger and satiety signals.

A great idea to use with young children is to have a 'grazing tray' available to them at all times. This is a container in which you put an assortment of healthy foods and to which your child has free access (without asking your permission or needing help to get into) throughout the day. Prepare the tray in the morning and leave it at your child's height so they can take what they want from it whenever they are hungry. Although it may not seem as if they are eating much, particularly if they do not sit and eat breakfast, lunch and dinner with you, if you take into account what they have eaten from their grazing tray (which you top up as needed and replace perishables with fresh items) over the course of the day you will be quite surprised. Good options to include are:

- cheese cubes

- raisins

- cucumber chunks

- cherry tomatoes

- egg slices

- strips of pitta bread and hummus dip

- sliced avocado

- strips of chicken or ham

- strips of yellow or orange pepper

- cold cooked baby potatoes

- cold cooked pasta shapes

- carrot sticks

- berries

- grapes

- orange segments

- apple chunks

- mini quiches

- sweetcorn kernels.

In addition to the grazing tray, sharing mealtimes with your child can really help, but do give some thought to how realistic your expectations are when it comes to wanting them to sit still and quietly, especially when you are eating out.

The following is a message I received from the mother of a toddler concerning her child's eating habits, and my response:

Q: *Is it asking for trouble in the future to offer your toddler different food options if they won't eat the meal you first put in front of them, regularly?*

A: Toddlers are wired to be neophobic, which means that they are predisposed to refuse novel foods – and it's important that they are wary in this way, as it stops them from accidentally ingesting something poisonous. We know that to keep on offering previously discarded food can really help with their preferences (which at this age are largely for sweet and salty flavours). However, it's important to understand that there will be food that your toddler genuinely does dislike (bitter tastes are the most common) and to respect that. Personally, I would offer several options on one plate, always including something you know that they do like, as well as new and previously discarded foods. Allowing the toddler the choice of lots of different foods is usually much more successful than giving them just one meal. If they genuinely seem to hate everything on the plate and are very hungry, then I would offer a fairly uninteresting food that they usually are happy to eat, such as porridge or toast, to ensure that they don't go hungry. Toddlers are too young to understand consequences and, as such, not giving them anything else to eat is punishing them for being a toddler.

Toilet learning

Perhaps the best tip I can give any parent on the subject of toilet learning is to always wait until their child is ready and allow them to decide, whenever that may be. Some parents believe that babies are born ready and are able to communicate their toilet needs from birth. This concept is commonly referred to as 'elimination communication' or 'baby-led toileting'. The idea behind this theory is that babies do not like the feeling of being soiled and are able to recognise their need for toileting and communicate it to their parents. This type of toileting requires a close connection between parent and child and, for this reason, is gaining popularity among parents who are also drawn to gentle parenting. Historically, however, babies have usually always been wrapped in some sort of cloth, wadding or plant material. There are also many mentions of early forms of potties, whereby babies were left sitting on straw or fashioned toileting chairs until they produced urine or faeces. For this reason, and given the constraints of modern-day life, for many people a more mainstream method of toilet learning, involving nappies in the early years, is preferable.

With patience a toddler will learn to use the toilet all by themselves, and if you allow your child the control of deciding when they are ready to do this, things will be infinitely easier. Many toilet-training troubles (I will use the term 'toilet training' in this section, as this is the one most commonly used in society today) are caused by trying to train the child before they are ready, physically, psychologically or both, resulting in lots of stress, many accidents and far more work than if you wait. The average age for showing readiness for toilet training is around twenty-four to twenty-five months, with daytime toilet training occurring, on average, just before the child turns three years of age. Night dryness often comes later and can take a while to achieve. It is certainly not an issue if your three- or four-year-old still needs nappies at night or has bed-wetting accidents, and is not considered a problem for a child to not be fully toilet-trained at night until the age of seven.

Here are some common signs of readiness to toilet train:

- Their nappies may be dry first thing in the morning.

- Your child may poo only in the daytime.

- Your child is aware of having a wee or poo.

- Your child may ask you to change their nappy.

- Your child may tell you (verbally or otherwise) when they need to go to the toilet.

- Your child may ask to wear pants or knickers.

- Your child may ask to use the potty or toilet.

- Your child may take an interest in other family members using the toilet.

When the time comes to begin toilet training, once again, giving your child as much control over the process as possible is key. Ways to do this include allowing them to:

- choose their own potty

- choose where in the house the potty should go

- choose their own pants or knickers

- choose to wear knickers/pants or a nappy each day.

In addition, try to normalise toileting as much as possible, sharing books about potty training, allowing your child to go to the toilet with you, observing older siblings using the toilet and talking about visiting the toilet or using the potty.

It should come as no surprise that I am not an advocate of rewarding wees or poos on the potty. In my opinion the act should be treated as normal, the ultimate aim being to teach your child to listen to their own body and the cues it gives them. Training a child to go to the toilet to get a sticker or a sweet treat does not do this, and may even teach them to override their body's signals in order to receive a reward. What's more, they can in time even regress in their toileting if you withdraw the reward that was initially on offer. I am also not a fan of praising children for toilet training, for most of the above reasons. That's not to say that your child shouldn't be encouraged to feel good when they successfully use the potty, but it is far better to say something like, 'I bet you feel proud of yourself for doing a poo in the potty', than, 'Good boy, you did a poo!' Our children are hard-wired to want to grow, explore and master new things. The reward of their own achievement is more than enough for them.

On a practical level, always make sure that you have lots of spare pants and knickers and one or two sets of clean clothes to hand, especially if you are out of the house. Many parents find it easier to leave their toddler naked from the waist down if they are at home, and for this reason toilet training in the warmer spring and summer months can be a good idea if they coincide with your child's cues.

Toileting troubles

One of the most common toileting problems, presuming that you have followed your child's lead in terms of when to start, is not making it to the potty in time. This is why it is so important for children to listen to their body's signals and learn when they need to go immediately or when they can wait a bit longer. Young children can often have trouble identifying the urgency of their need, especially when they are engrossed in play. It is fairly common, therefore, for them to realise when it is too late. One of the best things you can do is to watch for any clues that your child might need the toilet (holding their genitals, squirming and wriggling, bouncing up and down, becoming distracted in their play, grunting and humming) and asking them, 'Do you think that it may be time to use the potty?' when you notice these signs. This empowers them and can help them to recognise their body's signs of urgency, which will, in time, mean far fewer accidents.

When your child inevitably does have an accident, make sure that you never chastise them or refer to them as naughty. Remember that they are still learning and it is important that they view potty training as a normal and positive life event. So if your child doesn't make it to the potty on time, tell them, 'It's OK, it is tough always knowing when we need a wee or a poo. You will soon learn though.' Then clean up in a very matter-of-fact fashion and make sure that you never show any irritation over having to do so – however irritated you may feel!

It is very common for young children to have issues with poo, often related to discomfort. One of the simplest things you can do to make having a poo easier for your child is to ensure that their potty is comfortable and that their feet are resting flat on the ground or on a stool if they are using a seat on the big toilet. Humans are meant to poo in a squatting position, with their feet firmly on the floor – when they do this the muscles around the anus are loose, allowing for an easy poo; when little legs dangle from a toilet seat these muscles can tighten and make it more difficult for a child. Another issue around poo comfort is the possibility of constipation and also the memory and fear of previous constipation, which may make some toddlers reluctant to go and hold it in for as long as possible. This, of course, leads to a cycle of constipation, pain and fear. Aside from helping your toddler through their diet and encouraging them to drink as much liquid as possible, try to find comforting stories relating to toileting and fear, or make one up yourself. Lastly, some children are reluctant to poo in public and instead need privacy in order to go easily. If this is the case for your child, consider buying a second potty to leave in their favoured private place for this purpose.

Your child's brain between one and four years

By the end of this time period, the average child will have around twice as many synapses (connections) in their brain as the average adult. This is because an adult's brain has been 'pruned' of the weakest connections that were not reinforced in childhood. For this reason, the best chance of raising a happy, confident, emotionally and intellectually intelligent child is to reinforce those behaviours that you most want them to exhibit in later life. The best way of doing this is to treat your child in the manner you would like them to treat others – so communicate with them lots through speech and story reading and expose them to an environment that is as rich, in multi-sensory terms, as possible.

Your child's brain at this age has reached between 80 and 90 per cent of its fully grown adult size and the speed at which it processes information is increasing rapidly, although their frontal lobe – the thinking, decision-making part of their brain – is still extremely immature. This means their behaviour will still be anything but adult when it comes to making decisions, responding to situations and regulating their behaviour.

Sleep at one to four years

Although nobody sleeps through the night, not even adults, it is feasible to expect that at some point in this period your child may be able to sleep, on and off, throughout the night without needing your assistance to start a new sleep cycle. This, however, is definitely not the case for all children in this age range and night-waking requiring parental input still remains a common feature.

Toddler and preschooler sleep is complex. While most children should be able to last the night without needing milk, there may be many more reasons that cause them to wake up and require your assistance at this age than in the baby years: learning to be dry at night, night terrors, nightmares, diet, the effect of new siblings and starting preschool can all have a significant impact on a child's sleep. From a physical perspective avoiding artificial additives in food and medicines can play an important role, as can making sure your child had an adequate amount of omega-3 and magnesium in their diet.

Nightmares and night terrors are both fairly common at this age, the difference between them being that nightmares happen in a light phase of sleep and cause the child to wake, scared, often remembering the dream; whereas night terrors occur when they are very much asleep and they will have no recollection of them when they wake up.

Nightmares can be dealt with by identifying and removing the cause wherever possible. They may be due to anxiety surrounding a new event in the child's life, for example, or because of a story they have recently heard or something they have seen on television. Performing an elaborate 'monster hunt' before bedtime and making the child some 'monster spray' (water, food colouring and glitter in a clear spray bottle) can be very helpful. The child can use the monster spray in their room before bedtime and also have it close to hand in case they wake up scared. Similarly, asking your child to look after a cuddly toy at night, especially if they think the toy is scared, can be very effective as it allows the child to transfer their anxiety onto the toy and then work through their own emotions in a safe way.

Night terrors are harder to cope with as there is often no cause, aside from genetics (parasomnias – sleep disorders such as night terrors, sleepwalking and sleeptalking – often run in families). The most important consideration during a night terror is keeping your child safe. They may appear to be awake with their eyes open, violently thrashing around and lashing out, but they are very much asleep and need your help to ensure that they don't injure themselves. Stay with them during the terror, but don't try to wake them or talk to them – there is no point. In many ways night terrors are harder for the parents to cope with than they are for the child. If there is a pattern to your child's night terrors, waking them ten minutes before the time that they usually occur and keeping them awake for a few minutes before returning to sleep can help to break the cycle. Also, research has suggested that supplementing omega-3 oils may help.[18]

An important point to consider in relation to toddler and pre-schooler sleep is when they should go to bed. Research in Colorado, USA, has indicated that sleep problems may be due to parents trying to put children to bed too early in relation to their chemical indicators for sleep.[19] Looking at children between two and a half and three years of age, the researchers found that the average surge of melatonin did not happen until 7.40 p.m., around half an hour after most parents were trying to put their children to bed – and if the hormone has not risen sufficiently, then not only is bedtime going to be more challenging, but the child may wake more in the night too. So waiting until your child is chemically ready for bed, with a bedtime of around 7.45 to 8 p.m., preceded by a calming bedtime routine, can mean easier evenings for all.

The following is a message from the mother of a one-year-old concerning her son's sleep, and my response:

Q: *I have a question about sleep beyond the age of one. When is it reasonable to expect a child to get into bed awake and fall asleep? Is this called self-soothing? I am currently cuddling my son to sleep in the nursery chair. I then transfer him into his cot when he is asleep. If he wakes in distress in the night he comes into our bed. What's the next stage to progress to the skill of being able to sleep alone?*

A: Self-soothing indicates that the child is regulating their own emotions. For instance, if they are scared, they can remove the fear, if they are angry, they can calm themselves down, if they are sad they can cheer themselves up. All parents with toddlers will know that they can't do this in the daytime, let alone at night. Think, for example, about the last time your child had a tantrum: could he calm himself? A young child who gets into bed awake and falls asleep happily without parental input is not self-soothing, they are just in a happy and calm state in body and in mind and feel safe and secure enough to just drift off to sleep. No soothing has taken place. Some children do this naturally from a young age, but it's important to differentiate between putting them to bed and leaving them with whatever feelings they have and trying to regulate those themselves. Unfortunately, the development of self-soothing, or as psychologists call it 'emotional self-regulation' is a biological one. You need to wait until your son's brain is developed enough for this complex task, and until then he needs you to act as an external emotional regulator for him and to just keep on doing what you're doing.

Using the Seven Cs of gentle parenting from one to four years

How will you implement the Seven Cs of gentle parenting from one to four years?

Connection

Connection is absolutely vital at this age. A strong bond with your child will help them to be able to cope with their big emotions in the knowledge that you are always there to listen to them and comfort them when needed. Often, behaviour problems at this age can be a cry for more connection with their parent, particularly if a new sibling has recently been born, the parent has returned to work or the child has just started preschool.

Communication

In some ways communication becomes easier now, as by the end of this stage most children will be able to communicate many of their needs verbally. At the earlier end of the age range, however, children are far less verbal and behaviour remains their main form of communication. A child having a tantrum is not a 'naughty child', but one who is experiencing big feelings and trying to tell us that all is not right in their world.

Think about the way that you communicate with your child: get down on their level and use simple words that they understand and that are not ambiguous. Tell your child what you want them to do (for eample, 'Walk slowly please'), rather than what you don't want them to do ('Stop running'). Remember, too, that you are a role model for your child: how you communicate will be how they communicate. If you shout, you are teaching your child that it is acceptable to shout. Focusing on your own communication is, therefore, vital.

Control

The struggle for control is huge at this age. Toddlers, in particular, spend their days desperately attempting to gain some autonomy over their lives. They have an innate urge to master new tasks – indeed, it is how they grow and develop – but if we do not give them appropriate control, this can never happen. In addition, a toddler lacking enough control over their life will be forced to try to get some by behaving in a way that parents are not happy with. Common ways that children try to assert control over their lives at this age is through their sleep, eating and toileting. If you have concerns over any of these areas, look at the amount of control you are giving your child and how you can increase it.

Containment

Children at this age are like full pots of bubbling water with no lid: their volatile emotions commonly boil over if left unchecked, so it is a parent's job to regulate their emotional 'temperature'. We need to be big enough and mature enough to allow our child's big feelings to spill into our mature adult containers, diffuse them and give back space and love to our child. But we can only be effective containers if we have enough space ourselves. If we are too full up with the stresses of everyday life, we are not able to take on board our child's big feelings as well. Finding an external container for our own emotions, therefore, is vital, whether this is a partner, friend, relative, a network of fellow parents, a telephone helpline or writing a diary.

Champion

How can you champion your child's needs at this age? The list is almost endless, but must start with considering what is really for their benefit, not your own or somebody else's. Championing your child at this age can often mean ignoring advice from other people about what your child should or shouldn't be doing. It can also mean standing up for your child when others are commenting negatively about their behaviour, especially during a tantrum in public.

Confidence

Confidence here is twofold. Having confidence in your parenting abilities is vital. At this stage it is your child's job to test your boundaries and yours to gently enforce them; however, many parents question their choices when it feels as if their child is constantly testing boundaries and they wonder if their parenting style has perhaps caused their child to behave in a certain way. Confidence is also required to ignore comments from others and the disapproving looks thrown your way when your child tantrums in public. Remember that parenting gently does not mean that your child won't tantrum – they will and they may bite, hit, push and shove, too. These are all age-appropriate, normal behaviours.

The next facet to consider here is the development of confidence in your child. There is no magical age by which children should be expected to be confident, particularly when not around you or when conversing with others. If your child is more introverted and sensitive, then they will still need you as their secure base right through this age period and beyond. Confidence and independence cannot be forced, and coercing a sensitive and introverted child to separate from you, or to socialise, will not have the desired effect. Allowing them to explore the world from your safe base at their own time, will.

Consistency

You must stay focused and consistent with children of this age. It may feel as if your constant repeating of phrases such as, 'Ow, don't bite, it hurts; bite your special necklace instead' will never have an effect. Indeed, many parents expect results too quickly, when, in reality, it can take months to gently change your child's behaviour. This doesn't mean that your methods are not effective – it just means that you are working at your child's pace and that they are learning. Staying consistent with your approach here is vital, as is sticking with any boundaries and limits that you choose to put in place and enforcing them daily. Don't be tempted to ignore a behaviour that is normally unacceptable to you because you are tired, or to skip the bedtime routine because you got home late. Young children need predictability and this means that they need you to enforce any routines and boundaries consistently, otherwise life is highly confusing and quite scary for them.

Chapter 7

Growing Up –
Four to Seven Years

*We cannot always build the future for our youth, but
we can build our youth for the future.*

Franklin D. Roosevelt, former US President

Parenting a four-to-seven-year-old child is exceptionally rewarding. There are so many 'firsts' to experience and so much pride as you watch your child blossom and go out into the world. However, this age can bring many challenges for parents, both in terms of decisions that they must make and also knowing how to cope with their child's behaviour and relationships with others. Whether boys and girls should be treated differently at this age, for example, is one of many questions commonly discussed by parents, and this and other concerns are examined in this chapter.

Backchat

When researching this book I asked parents of four-to-seven-year-olds what their most common concerns at this age were, and 'backchat' topped the list. Just when you begin to think you know what you are doing with a toddler or a preschooler, they suddenly turn into a sassy five-year-old who answers back or questions everything you say.

But backchat isn't all bad. Most parents would like their children to grow to be free thinkers, challenging the status quo, especially if it is unjust. After all, assertiveness, persistence and ambition are all positive traits in adults, so why should we view them as negative in children? If your teenager was questioning her teacher over something she believed to be incorrect, or your son was questioning his boss about what he perceived to be the unfair treatment of a colleague, you would probably be proud. Similarly, if your teen was standing up to a bully or refusing to bow to peer pressure, you would be delighted. Yet when our children question our motives and directions, we consider it rude, disrespectful and inappropriate. We can't have it both ways.

A child who backchats a lot is one who may be feeling disrespected themselves. And the best way to teach a child to be respectful is to treat them with respect. Is your request or demand respectful? Have you explained yourself fully? Does your child understand why you are asking that they do something? All this can make a huge difference.

Take the following two scenarios:

- **Scenario One**: you have had a really hard day at the office and have a pounding headache. You collect your children from school, arrive home and remember you have a visitor that evening. You have to clean and tidy the very messy house and cook dinner in the space of two hours, ready to greet your guest. This is understandably stressful. Your children are chasing each other around the house, screeching in delight, making both the mess and your headache worse still. You yell, 'Stop it!' and then say, 'Go and tidy your rooms now', to which they reply, 'No, we're having fun.' You respond saying, 'No, I said now. This house is a mess and it needs tidying – we have visitors later.' And they say, 'We don't want to tidy up. You can't make us.' You quickly reach a stalemate which descends into yelling and threats.

- **Scenario Two:** you have had a really hard day at the office and have a pounding headache. You collect your children from school and in the car on the way home you say, 'Kids, I have a really bad headache. I'm sorry if I'm grouchy, but I'm in a lot of pain right now and it makes me grumpy. I'd really appreciate it if you could be a bit quiet this afternoon and help me to tidy the house ready for our visitor this evening. Could you do that, do you think?' When you get home you say, 'I bet you're really ready to play after a hard day at school, aren't you? How about you go outside and play for half an hour before we start the tidying and I'll call you when your time's up. Does that sound like a good idea?' After half an hour, you call the children back inside and say, 'Right, these are the jobs that need doing. How can we best get them done between us?', allowing your children to problem solve and share out the tasks. When the house is tidy you call your children and say, 'We did great team work, didn't we? Look how tidy the house is – we should be really proud of ourselves. Thank you so much for your help.'

Scenario Two treats the children with respect, which is far more likely to result in respectful behaviour back from them and little or no backchat. Avoiding backchat as much as possible means understanding your child's feelings and being empathic towards them.

Backchat is also commonly a child testing their parent's boundaries, and this is no bad thing. It is important for them to learn what is and what isn't acceptable. It is a child's job to test limits and a parent's job to enforce them. Not enforcing boundaries consistently can fuel backchat and, often, can indicate a child who is actually in need of more discipline, not less. But enforcing boundaries should be done with respect and understanding, with a focus on teaching the child, not punishing them. When it comes to enforcing boundaries and discipline, be sure to view yourself and your child as being on the same team, not opposing ones.

Backchat can often be an indicator of a relationship in need of a little more connection and understanding on both sides. When was the last time you took time to really enjoy your child? In the busy rush of school, homework, work, clubs and classes it can be easy to forget to really spend time together. Spending a day with your child doing nothing but having fun and chatting with each other can have a dramatic effect. The more fun and laughter the time involves the better. In addition, small measures should be taken every day to foster that connection with your child: a fifteen-minute chat in the bedroom while tucking them up for bed each night; a little note in their lunch box that says, 'I hope you have a nice day. I love you!'; drawing a little cartoon of the two of you together and pinning it on their noticeboard for them to find at a later time; and lots of hugs, cuddles and play, too.

When your child is in the middle of backchatting, responding with humour can be a great way to diffuse the situation. Put on a big, booming silly voice, raise your eyebrows and say, 'Oh, so you beg to disagree with the parent monster, do you? Well, let's see about that because it's coming to get you!' Then run after them, threatening to tickle them. This can have a great effect.

The following is a message I received from a mother of a six-year-old who struggles with her temper, and my response below:

Q: *How can we deal with a six-year-old girl who struggles with anger and frustration? Currently we use some coaching and reframing. The frustration seems to be getting worse. I really need a way to help my daughter understand and deal with these strong emotions.*

A: The most important thing you can do is to find out why she is so angry and frustrated. Is there something happening in her life that she feels unable to control? Does she have siblings? Does she have issues at school – with friendships or difficulty learning? Does she need more time with you at home? Is something in her diet affecting her, perhaps? Does she have too much screen time and not enough time playing outside to let off steam? Finding the cause is key.

Otherwise, it's important to help her to understand that there is nothing wrong with feeling frustrated or angry – everybody does at some point – and she just needs gentle steering to release these emotions in a more positive manner. Lots and lots of play and adding humour into her life can be really helpful, especially with you acting silly and roughhousing with her. The aim is to make her laugh, which, in time, will hopefully lead her to feel more comfortable to cry with you – because crying is what she really needs to do to release the emotions. Getting her to draw or paint her feelings can help, as can acting them out with toys. Try giving a name to her feelings: ask her to describe what it's like when she feels that way and see if you can work from there to choose a fun name. When you see her early-warning signs, ask if she is feeling the name you have chosen and if she needs some help to work through it. Working on her connection with you will really help – getting out for the day, just you and her, and really focusing on bonding with her. Help her to know that, no matter what she is feeling, you love her very much and are on her side.

Chores and pocket money

Many believe that chores and pocket money are linked, and that children only earn pocket money when they do their chores. I strongly feel that this is wrong. Pocket money is an important part of childhood. It teaches children about the value of money and the importance of managing it through budgeting, in order that they may have a good grasp of financial management when they are older – a vital life skill that many adults lack. I'd even say that giving children pocket money weekly or monthly, unconditionally, is as important as learning to read or write.

So from the age of four years old, all children should receive an appropriate amount of pocket money that is not linked to their chores or behaviour in any way. This means they do not get rewarded with more money if they are 'good' and they do not lose pocket money if they do not do their chores or behave in a way that is unacceptable to their parents. The amount of pocket money should remain the same each week or month.

When you start to give pocket money, you should discuss and agree with your child what the money covers. For instance, you may agree that it covers any sweets, magazines and toys your child wants to buy outside of Christmas and birthdays, but that you will still buy their clothes, stationery, books and presents for any parties that they attend. You may decide to give them an extra allowance to spend on holidays or day trips, or this may need to come from their pocket money. When you have decided on these rules it is important that you stick to them. This means you shouldn't buy something for your child that their pocket money is meant to cover, no matter how 'good' they have been.

If your child needs to earn extra money for something, you can offer them the opportunity through extraordinary tasks that are not part of their everyday expectations, such as washing the car or weeding the garden. As well as encouraging your child to save for big expenses, it is also good to encourage them to think about donating a proportion of their pocket money. This could be for a certain special charity event, a local collection outside a shop or giving a regular amount each month to a cause close to their heart.

How do you make children do chores?

The answer here is in the question: you shouldn't be 'making' your child do them. Chores are an essential part of everyday life – just like tooth-brushing, eating and sleeping. Everybody is expected to keep their environment clean and tidy. This is simply what happens, particularly when you are living in a house with other people. So chores are non-negotiable. They are not 'good' or 'bad', nor are they opportunities for rewards or punishments. Bedrooms should be kept tidy, everybody should put their rubbish in the bin, plates should be taken to the sink and the table should be cleared after dinner. We don't get paid for these tasks as adults, and neither should our children.

It is vital that your children know what is expected of them from an early age. I discussed earlier the idea of rewarding certain behaviours and how research shows that this makes children less likely to repeat these if the reward is no longer on offer (see page 138). Chores are no different. You can certainly show your appreciation and that you have noticed with a smile, but nothing else is required. For the child, feeling a part of the family and knowing that you are happy with them is enough.

So what happens if a child doesn't do their chores? Initially, they will need reminding – a lot – which requires plenty of patience on your behalf. Keep the reminders light-hearted and fun: 'Ooops, I see a plate on the table. Is it going to walk itself to the sink, do you think?' is much better than, 'For goodness sake, you left your plate on the table again. How many times do I have to tell you?' You can expect to repeat yourself every day for at least a month before the chore starts to become a habit. The reminder should be just that though, and not nagging, which is likely to have the opposite effect on your child. At the same time, you need to consider your own behaviour here: are you always consistent with putting your rubbish in the bin or taking your plate to the sink when you have eaten? If you are not, then you cannot insist that your child is. You are your child's role model. If you are messy, don't expect them to be anything but messy themselves.

Consequences

There are two types of consequences: natural and logical. A natural consequence is the natural reaction that takes place as a result of something the child has or hasn't done. For instance, if the child refuses to wear a coat when they go outside and they subsequently feel cold, then this is the natural consequence of their own decision. If they refuse to tidy up their bedroom and they step on a toy and hurt their foot, that, again, is the natural consequence of their decision.

Logical consequences focus on the outcome of a child's behaviour based upon the parent's reaction: for example, the child refuses to stop playing a game and so the parent decides to take it away from them for a certain number of days. In essence, logical consequences are just another form of punishment, used by the parent to teach the child a lesson. However, they rely on a certain degree of brain development that a child of this age does not possess.

So do consequences have a role in gentle parenting? I think they do, but at this age only if they are natural consequences. Natural consequences are one of the most important ways that children learn about the world, providing that they are safe and never used as a form of punishment or chastisement. In the case of a child refusing to put their coat on, for example, the parent could simply take it with them and when the child inevitably becomes cold they could say, 'It is cold when we don't wear our coat, isn't it? I brought yours with me, do you want to wear it now?' They should not say, 'See, I told you so. I said you would get cold if you didn't wear it.'

As for the 'lessons' of logical consequences, they generally do not have the desired effect and can cause friction and a lack of connection between parent and child. For this reason, they have no role in gentle parenting at this age.

Sensitivity and shyness

It is very common for children in this age range to be shy and sensitive, particularly around strangers, people they do not come into contact with regularly and new environments. Once again, the best way to encourage a child to be less reserved around new people or situations is to allow them to use us as an external regulator of their emotions, and not force their independence.

It can be incredibly hard for extroverted parents to cope with an introverted child. The personalities of parents and children can be hugely different and the adult can often struggle to empathise with their child. Try to understand that your child may not feel the same as you with regards to new people and situations and to respect this. The anxiety they feel is still very real,

even if you do not feel or fully understand it. Sensitive and introverted children need to be accepted for who they are, and
parents should not try to change them. This is almost impossible in any case, and will often only make the child's anxieties
worse, and place a strain on the relationship.

Try to view your child's sensitivities as a positive trait. Never
use the word 'shy' around them, as it is universally viewed in a
negative light. Instead, refer to your child as being sensitive or
feeling big feelings, and help them to view this as a good thing.
Some of the most introverted, sensitive children can be wonderfully compassionate, understanding and empathic. They can
make great listeners and fantastic friends, and their skills and
insight can be an asset in many job roles.

Once you have accepted your child's personality, the next
step is to help them to cope more in the world without you,
while respecting their limits, however extreme they may seem to
you. The way to do this is by very gradual exposure. For
instance, if your child does not like playing in the park away
from you, you could say, 'How about if I take some steps back
from you and you tell me when to stop?' The next time, they
may allow you to take one step further and another the next,
until eventually they may be happy with you sitting on a bench
twenty steps away from them. Comment positively on the
child's achievements: 'I bet you felt really grown up on the slide
today while I was on the bench, didn't you?' and so on. Also, try
to minimise any stress for your child wherever possible. So, if
they struggle with the school drop-off, for example, you could
arrange to arrive ten minutes early and wait with them in the
classroom, saying goodbye calmly before the other children all
come in. The noise and rush of the playground in the morning
can often be hard.

Here is a message I received from the parent of a sensitive
little boy, and my response:

Q: How do you encourage a four-year-old boy who lacks confidence in dealing with unknown adults? For example, the checkout lady in the supermarket asks him a question about the fancy-dress costume he is wearing and he hides behind me and won't interact.

A: He is still very little and obviously an introvert and does not feel confident in these sort of social interactions. I think it's important to respect that. For this reason I would allow him to do what he needs to help him to feel secure, which is to retreat back to you, his secure base. In this situation I would have crouched down to his level, asked him if he wanted me to reply to the lady's question for him and asked what he wanted me to say, before replying to the lady. This way you still respect his feelings, while also answering the lady who asked the question. Having left the store I would have said to him, 'It's scary sometimes when people you don't know talk to you, isn't it?', thereby validating his emotions. This may, at some point, spark a conversation where you can discuss ways that he may find it a little easier to cope with in future. Also be wary about how you, or his school, discuss 'stranger danger' with him. It's no wonder many children don't like speaking to unknown adults after they have had a 'stranger-danger' chat. We give them very mixed messages, telling them to not speak to strangers on the one hand, while getting frustrated on the other when they won't speak to them.

Free-range parenting and the importance of wings

Close your eyes for a minute and picture your childhood. Think about times when you had the most fun. Where were you? What were you doing? For many of us these scenes will be outdoors and involve other children, rather than our parents. How much freedom did you have as a child? Were you allowed to play out with your friends? Did you ride your bike to their houses? Did you go to the park with them? Now think about your own children doing this exercise in twenty years' time: will their memories be the same as yours or will they largely revolve around being indoors and at organised activities? Will they have recollections of freedom, playing with friends, or will you feature strongly in all of their memories?

Children today have significantly less freedom than we did. In turn, we likely had far less than our own parents or grandparents. And the area in which our children are allowed to play, if we are the nucleus, is ever decreasing. Why is this? Life today is no more dangerous than it ever was; there are no more child abusers or kidnappers than there were when we were children. In fact, if a child is abused or kidnapped, it is likely to be by a family member, not a stranger. There may be more cars on the roads today, but statistically speaking children are more at risk of a road accident the older they get – an eleven-year-old being twice as likely as a ten-year-old to be involved in one. This may be because parents think it's safe to let their high-school-aged child out alone, but not their younger children. If we don't allow children freedom and trust from a young age though, how can we expect them to suddenly be grown up enough once they are older?

When our children are young, our instincts often tell us to keep them as close as possible. Then, as they grow up, we can often be reluctant to 'let go' for fear of any potential harm that may come to them. So, when is the right time to let go? Being truly child-led means we must follow our children's needs for independence, as well as dependence. Or as the American journalist and author Hodding Carter put it in one of my favourite quotes:

There are only two lasting bequests we can hope to give our children. One of these is roots, the other, wings.

That's why I thought it would be appropriate to feature birds in flight on the cover. *Letting go can be so very hard though.* Just as we begin to feel at ease as parents, so it all changes again, and often it is so much easier to grow roots than to give wings. But the bestowing of wings (with age-appropriate levels of freedom) is vital if our children are to reach their full potential, and this age range is the right time for the roots-to-wings transition to take place. The true test of parenting at this stage comes in finding a balance between the two and, in doing so, setting the scene for the tween and teen years.

Boys vs girls: do they need different parenting?

Despite many people believing that there are significant differences between the male and female brain, particularly in childhood, this is not true, and while there are some dissimilarities, they are small. What may be more pertinent to consider is if any differences are caused by a child's biology or by our treatment of them.

Most behaviour is a result of the child's early experiences and environment, not their X and Y chromosomes. Whether we realise it or not, as a society we treat girls and boys differently, in everything from their clothing, to the books and toys we buy them, the way we play with them and the way we communicate with them. It is this stereotyped world that they grow up in that wires their brains more than any biological predetermination. In short, we are the cause of the most major brain differences, not Mother Nature.

From a gentle-parenting perspective, your child's chromosomes are irrelevant. All children, whether they are boys or girls, have a universal need for empathy, respect, understanding, compassion and connection with us. They all need to play, to learn through their senses and explore their environment, both inside and out. And they all need a champion. In short, if you are a truly gentle parent, you will focus on the uniqueness of each individual child, not a cliché of parenting based on their gender and perceived needs.

If boys' and girls' brains are not particularly different, then what about hormones? While it is true that hormones contrast hugely from puberty onwards, for most children before the age of ten any differences are minuscule and inconsequential when it comes to behaviour. Young boys do not experience a surge of testosterone that alters their behaviour making them more violent, active or boisterous. In fact, testosterone is an important hormone for both genders, playing a vital role in bone density and muscle mass, as well as the more obvious development of sexual characteristics. Immediately after birth the testosterone level of baby boys is approximately 120ng/dl – around half the level of an adult male – rising fairly significantly to around 260ng/dl between the second and third month, but then beginning to fall again very quickly after. By the time a baby boy is six months old, research shows that his testosterone levels will be extremely low and will remain so until he approaches puberty.[1] Girls' testosterone levels at birth are approximately one third of those of boys and decrease rapidly from then on, without the slight postnatal surge seen in boys. Our tendency to pathologise behaviour is alarming and does children a great disservice: if a parent feels that a child's behaviour is transient and due purely to biology – attributing a young boy's behaviour to a testosterone spurt, for example – then there is a danger that their real needs may not be met.

Violent play – guns, war and more

Children fashioning guns out of sticks or building blocks, chasing each other and shouting, 'Bang, bang – I'm going to shoot you', playing spy missions, goodies vs baddies, cops and robbers, zombies, monsters, soldiers and war games are commonplace in playgrounds around the world. This type of play can alarm many parents who struggle with feelings about its origins and step in to prevent it. In most cases children are probably modelling violence they have seen in the media, be it fictional or otherwise – because our children are bombarded with images of violence, however age-appropriate their screen time may be.

As much as we would rather our children played more gentle games, these violent games do have an important place in their development. Play is how children make sense of the world. It is a safe way for them to work with their feelings and release them. So when your child role-plays a murderous baddie, it does not mean that they will grow up to be a psychopath. In fact, working through feelings using their imaginations allows children to process them safely and diffuse any emotions which they might have otherwise retained and suppressed. Plus, parents can be reassured that researchers have found that gun play in childhood does not lead to more violence in adulthood.[2]

Not all children play violently, of course; some may not need to, perhaps because their exposure to violence, through real life or fiction, has not left them with any feelings to explore. For those that do, however, so long as nobody actually gets hurt and the games remain purely creative, then this is something that should be allowed to continue until the children eventually naturally outgrow it.

Screen time

The risks of screen time remain as children grow older. It is strongly linked to an increased risk of obesity, anxiety and depression, overall reduced wellbeing, negatively impacted sleep and a decrease in sociable behaviour.[3] Yet despite the many risks, almost half of children at the older end of this age range exceed the recommended limit of only two hours per day.[4]

It is vital that boundaries are put in place with regard to screen time – no more than two hours per day in total whether it is television, computer or electronic games – and that these are enforced consistently. When setting these family rules it is important to discuss them with your children and explain the reasons to them. If children understand why their screen time is restricted, they are far more likely to accept the rules and not challenge them. Once your rules are in place it is essential that they are stuck to unfailingly, no matter how tired or busy you may be and how tempting it is to allow your child 'just a few more minutes' to guarantee some peace for yourself.

What's more, the rules should apply to you too. Most adults have far too much screen time and the risks for children apply equally to adults. Remember that you are a role model to your child, and if you spend most of the day on your phone, laptop or tablet, then your child is going to follow suit. Introducing 'screen-free' days, perhaps once per week, is a wonderful idea for the whole family.

Along with setting rules about screen usage, you should also discuss e-safety at this age. Help your child to understand the risks of computer and game usage in terms of giving away any identifiable details to strangers. Ensure that you have a good parental-control system in place and frequently monitor your child's use of the internet. At this age the internet poses far more risk to your children than allowing them to play with some freedom away from you.

Nature-deficit Disorder

'Nature-deficit Disorder' is the term coined by journalist and author Richard Louv in 2005 in his book *Last Child in the Woods* to describe the possible consequences of children spending less and less time outside in nature and more time confined inside. These include the negative impact on health (including attention disorders and depression), obesity and growing levels of myopia (short-sightedness – caused, in this case, by a lack of exposure to natural light). In addition, Louv also discusses the negative impact a lack of time spent in nature has on a child's regard for their surroundings and environment. If they don't learn to appreciate nature, they are not inclined to protect it.

Children of this age are meant to spend much of their time in nature, making dens, climbing trees, fashioning rope swings, flying kites, skimming stones and pond dipping. For many children today though these activities feature only as special treats or holiday activities when they should be part of everyday life – nature is a separate entity from them to be viewed from a distance. For the children of generations past, on the other hand, it was intertwined with who they were: they could identify different species of trees, birds, wild flowers and the calls of different animals, whereas today's children resort to internet search engines for this sort of information. We have lost so much wisdom in such a short space of time.

There are moves to encourage children back into nature by Forest Schools and the like, but nothing can replace unorganised time spent playing in fields and woods and paddling in shallow streams where the children are fully in control. Allowing your children time in nature, alone or with their friends, as they grow, is an important part of their development.

Starting school

For many, preoccupations at this age inevitably focus on the impending school start. Thoughts turn to finding the best school for your child, and open days, reviews, policies, reports and scores all become increasingly important. Once your child's place is confirmed, it is time to prepare for their start, both practically and emotionally, with the following months devoted to their settling in.

A lot of parents don't realise that their choice when it comes to education is much wider than the standard state-versus-public-school decision, and many are also unaware of their legal rights regarding their children's schooling. In fact, there are numerous options, ranging from full-time traditional school, delayed entry to traditional school, flexi-schooling (a combination of part-time traditional school and part-time home education), alternative schools such as Steiner, Montessori, Democratic and Free schools and home education.

As ever, when it comes to parenting gently, the emphasis is on considering and respecting your child's individual needs and choosing a method that allows you to advocate for them as much as possible. This means the choice will be different for all families: some children will thrive in mainstream education, others will be much better off in an alternative setting, or remaining at home.

Delayed entry

UK law states that children should receive an appropriate education from the age of five (meaning the year they turn five). So currently, children start school at the age of four, and a lot of them will be only just four if their birthdays are in the summer. For many this is far too soon. They need time at home with their parents and are not emotionally or sometimes physically ready for full-time school.

It is possible to delay your child's start at mainstream school until after their fifth birthday. This does not just apply to summer-born children (those born between April and August), although research shows that they benefit the most from a delayed start.[5] The issue here, however, is that due to ambiguous guidelines, your child may then be required to start school in year one, rather than the reception class, which is clearly not in their best interests. The decision about the year group that your child will start in if entry is delayed is unfortunately made by the local school-admission authority, and may therefore depend on geographical area. However, there are likely to be changes to this, as it is under review.

Part–time start

Another option if you feel that your child is not quite ready to start school full-time can be to request that the school teach your child on a part-time basis for the first year, or for a certain number of months. This commonly takes the form of attending for mornings only. The school should consider your request, but unfortunately does not have to agree. For this reason, if you would like the option of your child attending part-time initially, this is an important point to consider when selecting schools.

Alternative schools

If you feel that mainstream school is not suited to your child or your family but you would still like your child to attend a school-based setting, there are several alternative schooling options available, although most do involve the payment of fees.

- **Steiner** The first Steiner school opened in 1919, based on the ideas of the Austrian philosopher Rudolf Steiner and the ethos of creating free-thinking, morally and socially responsible individuals. The focus is on learning through play and hands-on activities in early childhood, with learning stemming from sources such as art and storytelling and with the educator taking the part of a role model for the children. Children do not read until they are seven (an approach shared by Scandinavian countries) and standardised tests are rare to non-existent. The education provided is holistic and also focuses on Steiner's theory of anthroposophy, a system of wellbeing closely related to homoeopathy.

- **Montessori** Montessori education is based upon the beliefs of the Italian physician and educator Maria Montessori. The main elements here are independence, freedom within limits and respect for the child's natural psychological, physical and social development. Montessori settings feature mixed-age classrooms with children afforded freedom of movement and a choice of activities in order that they lead their own learning. Children learn experientially, that is through doing, rather than being instructed as is common in traditional education. Montessori places importance on a 'prepared environment' – one that is organised so as to facilitate the child's autonomy and learning within surroundings that are predominantly focused on beauty, harmony, cleanliness, order and nature. Environments are kept free of clutter and children are able to access all materials themselves without adult help.

- **Democratic schools** These focus on giving children autonomy and equality: their decisions are respected and they are given the freedom to organise their days and their own learning. Democratic education places great emphasis on trust, respect and values. Children are treated as equal to adults and the teacher is not in a position of authority over them. Class attendance is voluntary and no punishment or logical consequences exist if the child does not attend. The roots of democratic schools go back at least four hundred years and their philosophy is not attributed to any one person.

- **Free schools** These are a new addition to alternative education. Launched in 2010 in the UK, free schools are commonly set up by groups of parents, teachers, charities or religious groups and are funded by the state, but not regulated by the local authority. This allows those in management – usually parents – a great deal of control over the school's policies and curriculum, while providing the benefits of a fee-free education. Free schools also have the authority to decide their own school-day timings, term dates, how much teachers are paid and who to recruit as teachers and staff. They do not have to teach the national curriculum and are free to choose their own, providing it is 'a balanced and broadly based curriculum'. Free schools do, however, have to follow national-admissions criteria, which means entry must be free for all and not restricted in any way.

This mother describes why she chose a free school for her son:

We moved our son to a free school for Year 1 after a year in reception of being told 'He needs to be more like the other children' (he has Sensory Processing Disorder and possibly Autistic Spectrum Disorder). Now he's in a place where they value, celebrate and support individuality, and where we can discuss any concerns and feel listened to and supported.

HOME EDUCATION

In the UK, you must make sure your child receives a full-time education from the age of five. However, this does not have to be at a school and does not have to follow the national curriculum. Home education is a term used to describe learning for children who do not attend school, mainstream or otherwise. It can range from parents tutoring their children using the national curriculum at home, to 'unschooling' which provides the child with a great degree of freedom and autonomy to control their own learning, rather than following a school-based approach at home. Parents choose home schooling for many different reasons, such as the following:

> We're home educating. Largely because of the increased rigidity and formality of early-years education and the behaviourist approach of nearly all schools to discipline.

> We are home educating because we decided that a five-year-old suffering the symptoms of [school-related] stress was not worth it. We would rather live joyfully and allow his learning to happen as part of that. School subjects can be learned at any time in his life; his emotional wellbeing is important always.

> We are home educating because lack of council funding means my autistic son isn't eligible for the help he needs to get through the sensory

overload that a typical day in school was for him. Apparently he's not 'disabled enough' for statementing.

We started out with our two oldest daughters going to public school, but after watching my oldest struggle emotionally and mentally, I decided to go down a different road with all four of them. We now unschool all of them. It's more child-led, which means they learn based on their interests.

I chose to home educate when my seven-year-old was not doing well in school. I hated the system, it just never worked for our family. I found the curriculum inflexible and too basic, the teachers too tired or disinterested and very little to encourage a love of learning. It was about following pointless rules and passing tests, and there was a distinct lack of support for anything outside the 'norms'.

In the UK there is no requirement to tell your local council that you intend to home educate, unless you are taking your child out of a special school. So if your child is already attending a state school and you plan to remove them, you need only inform the headteacher. You can register voluntarily with your local council's home-education service if you wish, and they may be able to provide you with some support, although this will also mean that you will now be on their radar and they will want to visit you and inspect your plans.

Home education – FAQs

- **Can home-schooled children take exams?** You can arrange for your child to take exams as an external candidate with an exam centre. Examination boards can provide a list of centres near your home. Your child could also study through a reputable correspondence college who will be able to provide access to an exam centre.

- **Do you need qualifications to home educate your child?** No qualifications are necessary to educate your child at home. You have already taught your child for four years, nothing changes when they reach school age.

- **Aren't home-educated children disadvantaged socially?** There are a huge number of home-education support groups and networks. Home-educating families commonly meet several times per week and many share their child's learning, depending on their interests and skills. In addition, your child can attend many conventional after-school activities such as drama, music and sport clubs and classes. There are also summer camps each year for home-educating families. So in many ways it can be much more sociable than conventional schooling.

- **Can you home educate for infant and junior school only?** Many parents home educate until their child is slightly older and then integrate them into mainstream schooling, either when they are seven, at the end of the conventional infant period, or when they are eleven and starting secondary schooling, although some do choose to continue home education for high-school-aged children. In this case it is still possible to sit GCSEs and A levels.

- **Can you home educate for part of the week and send your child to school for the other?** This is known as 'flexi-schooling', and while it is possible to ask your local school if they would consider this arrangement they do not have to accept. There are a fair number of families who do successfully negotiate a flexi-agreement with their local school though.

Homework woes

Do you remember when you were first set homework? For most of us, homework was not a part of our lives until we reached secondary school. Life is very different for children today. If you have chosen a more traditional form of schooling for your child, homework will feature on the agenda at a very young age, often starting in Year 1 or Year 2. So while our evenings and weekends were spent bike riding, playing with friends and climbing trees, our children are expected to complete worksheets and online educational games and projects, in addition to learning times tables by rote, practising for spelling tests and regular reading.

There is no legal requirement for children to complete homework at this age and, significantly, a great deal of research has shown that it has no benefits either.[6] What's more, there are a great deal of negatives associated with the increasing amount of homework young children are given including frustration, exhaustion, anxiety and loss of their intrinsic desire to learn (or read for fun). Research also shows that children who are stressed by homework are more likely to be obese.[7] If you feel that your child should not be doing homework at this age, then a well-researched and well-constructed letter to your child's school informing them of your decision to permanently excuse your child from homework and the reasoning behind it should suffice.

The problem with school behaviour management

The vast majority of school behavioural-management techniques designed to motivate children and reduce unwanted behaviour (such as merit certificates, good-behaviour stickers, head teacher's awards, 'golden time' and class points) have major flaws and their efficacy is arguable, particularly when taking a long-term view. The meaningless proverbial carrots dangled by many schools in their outdated behavioural policies don't inspire anything, aside from a short-term behavioural change driven by compliance. But the focus of school behaviour management is not on the long term – it is aimed at controlling behaviour for as long as the child is at school, and largely for the benefit of others.

Significant scientific research supports the notion that the behavioural techniques commonly used in mainstream education today may have serious implications for our children's future learning and willingness to engage with their own education. The ever-growing current trend of 'rewarding the good' does not invoke long-term change, nor does it motivate children to behave better, work harder and concentrate more. What we really want is for our children to have a strong internal (intrinsic) drive to do well and learn more, and for this to happen they need to be in an environment that is conducive to learning, with age-appropriate activities (at this age largely focused on play and learning through the senses) and objects, tools and people to inspire their natural curiosity, desire for mastery and urge to explore the world. But with most teachers constrained by preparation for school inspections, tests and record keeping, all within the limitations of the national curriculum, and the children, meanwhile, confined within four walls, exposed to large amounts of screen time and made to sit still for far too long, is it any wonder they misbehave?

More alarming than rewards is the tendency for some schools to punish children for perceived wrongdoings by keeping them inside for part of their break time, despite this being in direct contravention of article 31 of the United Nations Convention on the Rights of the Child which states: 'Children have the right to relax and play, and to join in a wide range of cultural, artistic and other recreational activities.' Leisure time is vital for children and they should never be made to miss part of their break or lunch time for any reason.

The key to our children's success does not lie in certificates, awards, badges and 'special time'; it is already inside of them, just waiting to unlock their potential. For this reason, it is strongly advised that when considering schools for your child, you study their behavioural policies in depth before making a decision. This is perhaps one of the best ways that you can advocate for them and ensure that, if mainstream schooling is your choice, they will learn in an environment that is respectful of as many of their needs as possible.

School refusal

At some point all children will refuse to go to school. Just as we as adults need the occasional day off, so children are the same. I have always thought it terribly unfair that as adults we can choose to stay at home and curl up on the sofa on days when there is nothing physically wrong with us, but we just don't want to face the world for whatever reason, yet children are not allowed to do this. Which is why if my children have ever expressed a need for a 'duvet day', I have always honoured that and allowed them the break that they required.

There is a difference, however, between the occasional need to stay at home and a child refusing to go to school on a daily basis. Some children (between 1 and 5 per cent of all school-aged children) are so severely affected that they are diagnosed as having a 'school phobia'. In these cases the child will commonly cry in the morning before school or in the evening preceding the school day too. They may say that they feel sick or are in pain. They may plead to not go to school, throw tantrums or refuse to get dressed. Many experts advise that children with school phobia are referred to a medical doctor, but the problem is usually with the school itself – the environment or the people in it – or the lead-up to school and not with the child.

The following is a list of the most common reasons for children refusing to go to school:

- Friendship issues

- Bullying and teasing

- Clashes with their teacher or other member of staff

- Concerns over homework

- Worry over tests

- Worry over speaking in public, in front of the class, or in an assembly

- Not understanding the work

- An undiagnosed special educational need (SEN)

- Vision problems

- Hearing problems

- Sleep problems and feeling tired

- Anxiety around being separated from parents

- Anxiety around physical issues, such as going to the toilet

- Difficulty adjusting to the transition from home to school

- Generalised anxiety

- Response to a life or home event, such as a house move or arrival of a new siblings

- Simply being too young for school

- Exhaustion

- Difficulty adjusting to the increased noise and busyness of the school environment (some children experience school as a 'sensory overload', particularly those who are sensitive, or come from a smaller family where they may be the only child; for these children the school day can be draining until they adjust to the increased sensory experience).

The best way to handle school refusal is to find the underlying reason – there will always be one – and to work with the child and the school to resolve it. School refusal is not a problem that belongs solely to the child – very often it is an issue with the school and sometimes the parents, and resolution should not, therefore, focus exclusively on the child. In some cases the answer may be to find a new school or to consider alternative education options such as home schooling, delaying school entry and other kinds of schools.

Friendships

Once your child is in an environment with lots of similarly aged children, it is almost inevitable that they will develop friendship problems. Children can be very fickle and quite brutal with their honesty when it comes to their peers. Getting on and falling out with others is an important learning curve for children and also for their parents who play an important role in helping them to navigate the friendship minefield. In addition, parents can often find their own relationships with other parents become strained as a result of their child's interactions at school.

Firstly, remember that young children don't think like adults. They are still developing empathy and the ability to understand the thoughts and feelings of other people, and this often means that they don't mean to upset others, even if that is the outcome. Helping children to consider another person's point of view can be very helpful, as can empowering them to resolve their own friendship issues. As a parent it is very tempting to 'fix' your child's friendship problems – however, in the long run, this can be detrimental to them as they never learn how to resolve things on their own. Your role should be a listening and coaching one: your child definitely needs your help to navigate friendship issues; they just don't need you to step in and solve them.

Bedtime is a great time to chat with your child about their school day and any friendship concerns that have arisen. Listen to them without interrupting. When your child has finished telling you about what has happened, let them know that you have heard them and validate their experience and emotions – 'That must have been hard for you when she said that', or, 'I would have felt mad too if he stole the ball from me' – but make sure that you do not chastise them or tell them what you would have done instead. Next, ask them if they can understand why the other child may have acted in the way that they did. 'Can you think of any reasons why she was mean to you then?', or, 'I wonder how he was feeling before he took the ball from you?' This validates your child's feelings and also helps them to consider the other child's point of view without you taking sides. Lastly, ask your child if they can think of any resolution: 'I wonder if there was anything you could have done or said that might have helped?, or, 'If he tries to take the ball again, do you think that you could do anything that would make you both happier?' Allowing your child to brainstorm shows your trust in their ability to solve the situation themselves which, in turn, provides them with a great confidence boost. Although this approach is unlikely to help with the next friendship issue, with time, patience and practice your child will develop the skills to resolve social problems confidently on their own – something a lot of children still cannot do many years down the line and which quite a few adults have never developed the skills for either.

Sometimes, no matter how much you – and they – try, your child will not be able to resolve friendship issues. In these cases you need to stay empathic and patient, fulfilling your role as a container for their disappointment and anxiety. If the problem persists or escalates, then you should involve the school and, hopefully, they will react appropriately.

On a more general note, try to not steer your child's friendships, either towards those children you would prefer that they played with or away from those who you would rather they avoided, as hard as that may be for you. It's difficult for you, as a parent, if your child decides that they do not want to play with the child of a friend of yours, but that is their prerogative and you should respect their friendship choices.

Sibling relationships

Sibling relationships are closely related to friendship issues, but here it is even more important that you do not take sides. Once again, your role should be one of listener, mentor and sounding board. Even if you have one child who always appears to instigate arguments, you should always approach each occurrence with fresh eyes and ears and allow both children to have their say. Again, while the temptation may be strong to referee an argument, single out the instigator and 'fix' the problem, you should take a back seat. If you have to be actively involved in every argument that your children have, you will be setting a pattern for the future and they will not be able to resolve disagreements without you. Your role here should be to help the children to understand each other's points of views, to respect their differing opinions and come to a mutual compromise by way of a resolution.

In the scenario of two siblings arguing over one toy, for example, you might start by describing exactly what you see: 'I see two children who are both very angry right now.' This invites the children to tell you what is happening, but make sure that each of them is aware that you want to hear from both of them. Ask child one, 'Can you tell me what happened?' and then ask child two the same question. Ask child one, 'And how did that make you feel? and ask child two the same question. Then describe the situation again: 'So, you both wanted to play with the same toy and you are both sad and mad that the other one wants to as well.' Next, put the ball firmly in their court and ask, 'How do you think we can solve this problem?' Ask child one, 'What do you think we can do?', then ask child two the same question. You can then move on to discussing their suggestions. If they differ greatly, ask again: 'How do you think we can resolve this so that both of you are happy? Can we do a mix of what you have both suggested?' When the resolution has been ultimately reached let them know how proud you are of them for resolving the issue: 'I'm really proud that you both thought about each other's feelings and came to a good solution yourselves.'

Encouraging trust and co-operation between siblings can be

further enhanced by group family activities where everyone works as a team through something like den building. You can also buy special board games called 'co-operative games' that encourage children to work together to solve problems and win the game, rather than being in competition with each other.

If you have more than one child, it is of utmost importance that you have regular, good-quality one-to-one time with each of them on a daily basis. You should spend a bare minimum of fifteen minutes chatting with your children individually in a separate room from their siblings. An ideal time to do this is during the bedtime routine, when you're tucking them up in bed for the night. (If your children share a room, try to do their bedtime routines at a different time, so you have time with the youngest alone first, then time with the second and so on.) In addition, you should also arrange for larger 'top-ups' regularly. Ideally, this time will be spent doing an activity of the child's choosing. This could be a morning at the park with one child and a trip to the cinema or swimming with another; but it doesn't necessarily mean having to leave the house – doing jigsaws, building models or snuggling on the sofa watching a DVD are all great connection opportunities, but just make sure that they only involve the two of you. In each case no other siblings should be present, not even babies. One-to-one means exactly that – nobody else. Keeping this time consistent and adding extra top-ups is perhaps the best way to cope with any sibling rivalry.

Talking about growing up

When is the right time to talk to your children about sex, puberty and the differences between male and female bodies? Arguably, the answer is it's never too soon. Raising your child to know where they came from and to understand and accept the differences in human bodies when they are younger, in an age-appropriate manner, is perhaps the best way to prevent the need for awkward conversations when they are older. Raising a child who is not ashamed of their body or embarrassed by the changes that will soon be happening can smooth the transition through puberty.

Research has shown that children who have a good relationship with their parents when it comes to discussing sex and growing up tend to be less likely to engage in sexual activity at a young age and have a lower risk of teenage pregnancy, abortion and sexually transmitted infections.[8] So far from trying to keep children as innocent as possible for as long as possible, parents should be doing the very opposite. And the same is true with exposure to birth and breastfeeding. The earlier that these are normalised, the healthier the attitude and behaviours that the child will grow up with will be.

At this stage children should know the anatomically correct names for the genitalia, how the reproductive organs in the body work (including menstruation and breast milk), how a baby is made and how bodies change as we get older. And their questions should be answered simply and honestly. A good book can really help here and there are many on the market (I have listed some in the back of this book – see page 281). If your child is at mainstream school, then they will also receive sex-education lessons; but you should not rely on these alone to inform your child, as the quality is often highly dubious, and they should know that you are the person they can always come to with any questions.

Your child's brain between four and seven years

Your child's brain is still really busy at this stage. At the end of this age period the number of synapses (connections) in the brain are at a near peak, before the process of neural pruning starts to remove unused connections. The frontal lobe is still connecting, however, and it is this area that is the last to mature, which explains why a child's behaviour and understanding, particularly on a social level, are still not the same as an adult's. Size and weight wise, by the end of this period the brain is approaching near adult dimensions at around 85–90 per cent the volume of a mature adult brain.

While children start this age range extremely egocentric, towards the end of the period they become more sociocentric – that is, they begin to have much more of an appreciation of the thoughts and feelings of others and how these may differ from their own emotions. Grasping social rules also increases towards the end of the period. Understanding slowly becomes more intuitive and thought processes mature as children increasingly recognise logical concepts. It is still fairly crude, however, and children are generally only capable of thinking about one aspect of an object at one time; similarly, they are still unable to follow multiple instructions and classifications. So by the end of this age range children are still unable to think abstractly and metaphorically and still possess a degree of egocentrism.

What to expect of your child's sleep between four and seven years

From the ages of four to seven, experts agree that children need between eight and twelve hours of sleep per night, with most getting around ten to eleven hours. Bedtime is usually at around 8 p.m. with the average wake time being 7 a.m. Night waking is not very common at this age, but can still occur largely due to nightmares, night terrors and bedwetting.

Up to half of all children in this age range will experience lucid nightmares, requiring adult assistance to calm them, with around 6 per cent experiencing night terrors. At the start of this age range, approximately one in six children will wet the bed and still need nappies at night; by the end of this age range this figure is one in twenty. If your child still regularly wets the bed by the age of six or seven, then often medical help is required. This tends to focus on alarms and monitors to wake the child before the enuresis (bedwetting) occurs, although for some children there may be a physical cause behind it.

Children in this age range still need a consistent bedtime routine and most will still need adult assistance to fall asleep.

Using the Seven Cs of gentle parenting from four to seven years

How will you implement the Seven Cs of gentle parenting from four to seven years?

Connection

At a time when the majority of children are separated from their parents for at least six hours per day, five days per week, and when most are sleeping all night in their own bedroom, it can be all too easy to allow the connection to drop. This is only compounded by the arrival of new siblings and parents returning to work. So connection is vital here – taking time to reconnect one-to-one each day can transform behaviour.

Communication

At this age verbal communication is largely comparable to that of an adult as far as actual speech is concerned, but this can be misleading in terms of the comprehension of the words and processing of the information. Children of this age still do not think like adults and many difficulties can be down to our misunderstanding of this. As before, behaviour is a major form of communication at this age, from school refusal, to toileting, sleep, eating, backchat and tantrums. Looking for the cause of the behaviour remains the priority.

Control

If a toddler has little control over their daily life, then imagine how much control a child of this age in mainstream school has. They are only allowed to eat or drink when somebody else decides, and wear shoes and clothes that somebody else has chosen. Many children are prohibited from having free access to the toilet, and their play, their movement and their speech are all heavily restricted. To add to this, restrictions at home are only compounding the problem. Age-appropriate autonomy, freedom and trust are crucial. An over-controlled child will eventually protest in some way.

Containment

Children in this age range still have limited emotional-regulation abilities. They still need our help to act as their external emotional thermostats. And in order for us to adequately contain their emotions, they need to trust that we will listen to them, not belittle or chastise them, empathise with them, help them and, importantly, not share anything that they have confided to us in trust. In many ways children of this age need more containing than any other as they have so many transitions to cope with that evoke so many big feelings.

Champion

Children need a champion at all ages, but perhaps this is more pertinent now than at any of the other ages covered in this book. The issue of championing children is vital when selecting schooling for your child and even more so when the schooling begins.

Confidence

Your relationship and communication with your child at this age is a good predictor of their confidence in later life. Helping your child to learn that everybody is different, with their own strengths and weaknesses can be very helpful in terms of their education. This is why avoiding the overuse of praise and rewards is essential. Children need to retain an intrinsic drive for mastery and to learn, but not at the expense of their confidence if they find something challenging. From a parental perspective this age can bring quite a few knocks to your confidence as you leave the security of the baby, toddler and preschooler world that you have known for the last five years and enter new territory with new behaviours and new issues. Having faith in your parenting and, most importantly, your instincts is what will guide you through.

Consistency

Keeping consistent in your parenting is as necessary as ever at this age. Boundaries and limits remain key, now with a special focus on screen time. Setting a family limit on this and sticking to it religiously is imperative if you are to avoid problems with screens in the coming tween and teen years.

Chapter 8

Transitioning from Mainstream to Gentle Parenting

So many people have said to me, 'If we didn't make children do things, they wouldn't do anything.' Even worse, they say, 'If I weren't made to do things, I wouldn't do anything.' It is the creed of a slave.

From *How Children Fail* by John Holt, author and educator

I s it possible to change to a more gentle parenting style if you followed mainstream methods initially? Absolutely. And, for some, the change in parenting style comes as a welcome relief.

For many parents, learning about gentle parenting validates their own instincts and thoughts about raising their children. They finally feel free to parent in the way that they have always wanted to. I often speak with parents who tell me, 'This is how I felt that I wanted to parent instinctively, but I just didn't, as I thought I should be doing something else.' Understanding the gentle style, and all of the science that backs it, can be very liberating for parents. Similarly, children often take to the change quickly and extremely positively. It is not uncommon to see quite dramatic results with both parents and children thriving and flourishing after only a week or two of following more gentle principles.

For others, however, the transition can be harder and longer. Emotionally, it can be difficult for parents to learn about alternative and more positive ways of parenting, as this can create the realisation that methods they have previously used are not optimal and may carry unintended consequences for their child. This can mean there is an initial period of discomfort and unease as they come to terms with the past and resolve to make a difference in the future. But this process can also be quite cathartic, if you allow it to be, not only for you, but for your children too.

In some cases the change to a more gentle way of parenting can cause a temporary regression or worsening of behaviour. In many ways this is the most difficult part of the transition to deal with as it calls into question the efficacy of the new ethos. In addition, the newly emerged difficult behaviour can be challenging to manage in an already fragile family dynamic. But the good news is that these negative side effects are almost always temporary.

I like to talk about the transition to gentle parenting in terms of stages. Some families, those that find it really easy, move through these stages so quickly that they don't even notice that they are happening. But no matter how quickly or slowly you move through them, it is essential that you understand what may be happening in order to be prepared and also to be able to stay positive and focused on the end goal. If you are finding the transition particularly tricky it really helps if you understand that often your darkest hours are a sign that your efforts are working and that there is a brighter future ahead.

The five stages of transition to gentle parenting

Changing to a more gentle style of parenting goes through five different phases which may last anything from a day or two to several months each.

1. A feeling of a loss of control

This feeling is true for both parent and child, when all current methods of behaviour control disappear and nobody is sure what should be in their place. Children can find it hard to cope with changes in boundaries and a lack of predictability over resulting discipline. Adults struggle with not responding in their usual manner. This loss of control and the internal struggle experienced as a result is commonly reflected in the child's (and sometimes the adult's) behaviour.

2. A regression in behaviour

The lack of control from both sides can cause a big regression in behaviour. Children can suddenly tantrum, lash out, stop eating, stop sleeping, yell and generally become 'feral'. Adults have a tendency to follow suit and can become very 'shouty' and tense, with lowered tolerance levels, which, in turn, triggers even worse behaviour from the child. This is the stage at which many making the transition give up and declare that 'gentle parenting doesn't work'. In most cases, it most definitely does get a lot worse before it gets better, but regression is actually a very good sign that your family is becoming more authentic and emotions are being given permission to be felt and released.

3. Anger and sadness

Again, these emotions are commonly felt on both sides. Anger is often felt at the loss of control and worsened behaviour; sadness occurs most commonly for the parent as the realisation dawns that their child's behaviour is possibly a result of decisions that they did or didn't make. For children this stage is key. They need to get angry; they need to get sad. You are opening the gates to potentially years of suppressed emotion which needs to be released – from all of those times they sat in time out or on the naughty step, the times when emotions were covered up in order to gain a sticker or the nights when they didn't cry because nobody came. The fact that these emotions are appearing now is a very positive sign that the new parenting style is working for your family, even though it may seem unhealthy and abnormal and many believe that it is the gentle parenting that is causing these 'unacceptable' emotions. Rather, gentle parenting is allowing the emotions that have already been there to finally come out. At this stage you should encourage this raw emotion. Everybody needs to own their feelings and not be scared or ashamed of them. Crying is so healing, for both children and parents.

4. The need for reconnection

Once the repressed feelings are released, the need to reconnect and establish a bond of trust is vital. Your child needs to know that you will always be there for them. Sometimes you need to fall in love with each other all over again. Your attention in this period should be almost solely focused on rebuilding those invisible strings of love between you and your child, containing their big emotions and showing them that you will never leave them to cope with them alone again. This stage is also about loving yourself, making peace with your decisions and realising that, actually, you are a great parent, otherwise you wouldn't be at this stage. It takes a lot of courage to change your parenting and you have come so far already. You should be really proud of yourself.

5. The breakthrough

This is finally when things begin to fall into place, and could be months or sometimes even years after deciding to make the transition to gentle parenting. But one day something will happen and everything will click. It may be something your child says to another, it may be something you say to them or it may be a behaviour you observe. The breakthrough is different for everyone, but when it happens you will know, without a doubt, that you made the best possible decision for your family. From this point on it becomes solely about moving forward and not looking back.

How to cope with behaviour regressions

During the transition to gentle parenting, it is almost inevitable that your child's behaviour will deteriorate, albeit temporarily. Children need to explore their new boundaries and limits and you need to remember to consistently enforce them. This testing period is crucial for the whole family to be able to move forward. If your child is four years or older, then sitting down with them and discussing the change can be a good idea. You don't necessarily have to explain the whole ethos of gentle parenting, or why it matters to you, but taking time to sit together as a family to brainstorm and discuss the new boundaries is a great idea. Children respond really well when given ownership of something. Ask them what they think should be definite 'Nos' in your house and ask them to come up with some solutions for people who break the limit. For instance your family may decide that shoes should always be put away in the shoe cupboard. You may all decide that if anybody notices shoes have been left out, they should calmly tell the shoes' owner that this is the case and the owner should put them away. This, of course, applies to parents as well as children, and it is not unreasonable to expect your child to point out your contravention of the family rules and ask you to put your shoes away too.

As with all behaviour regressions, the key is in understanding the motivation and cause behind the behaviour. What is the child trying to communicate through their tears, tantrum, food refusal, hitting or resistance to going to bed? Once you understand this – and it may be as simple as the child feeling unsettled due to a new way of doing things – you can work to resolve the issue through reassurance and consistently enforcing boundaries. Remind yourself that this stage is normal and transient and a good sign that your new parenting style is becoming effective. Most of all though, try to stay as calm as possible yourself. Your response to any regressions in behaviour is vital. (See Chapter 10 for coping techniques for the tough days and exhausting nights.)

Coming to terms with your parenting mistakes

Stage three in the transition to gentle parenting – the stage of anger and sadness – is perhaps the most difficult to navigate, necessitating that we do some soul searching and coming to terms with our previous actions and decisions. This can be cathartic or painful, or often a mix of both. On days when I have found parenting tough, I have always wished that I didn't have to be an adult any more. How lovely it would be not only to not have to deal with the practicalities of being a parent, but also to not to have to live with the sea of churning emotions it evokes.

All parents make mistakes though. A vital part of the parenting journey is about learning and growing as an adult, and we can do neither without making mistakes. Parenting shapes your behaviour and personality almost as much as it does your child's. Becoming a parent is the final step in 'growing up' yourself. One of my favourite phrases in relation to parenting is, 'When we know better, we do better'. You can only do your best with the information that you believed to be correct at the time. The problem here is that we are presented with so much information, often from sources of authority, such as medical and childcare professionals, and it can be difficult to question the validity of their advice.

If we cannot process our parenting guilt, however, then we remain in a position of parental suspension. We experience the worst of both worlds: the constant nagging pain reminding us of a decision made at a time when we either didn't know or couldn't do better and the inability to move on using the experience to lift us to a new level of awareness. But as tough as it is to be the adult sometimes, it is the only way, for the sake of ourselves as well as our children. As the author and scientist Steve Maraboli writes: 'We all make mistakes, have struggles and even regret things in our past. But you are not your mistakes, you are not your struggles, and you are here now with the power to shape your day and your future.'[1]

If you have a bad day – and you will have because everybody does – remind yourself that it is just that: one bad day. Tomorrow is a chance to start afresh. And even though it may not seem like it at the time, a bad day is a great learning experience, helping you to understand what does and does not work for your family. So don't write off all your hard work for the sake of one day or one incident. It is vital that you are kind to yourself when progressing through this part of the transition to gentle parenting. Being gentle on yourself is as important as being gentle on your child. (We will cover the importance of self-nurturance in a Chapter 10 for just this reason.)

Why some parents can't – or don't – make the change to gentle parenting

Some parents can find the transition to gentle parenting too challenging, often because what they want is a 'quick fix' for their child's behaviour – there may be another baby on the way, a return to work or another deadline with the clock loudly ticking. Others are too engulfed by their busy lifestyles or lack of support to be able to persevere through all of the stages. And some simply decide that gentle parenting isn't for them.

The feelings of regret that emerge from learning that the way in which they were previously raising their children may not be optimal are overwhelming and, some parents cannot move beyond this guilt and remorse. It is fairly commonplace for these people to dismiss research and new information that is at odds with methods that they have used or are currently using. These are the people who often try to dissuade you from changing your own parenting, because it makes them feel too uncomfortable about theirs. Perhaps you have a friend or family member who scoffs at your parenting choices, instantly rejecting them out of hand? Perhaps they challenge you over your 'spoiling', 'softness' or 'mollycoddling'? In almost all cases their reaction is not really about you or your parenting at all, but rather is part of a process well known in psychology as 'cognitive dissonance'.

Cognitive dissonance

The American social psychologist Leon Festinger developed his theory of cognitive dissonance in the late 1950s. He described it as a two-step process, as follows:

1. The existence of dissonance, or feeling of being psychologically uncomfortable, will motivate the person to try to reduce the dissonance and achieve consonance.
2. When dissonance is present, in addition to trying to reduce it, the person will actively avoid situations and information which would likely increase the dissonance.

This process explains the tendency of individuals to avoid or be disdainful of situations or ideas that clash with their beliefs, no matter how accurate and reliable the information may be.

From a parenting perspective cognitive dissonance is unsurprisingly rife. The idea that you may have unwittingly caused harm to your child through your actions is perhaps the most uncomfortable feeling there can be, and it is much easier to dismiss new research as 'hippy rubbish' or with comments such as, 'What do these scientists know, anyway? I was smacked and I'm fine.'

In order to parent mindfully and as positively as possible, a certain amount of dissonance is inevitable. But a gentle parent would 'sit' with the dissonance, process it and move on, out of respect for their child and themselves. This is possibly the hardest part of parenting, particularly if you are changing to a different style, but it is something we all have to face at some point in time.

When others attack your gentle-parenting choices

As well as dealing with your own dissonance over your change to a more gentle way of parenting, you are quite likely to find that you spark dissonance in those around you too. Here it is important to recognise people's actions for what they are – namely, about themselves, not you. Stay focused on your own parenting and try not to let the opinions of others unsettle you.

Many parents remain in an uncomfortable limbo of dissonance throughout their entire parenting journey. Eventually, the guilt turns to bitterness which tends to manifest either as an internal attack upon themselves or as condemnation of others' parenting choices. Sadly, this criticism is usually directed towards those who are closest – friends and family. Again, remind yourself that it is not you, or your parenting, that is the real problem; the real problem is the uncomfortable feelings generated within the person who is judging you. And, unfortunately, the dissonance is so enormous for some people that they are long past being able to recognise these bitter feelings as their own guilt.

So be prepared that when you make the decision to parent in a more gentle manner, you can become the catalyst for dissonance in those around you if they do, or did, parent in a more traditional manner, which means that you open yourself to criticism. In response, many parents believe that 'proving' gentle parenting through articles and research is the answer to any condemnation, particularly from relatives. Sadly, it isn't. Each time you present them with a new piece of research, a new article or a new book, however well-executed, you are only compounding their state of dissonance. In fact, the more convincing the research, the more likely it is that you will increase their psychological discomfort and that they, in turn, will fight back even more.

What is the answer, then? Unfortunately, for some there isn't one. Sometimes new beliefs are too difficult for people to take on board due to the sheer amount of work required to accept them, in which case your best option is to afford them the same consideration and empathy that you do your own children. Understand how hard it must be for them to hear your message and the fact that you parent in a way that causes them discomfort. Softly and slowly, drip-feeding tiny pieces of information can help, but for many it may be a case of agreeing to disagree with mutual respect.

Moving forward – using our dissonance to good effect

All too often parents get stuck in a state of dissonance, unable to hear truths about the choices they made for their child's birth or in the early days of parenting. We must recognise and process our own guilt and we must not let it stand in the way of making a difference for those who follow in our footsteps. Just because a certain piece of information is hurtful for us to hear (whether it's about birth, breastfeeding, sleep training, discipline or anything else), we must not be slaves to the guilt and must use it as a driving force for good, for social change. When used in this way guilt becomes positive – it has a purpose, and it allows for healing, for both parent and child.

So when a piece of research is published that shows that a common parenting practice may cause harm, or may be less positive than we believed it was when we followed it with our own children, we must embrace it, no matter how it makes us feel. It's time to end the cycle of what obstetrician Dr Michel Odent calls 'cul-de-sac epidemiology':

This framework includes research about topical issues. Despite the publication of this research in authoritative medical or scientific journals, the findings are shunned by the medical community and the media. Cul-de-sac epidemiological studies are not replicated, even by the original investigators and they are rarely quoted after publication.[2]

Gentle parents understand the importance of embracing and not denying the validity of science because of how it makes them feel. Once again, when we know better, we do better, regardless of how tough that journey may be and how much it may challenge our beliefs and past behaviours. So if you ever feel those familiar feelings of guilt or regret slipping back in, tell yourself: 'I did what I did then, with the information I had at the time. Now I know better and I can do better.' Take one day at a time and be kind to yourself and your family. This is new to you all, and there will be hiccups and obstacles, but you have already completed the hardest part of the journey. Things will get better. Things will get easier. Remind yourself that anger, sadness and regressions in behaviour are all healthy stages to pass through and are, in many ways, responses to be welcomed. Everybody has tough days, even those who parented in this manner right from the start.

I have devoted the whole of the next chapter to getting through the dark days, and you will hear from many parents about their coping techniques. But first, I'd like to leave you with a few words from a mother who made the transition from a mainstream to a more gentle way of thinking in her work and in her own parenting:

I was a teacher, indoctrinated into behaviourism and adult-led activities. I learned how to become pupil-led but found it hard to remove myself from behavioural techniques altogether. When I became a mum, my heart changed my mind and I began to think differently about development, about behaviour, and mostly about myself – it has been a huge turnaround and I have struggled with it because I was convinced that was the way to go, and now I know that this is the way to go. But gentle parenting and being child-led is *hard work*, and behavioural approaches are all too easy to slip into. I work at it every day, but at the same time it feels like the most natural thing in the world, and I know it's all worthwhile.

Chapter 9

What to Expect in Terms of Results

*Don't judge each day by the harvest you reap
but by the seeds that you plant.*

Robert Louis Stevenson, novelist and poet

What does it mean when something works? In the case of an object, surely it means that it can perform the task it was purchased for – that it is 'fit for purpose'; in the case of a medicine, that the symptoms of a disease are cured or palliated; and in the case of a relationship, that there is a manifestation of happiness and contentment on both sides.

So what does it look like when gentle parenting works? Do we expect babies to not cry? Do we expect toddlers to not tantrum? Do we expect them to never bite, hit, throw, shove or push? Do we expect young children to share and not whine? Do we expect siblings to never fall out and friendships to never end? Do we expect that children will never answer back or refuse to tidy their rooms? And if any of these still occur, should we regard gentle parenting as having failed?

All too often I come across parents who proclaim that gentle parenting 'doesn't work'. They say, 'It's a nice idea, but my baby still cries all the time', or, 'We tried all of the recommendations and our toddler still tantrums and still hits his brother'. The obvious conclusion quickly drawn in these cases is that while the parents may understand and appreciate the theories behind gentle parenting, they're not so sure that they believe in it because it's just not working out for their family.

People will find all sorts of reasons why gentle parenting is not for them, saying it doesn't work if you have more than one child, if you have to go out to work, if you are a single parent or if you have twins or multiples. It is perfectly possible to parent gently in all of these situations and more. The problem lies in the level of investment that families make. And I am not talking about financial investments – you can buy all of the slings and cloth nappies in the world and it does not make you a gentle parent. I'm talking about time and a commitment to changing your choices and preferences to accommodate the new style of parenting. For many, however, these are investments that they are not willing to make.

Part of the problem is society's 'quick-fix' obsession, whether it's fast food, same-day pay loans, three-day weight-loss diets or celebrity nannies who claim they can fix any family's problems in one short visit. Because real life just isn't like that. Real life is messy. Real achievements take time and require a big re-evaluation of circumstances and a lot of commitment and willpower. Quick fixes come at a price, and that price almost always comes after the initially impressive results. But with gentle parenting the price comes before the results and that's something that our society just isn't used to.

So gentle parenting is hard: it is all too easy to slip into punishment or reward mode with toddlers, especially if these methods have previously produced the desired effects quickly.

And it is all too easy to sleep train for a few nights to get a child to sleep through. In the long term though, these shortcuts don't really resolve anything, they just mask the problem for another day.

As I've said, gentle parenting is a big investment. It can sometimes seem like thousands of hours are spent depositing into the bank of the future while fighting to survive day to day. This is a struggle so many parents face when transitioning to a more gentle-parenting style. Gentle parenting is not a quick fix; but it will pay out in time.

Gently parented babies still cry, they still get colic and they still wake frequently at night. Gently parented toddlers still bite, hit, kick and throw and refuse to eat their vegetables. Gently parented children still talk back, whine and fall out with their siblings. In time, however, a gently parented child will enjoy close relationships with their parents and siblings and will feel able to share their troubles. They are likely to turn into a teenager who resists peer pressure and doesn't lie to their parents and will, ultimately, be happy in their own skin, enjoying the confidence needed to form meaningful relationships with others. A gently parented child will grow up finding it easier to speak their own mind and be in control of their emotions and they will be ambitious and motivated to reach their full potential in life. Perhaps most exciting of all, however, gently parented children will go on to raise a whole other generation of emotionally intelligent children.

These parents describe the time that they knew gentle parenting was working for their family:

It was actually a friend who noticed … My three-year-old dropped her spoon in a restaurant. I gave her mine and was going to eat my dessert with a fork. She would not accept it as she didn't want me to go without a spoon. My friend noticed how worried my daughter was for me. The waiter brought another spoon and we were all happy.

My husband's mother wasn't very gentle with him. She spent years as a nanny, more or less making up for the pain she caused him, in fact, but when she came to visit our two-year-old last month she commented almost immediately on how happy, independent and well-behaved her granddaughter is, and thanked me for my patience and strength. There are still tantrums, and there is still angst and boundary pushing, but we see that applying kindness around those boundaries has reduced stress and tension.

When I was several weeks' pregnant, our twenty-month-old was suddenly a crazed lunatic. She's always been expressive with her emotions, but this was something else. I wondered if we were entering the terrible twos early or what on earth was to come if we weren't even there yet! Some might have started time outs or even spanking, but a few people suggested the cause was probably her recognition that something had changed with me, so I made extra time for just us with cuddles and hugs and activities like puzzles, colouring and books. The extreme behaviour has calmed down so much in the months that have followed.

I was crying and my girls, two and three, walked up really cautiously and laid a hand on my back and said, 'We are here for you, Mommy, when you are ready. We will always be here for you, no matter what.' Then they walked slowly backwards and stood against the wall not too far from me and waited – I don't know how long, five minutes roughly – and when I wiped my face and went to stand up off the floor, my two-year-old said, 'Are you ready?' I said, 'Yes, thank you for waiting so patiently'. And they ran up and covered me in hugs.

I always know that gentle parenting is *the* way to parent and I have so much joy with my three-year-old son every day. But one ordinary day at a restaurant, when I was actually a bit sick, a woman came up to us. She said she noticed us and how we interacted with each other. She said she loved our interaction. She turned to my baffled son and said, 'You are such a good boy'. It was one of the days when there was a conference on child abuse in town, so I wondered if she was an educator or in a related field.

Gentle parenting does work, just not in the time frame many expect, or want, it to. That first glimmer of hope, the first sign that it may be working, is one to grasp and hold onto, just like the parents above. Use it to keep yourself motivated on days when you question what you are doing. In time, you will experience many more similar events until you know, without a shadow of a doubt, that gentle parenting really works.

What to do if gentle parenting isn't working for you

Above all else, have you allowed enough time to pass? As a bare minimum, expect it to take eight weeks of sticking religiously to gentle parenting principles, although in reality it is likely to take a lot longer. Next, remember the Seven Cs of gentle parenting:

- connection
- communication
- control
- containment
- champion
- confidence
- consistency

Are you truly being mindful of all of these? People who are struggling with a transition to gentle parenting are often falling short on some of the Sevens Cs, communication, confidence and consistency being by far the three most challenging.

Communication

If we are stressed, or having a bad day, this is commonly reflected in our parenting and particularly in our communication with our children. Children, being great imitators, pick up on not just the words we say, but the meaning and intent behind them and the tone and volume of our voice. Sometimes, when gentle parenting isn't working, it is a sign that we need to adjust our communication a little. Take a deep breath and 'THINK' before you respond to your child:

T – Is it True?
H – Is it Helpful?
I – Is it Inspiring?
N – Is it Necessary?
K – Is it Kind?

Taking time to THINK before you speak can produce an amazingly different response from not only your child, but also your partner, other family members, colleagues and friends.

Confidence

Confidence is related to time. Parents who are new to gentle parenting tend to start second guessing their parenting abilities very quickly: 'She must be naturally calm, I'm not; it will never work for me', or, 'He's such a great dad; he's so patient and never yells. I could never be like that.' I can almost guarantee you that even the gentlest of parents, the earth mothers who make everything look easy, have struggled. As easy as they may make things look, they will still second guess their parenting every single day. You don't know what happens behind closed doors, or what goes on in their minds. The invisible part of their parenting is rarely as calm and ordered as the external projections.

Losing confidence in their abilities, or worse, their child's, is one of the first hurdles parents fall at. So if you find it hard now, that's OK – most people do. But just like others who have walked this path before you and not given up, so you will follow in their footsteps and one day inspire others. You *can* do it. You just need to have enough confidence to keep going.

Consistency

So you've really tried and you just can't do it. Your child is too energetic or strong-minded. Your best efforts are failing, you're too busy, too tired … Here I can almost guarantee that consistency is the key. Because when it comes to boundaries and limits, it is precisely the times when you are busy and tired – when you would rather do anything else than follow your child's new bedtime routine – that you should enforce them. Too many parents flit from one technique to the next without ever giving any of them time to work. Again, eight weeks is a good goal. Follow gentle parenting principles consistently every day for eight weeks as an absolute minimum before assessing any outcome. Lack of consistency ruins too many good intentions; don't let it ruin yours. In the next chapter we'll look at what you might need to change in your life to enable you to be more consistent.

How other parents cope with tough days

When researching this book I spoke with many parents about how they got through the tough days – the days when they could easily have lost hope in gentle parenting. These are some of their answers. I hope they inspire you as much as they did me:

> Just focus on this night, just focus on this day, just focus on this activity. The next night, day or activity doesn't need you yet.

> Remember there are parents all over the world with the same struggle as you. You are not alone.

> I think, let's start over; I'm not superhuman. I just cuddle my little one regardless. I try to stay calm and remind myself this will pass!

> One day you will forget how hard this is and will miss this little body curled up on yours, and that all it took was a hug. Every year is fast but every day is long.

> I tell myself, 'My daughter is strong-willed, determined, questioning, independent, spirited … These are all good qualities, these are all good qualities!'

> I remind myself that it's not their fault and it's not my fault. We're in this together and we'll get through this together.

I stop, look into the face of my gorgeous son, and think, I am so lucky to be his mommy.

When I'm in demand I remember that one day she won't need or want me as much and to enjoy this close time.

Slow down … when it's getting tough with a routine ask yourself, who is this bothering more: me or my child? Question who am I putting first with this routine and slow down. So what if they didn't get their bath or teeth brushed? It can happen tomorrow. So what if I'm late? This helps me to step back, go slow, get perspective and put my child first.

I just remember that I didn't sign up for convenience. I knew this role would be twenty-four/seven and wasn't one I could quit on. A good, long, tight cuddle, whatever hour of the day helps enormously too.

I always say to myself: 'This is so temporary.' Then I try to think of how things will be in the future when those difficult times won't be here any more. I also love to dream about a nice vacation I know can happen in the near future. Or I think about something nice that's been planned for the weekend or I come up with something good to focus on.

If you can't change the behaviour, change your attitude towards it.

I try to remember to respond rather than react. I can take the emotion out of it that way and think of my child's perspective, rather than how it's affecting me.

'It's their day too.' This is good for when you had a hundred things to do in the day and all you achieved was reading books and going to the park … makes you feel better that your child had a good day, even if you feel like you've been unproductive.

I think of the moment I first held them, and that amazing feeling. This always calms me down.

I remind myself she's doing this for a reason. This is a big deal for her. Big feelings, little body.

When I had my baby, an old friend of mine said, 'Remember, children need a lot of love, patience, and time.' That has gotten me through my toughest moments, and here's why: when you are ready to give all of the love you can, patience isn't so hard to have. Once you have patience, the time it takes to deal with a situation isn't so bad. That, and you can never love a baby too much.

It's never too late to turn *today* around and start being the parent I want to be.

I think that last quote is a fitting way to end this chapter. It doesn't matter what has happened in the past, or even what is happening in the present. The future is there for anyone to embrace and make a change. It's never too late.

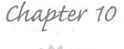

Chapter 10

Taking Care of Your Own Needs

I have come to believe that caring for myself is not self-indulgent. Caring for myself is an act of survival.

Audre Lorde, writer

If there is a secret to gentle parenting, it is surely taking care of yourself. If your emotional and physical needs are met, you will be calmer and more patient. If you are calmer and more patient, you are likely to be more peaceful and respectful. And if you are all of these things, then the way you respond to your children will have the greatest chance of being gentle.

How do you feel right now? Do you feel well rested? Is your mind fully in the present? Does your body feel calm? Do you feel that you have enough head space free to devote some to your child?

Or do you feel exhausted, with a mind that's racing and

worried about things that may not ever happen? Can you feel the tension in your body – a tightness in your chest, hunching of your shoulders and soreness in your neck? Is your head full of 'stuff'? And do you ever feel like you just can't cope any more – that you need a break from being an adult and a break from your child?

If you are tense, preoccupied, ill-nourished and poorly rested then, despite your best intentions, you will snap, yell at or ignore your child's concerns because you just don't have space for anything else. If you change only one thing today about your parenting, let it be the way that you care for yourself. Taking care of yourself isn't selfish; it isn't a luxury. It is a necessity – as vital as breathing and eating. And parents who recognise this need are better parents. After all, how is it possible to nurture anyone if you are in dire need of soul food yourself?

So many parents sacrifice their own needs in order to provide for their children. Parenting can be a selfless and thankless task. *You* matter too though. If you don't look after yourself, who will? And if you don't look after yourself and something bad happens to you, who will look after your children? I cannot stress the importance of this enough. Gentle parents need to nurture themselves – feed their bodies, their souls, their minds. So do whatever it is you need to do to be calm and relaxed. Find a hobby, take time out to read, go swimming, go to yoga classes, take up running, take long, thoughtful walks, meet up with friends, schedule time for a long bubble bath once a week with the door locked. Because when you are nurtured, everything is easier, and when you are calmer your children will be too. It is an ever-perpetuating circle and one that, sadly, can often be negative for many.

I asked some parents what they did to take care of their own needs, here is what they told me:

> I run. If I didn't run I may crack up! I also try and make sure I get time away from my son with my husband to keep our connection strong.

I signed myself up for a half marathon last year, despite never having run further than 5k, as I knew I needed a reason to justify going out running. Obviously, the real justification is to do something good for myself, by myself, but it is so easy to fall into the trap of putting yourself last and I found it easier to put myself first if I could say I was running for a reason.

I take baths at the weekend, encourage Daddy to have time with the kids without me at the weekends and have a babysitter look after my kids for a couple of hours one afternoon a week so I can get stuff done.

I try to stick to a fairly organised and early bedtime so that I get some time to myself in the evenings. My kids are both full-on all day, so I need a chance to indulge my hobbies (knitting, sewing, etc.) and recentre myself. If I don't get that time, I am a grumpy, impatient mummy and that helps no one.

I keep thinking I should give up teaching my hour-a-week salsa class, because it does take a bit of time to organise it and plan for it, and I already feel overwhelmed with the amount of stuff that always needs doing! But then I have to remind myself that it really is the one time of the week where I am not responsible for or thinking about the house or the kids, and for me I really need that.

I try to practise mindfulness techniques to keep me on an even keel. My husband and I are also honest now when we are having a tough parenting day. Just acknowledging parenting can have difficult times is helpful.

A nice soothing bath with Epsom salts and a good book. Or an hour watching one of my favourite shows while doing some knitting, while hubby takes baby for a walk.

Eating well

Is your diet healthy and nutritious or do you often sacrifice your own nutrition needs for those of your child, snatching a quick sandwich and too many takeaways while you steam organic vegetables for your baby? Do you focus on the ingredients in your child's food, but not so much on your own? Do you make sure to give your child a vitamin and mineral supplement every day, but not do the same for yourself? Perhaps you are trying to get your pre-baby body back and restrict your food intake a little too much?

Eating a healthy, well-balanced diet is vital not only for your children but for you too. This is especially important for breast-feeding mothers and all those who have recently given birth. Make sure you eat a good amount of a large variety of foods each day, including healthy fats and protein. Avoid 'diet' foods and drinks and focus on eating 'clean'. Clean eating means avoiding processed foods and instead eating simple, nutritious foods free from additives including sugar and artificial sweeteners. Many are concerned about the time taken to eat cleanly, however with a bit of forward planning it is very easy. Batch cooking and meal planning are two of the keys to eating well as a family and they are also good for your budget. So when you are cooking meals, see if you can make double and freeze half for another day, when all you have to do is to heat the food up. You can even pre-prepare raw ingredients and freeze them in freezer bags, so that the hard work is done and when it is time to prepare a meal, you just have to take out the bag and cook the ingredients. This works especially well if you have a slow cooker, when you can empty the defrosted, pre-prepared ingredients into the slow cooker in the morning, leave it all day and then sit down to a nutritious meal in the evening.

For many, particularly new mothers whose bodies need time to recuperate from growing and birthing a baby, certain vitamins and minerals can be lacking in their diet, and some deficiencies can make you much more likely to feel exhausted, anxious and depressed, as well as negatively affecting your immune system.

Vitamin B12

A deficiency of B12 can cause feelings of extreme tiredness and exhaustion, irritability, depression, confusion, pins and needles, mouth ulcers and a sore tongue. There are different forms of B12 available including cyanocobalamin and methylcobalamin. The former is usually the cheapest, however methylcobalamin is much more efficient and more easily absorbed.

Vitamin D

A deficiency of vitamin D has been linked to many diseases including certain types of cancer, diabetes and glucose intolerance, hypertension (high blood pressure), as well as muscle weakness and joint aches. If you are pregnant or breastfeeding, you should take a vitamin D supplement. (There is a fairly strong argument that supplementation would benefit most of the population, especially if you are not exposed to much natural sunlight on a daily basis.) When selecting a supplement look for one that contains Vitamin D3 (or cholecalciferol), which is the natural and best-absorbed form of the vitamin.

Magnesium

A deficiency of magnesium can cause difficulty falling asleep and relaxing, feelings of anxiety and depression, muscle cramps and spasms and twitchy eyes. Magnesium deficiency is fairly common and can be remedied by supplementing magnesium using a transdermal spray, otherwise known as 'magnesium oil' which you simply spray on your skin once or twice a day. This form is much more easily used by the body than the more common, cheaper tablets usually found on the high street. Another good way to introduce more magnesium is by taking a bath with a cup or two of Epsom salts added to the water once or twice per week.

Zinc

Zinc is essential for a healthy-functioning immune system, so those who are deficient can therefore be more inclined to catch colds and other viruses. A deficiency in zinc can also contribute to hair loss, a decreased appetite and sex drive and skin rashes. Zinc can be easily supplemented in tablet form.

Sleeping well

The old advice to 'sleep when the baby sleeps' is very wise, however frustrating it may be. And it applies as much to parents of toddlers and older children as it does to those with babies. Yet many parents don't heed the advice and rush to clean and tidy the house when their children sleep. The housework can wait – it doesn't matter if your house is messy, but it does matter if you are too exhausted, through lack of sleep, to parent in the way that you would like. Getting enough sleep is vital, and although if your children are young, you may not get that sleep in a seven- or eight-hour block overnight, you can – and should – top up with naps during the day and early bedtimes.

If you live with a partner, it can also be very effective to each have a 'sleep-tank' day per week. This is where one partner looks after the children overnight and for a fair amount of the next morning while the other sleeps and tanks up on sleep. I find this works really well if it happens on a Friday and Saturday, with one parent taking the Friday night and the other 'tanking up' and then swapping on the Saturday night. Other parents do a similar thing, but just with the mornings, giving each other the chance of a lie-in at least once per week.

Ironically, many parents can find it hard to sleep even if their children are sleeping. If this is true for you, I would suggest you consider the following:

- Check your diet – are you consuming too much caffeine? Do you have enough magnesium or do you need to supplement?

- Make sure your bedroom is cool enough – 18°C is the optimum temperature for sleep.

- Remove all screens from your bedroom – so no TVs, laptops, tablets or smartphones.

- Be careful about the lighting in your bedroom, switching regular light bulbs to ones with a red hue in order to not inhibit the sleep hormone melatonin.

- Try to follow your own bedtime ritual, which could start with 'unplugging' from all devices two hours before bedtime, then a bath or shower, followed by a warm drink and curling up in bed with a book.

When you are in bed don't focus on trying to fall asleep; focus instead on feeling your body and mind relax. Sleep will follow, but is far less likely to do so if you think too much about it. Interestingly, something known as 'Coué's Law of Reversed Effort' states that the harder we try to do something, the more difficult it becomes. So the more you focus on your inability to get to sleep, the more stressed you will become and the less likely it is to happen. The tips under the heading 'What to do when you feel like yelling' (see page 249) can really help you to relax and become calm enough to drift off to sleep fairly quickly.

Moving well

When you are exhausted and desperate for a rest, it can seem counterproductive to exercise. Often, however, this is precisely what can help the most. When you exercise, you release feel-good brain chemicals known as endorphins. These endorphins can help to reduce stress and depression and also act in an analgesic, or pain-killing, capacity. So exercise resulting in the release of endorphins can help you to think more positively and also to feel more energetic, even if it was the last thing you felt like doing initially.

Exercising doesn't have to happen in the gym. Walking is fantastic for the body and the mind, as are swimming and dancing. Gardening too is a great form of exercise and doubles up as an excellent way to increase vitamin D absorption too. Moving your body more can really help you to stay calm and relaxed and can also help to boost your energy.

What to do when you feel like yelling

How often do you shout at your children? For many the answer is probably, 'Too often'. Inevitably, shouty parents lead to shouty children. Children model others' behaviour, so if your child is shouty and angry, it is worth considering whether he or she is reflecting your own behaviour.

If your boss yelled at you because you did something wrong

in your job, would you listen to him and really think about the point he was trying to make? Or would you close your ears to his yells and ignore the majority of what he was saying? Most people would certainly vouch for the latter. And the same applies to communicating with your children: the more you yell, the less they will listen to you; the more you yell, the less they will communicate with you for fear of your response.

A good way to reduce any yelling, aside from taking care of your own needs, is to create a 'yelling jar' to use for a week. Each time you yell you should place a coin in the jar (at a value of your choice). At the of the week count up the coins in the jar (you may well be shocked at how many there are) and use the money to put towards something for yourself in the way of 'me time' – a magazine, new book, bubble bath or chocolate bar. Start afresh each week and, hopefully, you should notice your coin count gradually decreasing as you become more aware of your behaviour, the positive here being that when you need self-care the most is when you will have the most money to put towards it.

In addition, think about what you could do instead of yelling? Perhaps one of the following tips may help:

- **Slow your breathing**. Close your eyes, take a deep breath in through your nose to a count of seven and exhale, again through your nose to a count of eleven.

- **Breathe like a yogi**. Once again, close your eyes. Place your right thumb over your right nostril, then hover the middle finger of the same hand over your left nostril. Now take a deep breath in through your nose with your right nostril closed off. Hold it for a second, release your thumb and place your middle finger down onto your left nostril, closing it off, then exhale through your right nostril. Hold the breath for a second and then close off your right nostril again and inhale through your left. Repeat until you feel calm.

- **Picture your haven**. Is there a spot in nature that really resonates with you? A beach, a forest, mountains, a lake or waterfall? Close your eyes and picture yourself there for a few moments until you feel calm.

- **Imagine turning your anger thermostat down**. Close your eyes and imagine you have a thermostat in your head – like the one that controls the temperature on a central-heating system, only in this case the numbers reflect your anger levels. See yourself turning the dial or pressing the button to lower the thermostat and feel your body respond as you do so.

- **Do something unexpected**. Sing, jump up and down, blow raspberries or hum. Allow your actions to act as an escape valve for your emotions.

- **Create an awareness band**. Wear an elasticated band on your wrist, as tight as you can bear. When you feel the urge to yell, gently ping the band on your wrist and repeat 'I am calm, my voice is calm' in your head as you do so.

- **Leave the room**. Put a space between your child's action and your reaction, geographically speaking. In a sense, this is 'time out' for adults. You are not punishing your child by your absence though – rather, you are showing respect for them by removing yourself from a situation where you may say or do something you do not really want to do. Tell your child why you are leaving and ask that they allow you a minute to calm down. Tell them you will be straight back though, as soon as you are calm.

- **Use a stress-reduction object**. A stress ball, putty or similar – just something to squidge in your pocket – can allow the stress to leave your body via your hands.

Mindfulness

Mindfulness may sound complicated, or 'alternative', but in reality it is a very simple scientific concept. Mindfulness is simply focusing all of your attention, without prejudice or judgement, on the sensations within your body, your emotions and your surroundings at any given moment in time. It is focusing on the now without regard for the past or the future: living fully in the present moment. Practising mindfulness means full awareness of your own being and the environment around you, without concerns about things or people who are elsewhere.

Young children are naturally mindful, but as we age we lose focus on the things that really matter and create all sorts of artificial realities around us, based on things that may never happen or things that have happened that we can never change. Mindfulness is accepting where and who you are right now and learning that at this present moment that is all you need. The more mindful you are, the stiller your mind becomes and the more relaxed your body will be.

Although much of modern-day mindfulness stems from Buddhist teachings, there need not be any religion or spirituality attached to its practice. Mindfulness today is embraced by the scientific community and recommended by doctors and psychologists the world over. It has been proven to aid a multitude of complaints from anxiety and depression to bowel and skin conditions, as well as helping with sleep, childbirth and learning and behaviour in children.

Anybody can learn and practise mindfulness. There are many different courses and workshops available, but it can also be easily learned from a book, CD or an online class (see page 281 for some suggestions). Mindfulness is perhaps one of the best ways to get some 'me time', and only ten to fifteen minutes every day can revolutionise your parenting.

Support network

Right at the very start of this book I mentioned the importance of creating a support network around you. This is vital to your self-care, so if you don't yet have one, it is crucial that you build one. Your network could consist of family, friends, voluntary organisations or, if funds stretch, paid help. (See pages 27–9 for ways that you can form a network if you don't have anything in place already.)

When it comes to utilising your network to best help you parent gently, the following suggestions may inspire you:

- Pick up the phone and call somebody if you are having a bad day. This needn't be a friend or relative – it could be a parenting-related helpline.

- Chat with a friend online who is going through something similar to help you realise that you are not alone.

- Arrange a play date; entertaining your child and also giving you somebody to chat with.

- Ask someone in your network if they can sit with your child for an hour or two while you get some time to yourself.

- If you have family or friends who are close enough and children who wake regularly at night, ask if they could possibly do one night shift to enable you to top up on sleep.

- Organise a reciprocal babysitting arrangement on a regular basis.

- Consider organising a big get-together for the day – externally, so you don't feel obliged to tidy and clean your house.

How can you apply the Seven Cs of gentle parenting to yourself?

Many parents spend so much time focusing on their parenting and treating their children with respect that they forget to afford themselves the same privilege. Would you talk to anybody else the way you talk to yourself? Would you stay in a relationship if your partner treated you the way you treat yourself? Do you want your children to grow up with respect for their own bodies, minds and needs? If so, then you need to treat yourself in the same way. Applying the Seven Cs to yourself is important here.

Connection

How can you connect with your pre-child self? In many ways becoming a parent can reveal gaps and flaws in the way you were parented. To heal, sometimes you need to parent yourself to be able to move on. Are you in connection with your own needs? Or have you neglected them for so long you no longer understand what they are? Perhaps you need to connect more with friends, relatives or your partner?

Communication

What is your body telling you? Do you pay attention to the subtle cues of *dis*-ease within yourself? Aches, pains, niggles, food cravings all indicate that something is amiss. What is your body telling you? Do you communicate your feelings enough to others? Or do you repress them and then put yourself at risk of 'snapping' at some point in the future when you can no longer do this? Do your repressed feelings make you irritable and short-tempered with your children? Practising mindfulness is a wonderful way to step up communication within yourself.

Control

How much control do you have over your own life? Is there any way that you can regain a little more? Or perhaps the opposite is true and maybe you need to 'let go' a little? Mindfulness can be a wonderful tool to help you to relax and live in the moment, rather than worrying about everything that you cannot control.

Containment

Who or what contains your feelings? Do you try to keep them all inside? Do you need to make space in your container in order to contain your child's needs? If so, then you need to find somebody (or something) to contain your own feelings. This could be your support network, it could be a sport, it could be a hobby or it could be a support organisation. Don't allow your container to become so full that you are no use to anybody else.

Champion

Who champions your needs? While you are busy championing the needs of your family you often relegate your own to the bottom of the pile. Who or what helps you to feel good about your parenting skills? It's so rare that we compliment other parents on their skills, or indeed compliment ourselves. Don't be afraid to ask for help, or to take a day to nurture yourself whenever possible – your needs matter too.

Confidence

How can you improve your confidence as a parent? Do you have issues with confidence generally? How can you improve this? Surround yourself with people who inspire you and help you to feel good about yourself and remember that criticism from others is often rooted in cognitive dissonance and actually nothing to do with you.

Consistency

Do you lack consistency? Do you find it difficult to enforce boundaries? Do you find it hard to say 'No'? Similarly, are you consistent enough in your self-care efforts? Or do you make a half-hearted start and not continue? Conversely, perhaps you need to be a little more flexible? Loosen your routines and expectations and relax a little more into being led by life, rather than always trying to steer it in a certain direction.

I'd like to end this chapter with a message I received from a mother about taking care of herself, and my response:

Q: *How do I gentle-parent myself? I have some level of post-natal anxiety and I am constantly doubting and questioning everything I do. How am I gentle on myself?*

A: Treating yourself with the same empathy and respect that you treat your child with is important – realising that you have needs that should be met and doing what is necessary to meet them. If you haven't already, I would seek help with the anxiety that you are experiencing; it is very common, but there is help available and you don't need to carry on as you are. All mothers doubt and question everything they do – I certainly do – and that's something that never goes away. In a way it's a sign of being a great mother. Imagine if you never doubted yourself – that would be quite dangerous! The key is trying to keep it under control and learning to trust your instincts a little more and grow some confidence in your mothering abilities. Surrounding yourself with a great network can really help, particularly other mothers who you can share your feelings with, so I would be looking for ways to form that network if you don't have it already. I would also really recommend learning mindfulness, it can be so helpful in the transitioning into parenthood and can be very good for anxiety in general, not just parenting-related.

Chapter 11

Gentle Parenting in Special Circumstances

*Kids don't remember what you try to teach them.
They remember what you are.*

Jim Henson, screenwriter, director, puppeteer

Gentle parenting is not exclusive. Gentle parents come from all walks of life. They are parents to one and many. They can be foster and adoptive parents, as well as biological parents. They can be single, separated, in a same-sex or heterosexual relationship. Gentle parenting is not only suited to a certain group of children – it applies to all, no matter what their needs may be.

Likewise, applying the 'Seven Cs' does not exclude anybody, whether parent or child. The ethos of gentle parenting is based upon individuality, and so it is up to you as a parent to apply them to your own unique situation and to ensure you practise enough self-care to be able to follow them.

Gentle parenting with twins and multiples

It is a popular misconception that twins and multiples must be parented to a schedule with strict behavioural-control methods. While it is undoubtedly more work to parent more than one baby at a time, it is not impossible to do so gently.

Twins, triplets and more are too often treated as one. This is one of the most common mistakes that traditional multiple-parenting methods make. If you have twins, you have two children with very distinct needs in just the same way that you would if you had two children born at different times. This means that twins are likely to need different bedtime routines, different approaches to tackling their behaviour, different levels of need for connection and separation and different preferences when it comes to eating, play and activities. Although it may seem easier to treat the twins as a pair and create 'a twin schedule', this often creates more issues in the long term, as does comparing your children to each other.

These parents discuss why they parent their twins gently and how they believe that, ultimately, it is easier:

> I have twins and the first year was very hard. There was far more crying (from them and me!) than I would have liked. I think gentle parenting is essential with twins though because they always have to share the most important thing in their lives – you! The fact that I always empathise with them and acknowledge how hard it can be to take turns or share really does help, I think. They are starting to empathise with each other (at two and a half) and it's lovely to watch.

I have twins and if I wasn't going down the gentle-parenting route I think I'd be totally overwhelmed by parenting and feel out of control. I'm very relaxed with the boys, choose my battles very carefully and find I'm very rarely stressed. One of my boys is quite boisterous and I have to watch him constantly and the other is incredibly empathic and gentle for his age (seventeen months). I find myself repeating myself lots, but am confident it will pay off. I believe that due to the way we parent, our boys are very happy and that it will ultimately help them be independent and confident individuals. The fact they share a mummy makes it all the more important to come alongside them and nurture their feelings.

The key to fostering individuality and respect for the differing needs of your children is to give yourself enough self-care and to build the best support network possible. Help of the practical kind, such as a postnatal doula or mother's help or even a cleaner is ideal (and finances needn't preclude this as many charities offer help for free or for a very minimal fee). In the early days it is likely that you will need two people for bedtime routines, for instance; and as the children grow, their need for 'one-to-one' time with you, without their sibling involved, will also increase, again necessitating an extra pair of hands.

Emotional support is vital too. Meeting with parents of multiples in your area via local support groups can be a life-saver. Even if the style of parenting used by them differs greatly from your own, you can still gain so much from spending time with other parents of multiples. The sense of shared experience and understanding can go a long way to helping you to cope and parent your children in the way that suits you best.

Pre-birth planning when expecting twins or more

Preparing for the arrival of twins, triplets or more is an exciting time, but one that may need slightly more preparation and thought than if you were expecting a singleton. Two of the biggest decisions that you will need to make initially are surrounding the birth and feeding of your babies. Depending on the health and positioning of your babies and their placentas, it is very possible for you to have a natural vaginal birth and even a home or water birth if that is your wish, although this may not be what your consultant advises. If you do decide that you would like a natural birth, then possibly the best investment that you can make is to hire a birth doula or independent midwife who specialises in multiple births and who will help you to fully explore your options.

When it comes to feeding your babies, it is possible to exclusively breastfeed twins, triplets and more, and many mothers of multiples do just this every day. Once again though, you may find that you need to seek expert support from a breastfeeding counsellor or lactation consultant who can show you special positions for feeding two babies at the same time. Before the birth, meeting with a mother who breastfeeds twins or more is also a wonderful idea.

When parenting baby twins, do invest in a good baby carrier or two, and a visit with a babywearing consultant is time well invested. Learning to carry both babies can prove invaluable, especially if you also have older children. Although there are many videos online showing multiple carriers, in this instance it really is better to have some hands-on expert guidance.

Lastly, when thinking about sleeping arrangements, consider how your babies felt in the womb. As well as contact with you, they had constant contact with each other. For this reason, sleeping the babies together in a cot or Moses basket can help to keep them calm. If you wish to bedshare, then follow safe bedsharing guidelines (see page 55) and situate a baby either side of you on the bed; nobody else should share the bed with you and a mattress on the floor to sleep on is preferable to prevent the babies from falling.

Gentle parenting after fostering or adoption

Too much lip service is paid to attachment in social work. It is a 'buzz term', but very often the advice given is actually at odds with it. A child who has previously been cared for is in desperate need of connection and containing, through physical contact and otherwise. They need their story heard, but only when they feel safe enough to communicate it with you. For these children the ethos of gentle parenting is perhaps most important. Unless you are fostering or adopting a newborn baby, which is highly rare, the child you will be welcoming into your home is likely to have come from an environment where their caregiving was suboptimal. And even if the child's upbringing until that point has been optimal, you will still need to help them to adjust to the trauma of being removed from their birth parents and, potentially, grief over the removal from previous foster parents.

This grief and trauma and, possibly, having lived in an abusive or neglectful environment may result in a child who is more sensitive or emotionally immature – one who externalises their emotions through violence or who internalises their emotions and exhibits signs of anxiety or depression. Cared-for children need huge amounts of empathy and patience, along with unlimited, unconditional love. It is important to not label them, or their behaviour as 'naughty'. A large proportion of cared-for children will exhibit behavioural problems; however, these are a symptom of the big and uncomfortable feelings that they are experiencing and have probably been experiencing for a very long time. Conventional behavioural-control measures should be avoided here more than ever. Anything that causes the child to internalise and repress their emotions further still, such as time out or the naughty step, can cause irreparable harm.

Similarly, avoiding the standard advice, given by so many fostering and adoption agencies, to 'reward and praise the good as much as possible' can help the child to build on some much-needed intrinsic motivation, which is likely to be severely lacking in almost all cases. Superficial praise and rewarding 'good' behaviour suggest to the child that they are only lovable when they behave 'well', and that they cannot be authentic and share how they really feel through their speech or actions. It is the latter that is so vital for cared-for children, and any-thing that represses this, such as rewards and praise, should be avoided.

The cared-for child needs a champion, they need consis-tency by the bucketload and they need some control over their previously out-of-control life. What they need more than any-thing, however, are patience and understanding. Don't try to rush the bond – in order to bond the child first needs to trust, and for that trust to develop they need to know that they are loved, even in their most unlovable moments. In fact, it is when they behave the worst that they need your love, attention and understanding the most.

For those fostering or adopting young babies and toddlers, building on the bond via close proximity – babywearing and bed-sharing and infant massage – can be hugely helpful. Skin-to-skin contact and the constant reassurance of your presence can help to heal separation-anxiety issues and insecure attachment. Unfortunately, advice from fostering agencies is usually that bed-sharing should be avoided, largely for safeguarding reasons. Here, it is important to question whose needs matter the most and who the policy is really protecting.

Adoptive and foster parents need to consider their own needs too – self-care and support here are vital. Taking in a cared-for child, whether the home you are offering them is temporary or permanent, is a huge job and can take its toll on you physically and emotionally. Ensure you have a good support network in place – one that includes other foster or adoptive parents in particular (see Resources, page 280) – and allow yourself adequate time to rest and recuperate regularly. If you are fostering, you should allow a break of at least a month or two in between placements, wherever possible, for this reason.

Adjusting to parenting after fertility treatment or previous loss

Welcoming your first baby after a long struggle to conceive will no doubt be one of the (if not *the*) best moments of your life. The minute you hold your baby in your arms, you will quickly realise that they were well worth the wait. Many parents will adjust easily to the transition, taking each day in their stride, filled with gratitude for being blessed with a healthy baby. For others, however, their determination to be grateful and to fully accept how lucky they have been can often cause a great deal of stress and anxiety.

It is not uncommon for those who become parents after a previous loss or fertility treatment to struggle with feelings of guilt when they feel resentment towards their child or admit to themselves that actually they are not enjoying the experience as much as they thought they would. All parents feel like this at some point in their parenting journey, but for those for whom the journey has been more demanding and longer, these feelings can hit doubly hard. Knowing what it felt like to be desperate for a child, they can think that they should never complain or admit to anybody that life is not the bed of roses that they'd hoped for.

If you find yourself in this situation, rest assured that your feelings are entirely normal and perfectly understandable. You are not superhuman and your child isn't an unrealistic one from a television advert or greetings card who never cries and never tantrums. You are both real and your emotions are too. Go easy on yourself and allow yourself to feel whatever you need to feel; you are not a bad person for occasionally wondering why you did this. Just because it took you longer to reach your destination, doesn't mean that you should be more grateful than anybody else.

Parenting children with special needs gently

If you have a child with special educational needs (SEN), there is a good chance that you will have been recommended behaviour-control methods that focus on rewarding good behaviour and ignoring the child when they are 'naughty'. There is currently a worrying trend of treating children with special needs quite harshly. Behavioural-control methods are rife, particularly when it comes to sleep and yet children with special needs can often find it harder to sleep due to their developmental levels and cognitive abilities. For some reason, however, many of the large organisations supporting parents of children with SEN advocate sleep training that hinges on some form of controlled crying, rapid return (where parents are advised to put their child in their cot or bed and leave the room, returning briefly to settle them if they cry, then leaving again – repeating until the child is asleep) or cry it out. This is despite the fact that these methods are at odds with their children's needs and abilities.

Instead of helping parents to understand the psychological and biological processes behind their child's behaviour, which should be paramount, discipline advice commonly includes the use of naughty steps, time out and lots of praise and rewards when the child is 'good'. Extrinsic motivation is encouraged to the detriment of the child's intrinsic motivation, while often ignoring their neurological capabilities. For instance, some children with special needs may have more difficulty with Theory of Mind acquisition (see page 132), but this does not mean that they can never develop sociable behaviour – it's just unlikely that you will encourage it by punishing them for antisocial behaviour. The best way to help a child with SEN to develop appropriate social behaviour is the same as it is for any other child, namely, by modelling respect and empathy ourselves. Inevitably, this means resetting expectations of the child's abilities and lessening the desire to train and control. Of course, to do this, again, requires an incredibly supportive network, including, in particular, other parents of children with SEN, and lots of self-care.

This mother explains why she prefers to gently parent her son and avoid the 'carrot-and-stick' approach commonly advocated by the professionals who care for him:

> My little boy has Down's Syndrome. He's five. I try to use gentle techniques with him, which I find work much better than rewards and punishments. Unfortunately, most of the therapists involved have got praising verbal tics: 'Good sitting!', 'Good standing!', 'Good listening!', 'Good singing!', 'Good talking!', 'Good helping!' – along with the occasional 'Good boy!' (to which I normally respond, 'Woof, woof'). I'm hoping that one day he'll respond to all this praise with 'Good praising!' in the same tone of voice.

This mother explains why she uses gentle parenting with her daughter and brilliantly explains why empathy is so important:

My daughter has medical conditions that leave her with pain, fatigue and on medication that can leave her feeling sick and nauseous. Add that to the normal four-year-old behaviour, and it can lead to some big meltdowns. Gentle parenting is the only way we can help her control her feelings and emotions without leaving her too afraid to show them.

And this mother explains her parenting choice for her son, and in particular why she feels he is entitled to some control over his own discipline:

I have an autistic son and gentle parenting is the only way things work. For him to function he has to understand my decisions and how they are of benefit to him, so by allowing him to be part of his parenting it is like giving him wings to soar.

Can single parents be gentle parents?

Gentle parenting isn't solely the domain of two-parent families. Nothing in the Seven Cs suggests that two parents are required. Raising children with compassion, respect and empathy only takes one person, and far better a consistent approach from one parent than conflicting approaches from two. The consistent message given here can be really positive for the child. I also don't agree that children need different things from a mother and a father. Mothers are perfectly capable of providing rough-housing and sporting activities and related chat, while fathers are perfectly capable of providing emotional contact, conversation and cuddles, and the stereotyped view of parenting that says otherwise is derogatory to all. It is simply a question of a parent being responsive to their child's needs.

Of course, this responsivity does require a large amount of self-care, as well as a solid support network (there are some good support organisations for single parents, see the Resources section, page 280). Do make sure that you book some 'me time' for yourself. This could be in the form of a regular night out with friends, a day doing an activity you love once or twice a month or the occasional weekend where your child stays with friends or family for you to top up your self-nurturance tank. All parents need to be mindful of self-care, but when you are the sole carer for your child this is doubly important.

If you are a single parent, whatever your gender, it is important to look at the way you are with your child and try to pinpoint any gaps that other people might fill to benefit your child. For instance, if you find it difficult to rough play, or 'roughhouse' with your child, it could be worth finding a friend or family member to whom it comes more naturally, rather than trying to force yourself to be something you are not. If you are not a great nature lover and recoil in horror at the thought of mud play, puddle jumping and tree climbing, again, finding friend or relative who can ensure your child gets plenty of these types of activities if they want them is a good idea. Remember, it's not easy for any parent to be all of the things that a child needs; this isn't a flaw on your part – you are only human – so don't beat yourself up if you need to 'outsource' some elements of child-raising.

When parents are divorced or separated

Separation can be incredibly difficult for children, long after the initial event has taken place; however, living in a home with warring parents can be even harder on them. Perhaps the worst decision parents can ever make is to stay together for the sake of their children when the relationship has broken down for good. For those who are not yet at that stage, couples counselling can be a really positive step to take (it can be very useful in aiding you all through a separation too). If your relationship is past saving though, it is far better for your child to have two happy parents living separately from each other than two miserable parents living together.

How to tell a child you are separating

Ideally, the news should be delivered by both parents at the same time, but if the relationship has broken down to such a degree that the parents cannot be amicable with each other, it is better for the child to hear the news from just one of them.

Try to speak to your children about the planned separation on a Friday afternoon or Saturday when everybody is home from school or work for the weekend, but not the day before you have an event or activity planned. Try to use simple words and stay neutral about your partner, no matter what your feelings are towards them. Reassure your child that while you may not want to live together any more, it is nobody's fault, especially not theirs, and reinforce the fact that you both love them just as much as you ever did.

Next, be ready to answer any questions that they may have; some of these may be quite awkward and perhaps ones that you may not want to address, but you should be prepared to answer anything they may ask you honestly. Reiterate that you are always happy for them to ask you questions at any point and suggest that if there are some they don't want to ask right now, they can write them down in a special book, or on a piece of paper, and post them in a 'worry box' (an old shoebox with a hole cut out) that you will leave in a special place and check regularly.

There are many good books and resources for helping children to cope with parental separation and it would be good to have one on hand to give your child for them to refer to in their own time (see Resources, page 280). Above all, though, accept whatever reaction your child has and be prepared to comfort them however they need. It is very common for behaviour, including sleep and eating, to regress, so be prepared for this in advance, and if your child is at school or nursery, then be sure to inform staff there of the change in your family circumstances, so that they may help your child.

Moving forward

If either parent has a new partner, it is advisable to wait for as long as possible before introducing him or her. It is important that your child doesn't view the new partner as the cause of splitting up their family, which can happen if they meet them too soon. A gap of six months between the separation and the introduction of a new partner is preferable. Even then, bring them into the child's life at the child's pace. Gauge their reaction and take things as slowly as they need, no matter how quickly you may wish things to progress. This is especially true for introducing your child to any children that the new partner may have.

Try to remain neutral about your ex-partner's new partner in front of your child. If you are negative about the new person in their other parent's life, they can often react negatively towards them to try to please you, which, ultimately, is not good for anybody. The new partner may be in your child's life for a very long time and, despite your feelings, it is far better that they can forge a good relationship with each other.

Many children of separated parents benefit hugely from professional counselling, even if they are not showing any particular signs of distress. Speaking to somebody impartial without worrying if they are making them sad or angry can help them to process their feelings much more quickly and is crucial in terms of moving forward. It is not only children who benefit from professional guidance however – parents often find the neutrality and listening ear invaluable too.

From a gentle-parenting perspective, the most vital element to bear in mind is that all decisions are made out of respect for your child as well as yourself. Often this means that parents may need to reset their expectations of custody and visitation. A good example here is a recently separated couple who are parents to a breastfed baby or toddler. In this instance, overnight contact away from the breastfeeding mother is inappropriate and not considerate to the child's needs. Forcing the separation of a well-connected dyad is not in the best interests of the child. There are many years to come for overnight stays and visits, but now is not the time for them. For young children, then, it may be decided that the mother retains primary custody and the partner initially has them for daytimes only, until they are older and more capable of spending time away from their primary attachment figure. This may not be what the partner would choose, but making the choice that is best for the child now is surely the way forward and, ultimately, the best for the future relationship between them and both parents.

Communication between separated parents is vital. Although you may feel anything but respect for the other parent, you still need to convey respect, especially in your child's presence, remembering that children learn from our example, not our words. While you may be angry with your partner, it is crucial that your child does not pick up on this and feel insecure in their relationship with them as a result. Family-wide counselling during and after a separation, even if it is progressing with relative ease, is a very good idea to prevent a breakdown in communication and negative consequences for children.

Lastly, again, is the importance of self-care is. It is essential that you have a container for the big emotions that you will be feeling during and after the separation, so that you can remain emotionally calm and present for your child. Make sure that you allow yourself enough head space to think and explore your emotions and take time to nurture your body too. A break-up is tough even without children; with them, it can be exhausting and, if not in check, this exhaustion can all too easily reflect in your parenting at a time when your child is already very delicate and in need of compassion from you.

A few closing words

I started this book with the following words from the anthropologist Margaret Mead:

> Never doubt that a small group of thoughtful, committed citizens can change the world. Indeed, it is the only thing that ever has.

This quote is one of my favourites, in part because it inspires me to want to be better and do better, empowering me in the knowledge that I can make a difference. It also inspires me for the simple fact that I happen to believe it to be true. Throughout history, major change has almost always been brought about by a small but determined group of individuals, sometimes for the good and sometimes otherwise.

Never think that your efforts won't make a difference; they can and they will – not only to your children, but your children's children and their children in turn, along with everybody they come into contact with. When you think of it in this way you see how quickly compassion can grow and how the efforts of just one family have the potential to change the lives of thousands. The world as we know it now is crying out for social change. Imagine a world where the majority of children were parented in a more gentle manner. Well, right here, right now we have the opportunity to make that happen. The future lies in our children and in how we raise them.

On a less global scale, how you raise your child will also dictate your own future. Remember the old joke that one day your child will choose your nursing home when you are old? If you treat your child with compassion now, they are likely to return the favour in the years to come. But before then, a gently parented baby, toddler or child is far more likely to be kind, thoughtful and closer to you as they grow up. Indeed, the seeds you sow today will be those that you reap when your child is a tween or teen.

All that remains now is to wish you good luck on your journey, whether it is a short island hop or a major voyage to faraway lands. Keep the Seven Cs in mind at all times (on pages 274–6 you will find a short reminder with space for you to make notes), and if at any point you question the efficacy of your efforts, stay mindful of what matters the most: your family – not the opinions or, indeed, criticisms of others. Don't allow their dissonance to erode your confidence. Be kind to yourself, especially when you feel you least deserve it, because that is surely when your need for self-compassion is the greatest. Build a network to support and to hold you, to allow you to hold your child.

Last of all, remember that the best parents aren't perfect, they are 'good enough', and I suspect that having chosen to read this book in the first place, you are already more than 'good enough'.

Bon voyage!

The Seven Cs – a reminder

This section includes blank spaces for you to write notes unique to your family situation. Work through each point in turn and record ways in which you think you can apply them. This will then serve as a reminder and checklist for you to refer back to. Do use it often.

Connection

Communication

Control

Containment

Champion

Confidence

Consistency

Resources

Sarah Ockwell-Smith

Sarah's website: www.sarahockwell-smith.com

Sarah's Twitter: www.twitter.com/TheBabyExpert

Gentle parenting

The Gentle Parenting website: www.gentleparenting.co.uk

Gentle Parenting on Facebook
www.facebook.com/GentleParentingUK

Gentle Parenting on Twitter: www.twitter.com/GentleParentUK

Gentle Parenting Book website: www.gentleparentingbook.com

Gentle Parenting Book Facebook:
www.facebook.com/GentleParentingBook

The Gentle Sleep Book website: www.gentlesleepbook.com

The Gentle Sleep Book on Facebook:
www.facebook.com/SleepCalm

Gentle Sleep Training website: www.gentlesleeptraining.co.uk

Pregnancy and birth

Primal Health Research Database: www.primalhealthresearch.com

Doula UK: www.doula.org.uk

Homebirth: www.homebirth.org.uk

AIMS (Association for Improvement in Midwifery Services): www.aims.org.uk

Birth Trauma Association: www.birthtraumaassociation.org.uk

PANDAS (Pre & Postnatal Depression): www.pandasfoundation.org.uk

Independent Midwives: www.imuk.org.uk

Babies

Baby Massage: www.iaim.org.uk

Baby-led weaning: www.babyledweaning.com

Babywearing UK: www.babywearing.co.uk

Association of Tongue-tie Practitioners: www.tongue-tie.org.uk

Infant Sleep Information Source: www.isisonline.org.uk

Mother-Baby Behavioral Sleep Laboratory (co-sleeping information): www.cosleeping.nd.edu

Homestart: www.home-start.org.uk

Breastfeeding

Lactation Consultants of Great Britain: www.lcgb.org

Biological Nurturing: www.biologicalnurturing.com

The Breast Crawl: www.breastcrawl.org

La Leche League: www.laleche.org.uk

Association of Breastfeeding Mothers: www.abm.me.uk

Breastfeeding Network: www.breastfeedingnetwork.org.uk

UNICEF: www.unicef.org.uk

Toddlers and preschoolers

Help for children in stressful situations – Relax Kids: www.relaxkids.com

Forest Schools: www.forestschoolassociation.org

Montessori: www.montessori.org.uk

Older children

E-safety: www.thinkuknow.co.uk

Sex education: www.fpa.org.uk/help-and-advice/advice-for-parents-carers

Bullying: www.bullying.co.uk

Enuresis (bedwetting): www.eric.org.uk

Alcohol advice: www.drinkaware.co.uk

Home education: www.home-education.org.uk; www.educationotherwise.net

Steiner: www.steinerwaldorf.org

SEN

Support for families of disabled children – Contact a Family: www.cafamily.org.uk

Advice on education for children with SEN – IPSEA: www.ipsea.org.uk

For children with speech and language difficulties – ICAN: www.ican.org.uk

LGBT

Stonewall: www.stonewall.org.uk

LGBT Foundation: www.lgbt.foundation/parenting

LGBT adoption/fostering (New Family Social): www.newfamilysocial.org.uk

Single parents

Advice and support for single parents – Gingerbread: www.gingerbread.org.uk

Parental separation

Representation of children's interests in family courts – CAFCASS: www.cafcass.gov.uk

Twins and multiples

TAMBA: www.tamba.org.uk

Adoption and fostering

BAAF (British Association for Adoption/Fostering): www.baaf.org.uk

Adoption UK: www.adoptionuk.org

Fosterline: www.fosterline.info

The Foster Network: www.fostering.net

Self-care

Mindfulness – Headspace: www.headspace.com

Anxiety UK: www.anxiety.org.uk

MIND: www.mind.org.uk

Recommended reading for children

Growing up Books

What's Happening to Me? (Boys), Usborne (2006)

What's Happening to Me? (Girls), Usborne (2006)

Dr Christiane Northrup, *Beautiful Girl: Celebrating the Wonders of Your Body*, Hay House (2013)

For the Arrival of a New Baby

Giles Andreae and Vanessa Cabban, *There's a House Inside My Mummy*, Orchard Books (2012)

Jenni Overend, *Hello Baby*, Frances Lincoln Children's Books (2009)

Kate Evans, *Bump: How to Make, Grow and Birth a Baby*, Myriad Editions (2014)

Coping with Big Feelings

Elaine Whitehouse and Warwick Pudney, *A Volcano In My Tummy*, New Society Publishers (1998)

Virginia Ironside and Frank Rodgers, *The Huge Bag of Worries*, Hodder Children's (2011)

Carol McCloud, *Have you Filled a Bucket Today?* Nelson Publishing (2013)

Help with Divorce

Hilary Robinson and Mandy Stanley, *Tom's Sunflower*, Strauss House Publishing (2015)

Claire Masurel and Kady MacDonald Denton, *Two Homes*, Walker Books (2002)

Kes Gray and Lee Wildish, *Mum and Dad Glue*, Hodder Children's Books (2010)

Vicki Lansky and Jane Prince, *It's Not your Fault, Koko Bear*, Book Peddlers (1998)

Jeanie Franz Ransom and Kathryn Finney, *I Don't Want to Talk About It*, Magination Press (2000)

Bibliography

Sara Bennett and Nancy Kalish, *The Case Against Homework: How Homework Is Hurting Our Children and What We Can Do About It*, Three Rivers Press (2007)

Angela Davis, 'Experts and childcare "bibles": mothers and advice literature', in *Modern Motherhood*, Manchester University Press (2014)

Truby King, *Feeding and Care of Baby*, (1913)

R. A. Lawrence and R. M. Lawrence, *Breastfeeding: A Guide for the Medical Profession*, Elsevier (2011, 7th edition)

Penelope Leach, *Your Baby and Child: From Birth to Age Five*, A. A. Knopf (1977)

Richard Louv, *Last Child in the Woods: Saving Our Children from Nature-deficit Disorder*, Atlantic Books (2010)

Gill Rapley and Tracey Murkett, *Baby-led Weaning: Helping Your Baby to Love Good Food*, Vermilion (2008)

Rima Shore, *Rethinking the Brain: New Insights into Early Development*, Families and Work Institute (1997)

Benjamin Spock, *The Common Sense Book of Baby and Child Care*, Duell, Sloan and Pearce (1946)

Daniel Stern, *The Motherhood Constellation*, Karnac Books (1995)

John B. Watson, *Psychological Care of Infant and Child* (1928)

References

Introduction

1. Winnicott, D., *Getting to Know Your Baby*, Heinemann (1945).

2. Bowlby, J., *Maternal Care & Mental Health*, Jason Aronson (1950).

3. Baumrind, D., 'Effects of authoritative parental control on child behavior', *Child Development*, 37(4) (1966), pp. 887–907; Baumrind, D., 'Child care practices anteceding three patterns of preschool behavior', *Genetic Psychology Monographs*, 75(1) (1967), pp. 43–88.

Chapter 2

1. Mittendorf, R., Williams, M. A., Berkey, C. S. and Cotter, P. F., 'The length of uncomplicated human gestation', *Obstetrics and Gynecology*, 75(5) (1990), pp.929–32.

2. Birthplace in England Collaborative Group, 'Perinatal and maternal outcomes by planned place of birth for healthy women with low-risk pregnancies: the Birthplace in England national prospective cohort study', *BMJ*, 343 (2011).

3. Hodnett, E. D., Gates, S., Hofmeyr, G. J. and Sakala, C., 'Continuous support for women during childbirth', *Cochrane Database of Systematic Reviews*, issue 3 (2007).

4. Keenan, P., 'Benefits of massage therapy and use of a doula during labor and childbirth', *Alternative Therapies in Health & Medicine*, 6(1) (2000), pp.66–74; McGrath, S. K. and Kennel, J. H., 'A randomized controlled trial of continuous labor support for

middle-class couples: effect on cesarean delivery rates', *Birth*, 35(2) (2008), pp. 92–7; Campbell, D. A., Lake, M. F., Falk, M. and Backstrand, J. R., 'A randomized control trial of continuous support in labor by a lay doula', *Journal of Obstetric, Gynecologic & Neonatal Nursing*, 35 (2006), pp. 456–64; Campbell, D., Scott, K. D., Klaus, M. H. and Falk, M., 'Female relatives or friends trained as labor doulas: outcomes at 6 to 8 weeks postpartum', *Birth*, volume 34(3) (2007), pp. 220–7.

5. Newton, N., 'The Fetus Ejection Reflex Revisited', *Birth*, article first published online 31 March 2007.

6. See http://www.wombecology.com.

7. Jordan, S., Emery, S., Watkins, A., Evans, J. D., Storey, M. and Morgan, G., 'Associations of drugs routinely given in labour with breastfeeding at 48 hours: analysis of the Cardiff Births Survey', *BJOG* 116(12) (2009), pp.1622–9.

8. Rabe, H., Diaz-Rossello, J. L., Duley, L. and Dowswell, T., 'Effect of timing of umbilical cord clamping of term infants on mother and baby outcomes', Cochrane Database of Systematic Reviews (2012).

9. Boulvain, M., Marcoux, S., Bureau, M., Fortier, M. and Fraser, W., 'Risks of induction of labour in uncomplicated term pregnancies', *Paediatric Perinatal Epidemiology*, 15(2) (2001), pp.131–8; Dunne, C., Da Silva, O., Schmidt, G., Natale R., 'Outcomes of elective labour induction and elective Caesarean section in low-risk pregnancies between 37 and 41 weeks' gestation', *Journal of Obstetrics and Gynaecology Canada*, 31(12) (2009), pp. 1124–30.

10. Stuebe, A., 'The risks of not breastfeeding for mothers and infants', *Reviews in Obstetrics and Gynecology*, 2(4) (2009), pp. 222–31.

11. Boyd, C. A., Quigley, M. A. and Brocklehurst, P., 'Donor breast milk versus infant formula for preterm infants: systematic review and meta-analysis', *Archives of Disease in Childhood*, 92 (2007), pp. 169–75; Williams, A. F., Kingdon, C. C. and Weaver, G., 'Banking for the future: investing in human milk', *Archives of Disease in Childhood*, 92 (2007), pp.158–9; Arnold, L. D. W., 'Global health policies that support the use of banked donor human milk: a human rights issue', *International Breastfeeding Journal* 1:26 (2006), pp.1–26.

12. Blyton, D. M., Sullivan, C. E. and Edwards, N. 'Lactation is associated with an increase in slow-wave sleep in women', *Journal of Sleep Research*, 11(4) (2002), pp. 297–303; Doan, T., Gardiner, A., Gay, C. L. and Lee, K. A., 'Breastfeeding increases sleep duration of new parents', *Journal of Perinatal & Neonatal Nursing*, 21(3) (2007), pp. 200–6; Dorheim, S. K., Bondevik, G. T., Eberhard-Gran, M. and Bjorvatn, B., 'Sleep and depression in postpartum women: A population-based study', *Sleep*, 32(7) (2009), pp. 847–55; Gay, C. L., Lee, K. A. and Lee, S.-Y., 'Sleep patterns and fatigue in new mothers and fathers', *Biological Nursing Research*, 5(4) (2004), pp. 311–18.

Chapter 3

1. Okami, P. and Weisner T., Olmstead, R., 'Outcome correlates of parent-child bedsharing: an eighteen-year longitudinal study', *Journal of Developmental Behavioural Pediatrcs*, 23(4) (2002), pp. 244–53.

2. Hunziker, U. A. and Barr, R. G., 'Increased carrying reduces infant crying: a randomized controlled trial', *Pediatrics*, 77(5) (1986), pp. 641–8.

3. Dwyer T. and Ponsonby, A. L., 'Sudden Infant Death Syndrome and prone sleeping position', *Annual of Epidemiology*, 19(4) (2009), pp. 245–9.

4. Gessner, B. D., Ives, G. C. and Perham-Hester, K. A., 'Association between sudden infant death syndrome and prone sleep position, bed sharing, and sleeping outside an infant crib in Alaska', *Pediatrics*, 108(4) (2001), pp. 923–7.

5. Arnon, S., Diamant, C., Bauer, S., Regev, R., Sirota, G. and Litmanovitz, I., 'Maternal singing during kangaroo care led to autonomic stability in preterm infants and reduced maternal anxiety', *Acta Paediatrica* (2014).

6. Daniels, L. A., Mallan, K. M., Nicholson, J. M., Battistutta, D. and Magarey, A., 'Outcomes of an early feeding practices intervention to prevent childhood obesity', *Pediatrics* 132(1) (2013), pp.109–18; Iacovou, M. and Sevilla, A., 'Infant feeding: the effects of scheduled vs on-demand feeding on mothers' wellbeing and children's cognitive development', *Eur J Public Health*, 23(1):13 (2013).

Chapter 4

1. Vandell, D. L. and Wilson, K. S., 'Infants' interactions with mother, sibling, and peer: contrasts and relations between interaction systems', *Child Development*, 48 (1988), pp. 176–86.

2. Montessori, M., *The Absorbent Mind* (1949).

3. Mampe, B., Friederici, A. D., Christophe, A. and Wermke, K., 'Newborns' cry melody is shaped by their native language', *Current Biology*, 19(23) (2009), pp. 1994–7.

4. Singh, L., Best, C. and James, M., 'Infants' listening preferences: baby talk or happy talk?', *Infancy*, 3 (3) (2003), pp. 365–95; Singh, L., Nestor, S., Parikh, C. and Yull, A., 'Influences of infant-directed speech on early word recognition', *Psychology Press*, 14(6) (2009); Schachner, A. and Hannon, E., 'Infant-directed speech drives social preferences in 5-month-old infants', *Developmental Psychology*, 47(1) (2011), pp.19–25; Kaplan, P., Jung, P., Ryther, J. and Zarlengo-Strouse, P., 'Infant-directed versus adult-directed speech as signals for face', *Developmental Psychology*, 32(5) (1996), pp. 880–91.

5. Goldschmied, E. and Jackson, S., *People Under Three: Young Children in Day Care*, Routledge (2004).

6. Feldens, C. A., Faraco, I. M., Ottoni, A. B. and Vítolo, M. R. J., 'Teething symptoms in the first year of life and associated factors: a cohort study', *Clinical Pediatric Dentistry*, 34(3) (2010), pp. 201–6.

7. Wake, M., Hesketh, K., Lucas, J., 'Teething and tooth eruption in infants: a cohort study', *Pediatrics*, 106(6) (2000), pp. 1374–9.

8. Beasley, R., Clayton, T., Crane, J., von Mutius, E., Lai, C. K., Montefort, S. and Stewart A., 'Association between paracetamol use in infancy and childhood, and risk of asthma, rhinoconjunctivitis, and eczema in children aged 6–7 years: analysis from Phase Three of the ISAAC programme', *Lancet* 372(9643) (2008), pp. 1039–48.

9. Clayton, H., et al., 'Prevalence and reasons for introducing infants early to solid foods: variations by milk feeding type', *Pediatrics*, 131 (2013), pp.1108–14.

10. Ibid.

11. Nevarez, M. D., Rifas-Shiman, S. L., Kleinman, K. P., Gillman, M. W. and Taveras, E. M., 'Associations of early life risk factors with infant sleep duration', *Acad Pediatrics*, 10(3), (2010), pp.187–93.

12. Sadler, S., 'Sleep: what is normal at six months?', *Professional Care Mother Child*, (6) (1994), pp.166–7.

Chapter 5

1. Mandel, D., Lubetzky, R., Dollberg, S., Barak, S. and Mimouni, F. B., 'Fat and energy contents of expressed human breast milk in prolonged lactation', *Pediatrics*, 116(3) (2005), pp. 432–5; Buckley, K. M., 'Long-term breastfeeding: nourishment or nurturance?', *Journal Human Lactation*, 17 (2001), p. 304; Karra, M. V., Udipi, S. A., Kirksey, A. and Roepke, J. L., 'Changes in specific nutrients in breast milk during extended lactation', *American Journal Clinical Nutrition*, 43 (1986), pp. 495–503; Dewey, K. G., Finley, D. A. and Lonnerdal, B., 'Breast milk volume and composition during late lactation (7–20 months)', *Journal Pediatric Gastroenterology and Nutrition* (5) (1984), pp. 713–20.

2. Rosenblatt, K. A., and Thomas, D. B., 'The WHO collaborative study of neoplasia and steroid contraceptives: lactation and the risk of epithelial ovarian cancer', *International Journal of Epidemiology*, 22 (1993), pp. 192–7; Brock, K. E., et al., 'Sexual, reproductive and contraceptive risk factors for carcinoma-in-situ of the uterine cervix in Sydney,' *Medical Journal of Australia*, 150(3) (1989), pp. 125–30; Jernstrom, H., et al., 'Breast-feeding and the risk of breast cancer in BRCA1 and BRCA2 mutation carriers', *Journal National Cancer Institute*, 96(14) (2004), pp. 1094–8; Lee, S. Y., Kim, M. T., Kim, S. W., Song, M. S. and Yoon, S. J., 'Effect of lifetime lactation on breast cancer risk: A Korean women's cohort study', *International Journal of Cancer*, 105(3) (2003), pp. 390–3.

3. Wiklund, P. K., et al., 'Lactation is associated with greater maternal bone size and bone strength later in life', *Osteoporos International* (2011); Yazici, S., et al., 'The effect of breast-feeding duration on bone mineral density in postmenopausal Turkish women: a population-based study', *Archive Medical Science*, 7(3) (2011), pp. 486–92; Grimes, J. P. and Wimalawansa, S. J., 'Breastfeeding and postmenopausal osteoporosis', *Current Women's Health Rep.*, 3(3) (2003), pp.193–8.

4. Oddy, W. H., et al., 'The long-term effects of breastfeeding on child and adolescent mental health: a pregnancy cohort study followed for 14 years', *Journal of Pediatrics*, 156(4) (2010), pp. 568–74; Duazo, P., Avila, J., Kuzawa and C. W., 'Breastfeeding

and later psychosocial development in the Philippines', *American Journal of Human Biology*, 22(6) (2010), pp. 725–30.

5. Oddy, W. H., et al., 'Breastfeeding duration and academic achievement at 10 years', *Pediatrics*, 127(1) (2011), pp.137–45; Mortensen, E. L., Michaelsen, K. F., Sanders, S. A. and Reinisch, J. M., 'The association between duration of breastfeeding and adult intelligence', *JAMA*, 287 (2002), pp. 2365–71; Richards, M., Hardy, R. and Wadsworth, M. E., 'Long-term effects of breast-feeding in a national birth cohort: educational attainment and midlife cognitive function', *Public Health Nutrition*, 5(5) (2002), pp. 631–5.

6. Gooze, R. A., Anderson, S. E. and Whitaker, R. C., 'Prolonged bottle use and obesity at 5.5 years of age in US children', *Journal Pediatrics*, volume 159, issue 3 (2011), pp. 431–6.

7. Ibid

8. Koranyi, K., Kaye, L., Rasnake, K. J. and Tarnowski, H. J., 'Nursing bottle weaning and prevention of dental caries: a survey of pediatricians', *Pediatric Dentistry*, volume 13, number 1 (1991).

9. Groeneveld, M. G., Vermeer, H. J., van Ijzendoorn, M. H. and Linting, M., 'Stress, cortisol and well-being of caregivers and children in home-based child care: a case for differential susceptibility', *Child Care Health Development*, 38(2) (2012), pp. 251–60.

10. Belsky, J., Vandell, D. L., Burchinal, M., Clarke-Stewart, K. A., McCartney, K., Owen, M. T. and the NICHD Early Child Care Research Network, 'Are there long-term effects of early child care? *Child Development*, 78(2) (2007), pp. 681–701.

11. Vermeer, H. J. and van Ijzendoorn, M. H., 'Children's elevated cortisol levels at daycare: A review and meta-analysis', *Early Childhood Research Quarterly*, 07/2006.

12. Elford, L. and Brown, A., 'Exploring child-feeding style in childcare settings: how might nursery practitioners affect child eating style and weight?' *Eating Behaviour*, 15(2), (2014), pp. 314–17.

13. Stein, A., Malmberg, L. E., Leach, P., Barnes, J., Sylva, K. and FCCC Team, 'The influence of different forms of early childcare on children's emotional and behavioural development at school entry', *Child Care Health Development*, 39(5), (2013), pp. 676–87; Loeb, S., Rumberger, R., Bassok, D., Bridges, M. and Fuller, B.,

'The influence of preschool centers on children's development nationwide: how much is too much?', *Economics of Education Review*, 26 (2007), pp. 52–66.

14. Sun Y. and Sundell, J., 'Early daycare attendance increase the risk for respiratory infections and asthma of children', *Journal of Asthma*, 48(8) (2011), pp. 790–6.

15. Sadler, S., 'Sleep, what is normal at 6 months?', *Professional Care of Mother and Child*, 4 (6) (1994), pp. 166–7.

Chapter 6

1. Baron-Cohen, S., Leslie, A. M. and Frith, U., 'Does the autistic child have a "theory of mind"?', *Cognition*, 21(1) (1985), pp. 37–46.

2. Yirmiya, N., Solomonica-Levi, D., Shulman, C. and Pilowsky, T., 'Theory of mind abilities in individuals with autism, Down syndrome, and mental retardation of unknown etiology: the role of age and intelligence', *Journal Child Psychology Psychiatry*, 37(8) (1996), pp. 1003–14.

3. Rosenblum, K. L., McDonough, S. C., Sameroff, A. J. and Muzik, M., 'Reflection in thought and action: Maternal parenting reflectivity predicts mind-minded comments and interactive behavior', *Infant Mental Health Journal*, 29 (2008), pp. 362–76.

4. Warneken, F. and Tomasello, M., 'Extrinsic rewards undermine altruistic tendencies in 20-month-olds', *Developmental Psychology*, 44(6) (2008), pp. 1785–8.

5. Fabes, R. A., Fultz, J., Eisenberg, N. and May-Plumlee, T., 'Effects of rewards on children's prosocial motivation: a socialization study', *Developmental Psychology*, 25(4) (1989), pp. 509–15.

6. Henderlong, J. and Lepper, M. R., 'The effects of praise on children's intrinsic motivation: a review and synthesis', *Psychological Bulletin*, 128(5) (2002) pp.774–95.

7. *Schubert, E. and Strick, R., Toy-free. Kindergarten. A Project to Prevent Addiction for Children and with Children* (1990).

8. Kasey, S., Buckles, L. and Munnich, E., 'Birth spacing and sibling outcomes', *Journal Human Resources* (2012), pp. 613–42.

9. Werner, E. E., 'The children of Kauai: resiliency and recovery in adolescence and adulthood', *Journal Adolescent Health*, 13(4) (1992), pp. 262–8.

10. Ball, S., Pereira, G., Jacoby, P., de Klerk, N. and Stanley, F., 'Re-evaluation of link between interpregnancy interval and adverse birth outcomes: retrospective cohort study matching two intervals per mother', *BMJ*, 349 (2014).

11. McDonough, P., 'TV viewing among kids at an eight-year high', *Nielsenwire*, 26 October 2009. Available at: http://blog.nielsen.com/nielsenwire/media_entertainment/tv-viewing-among-kids-at-an-eight-year-high/.

12. Bickham, D. S. and Rich, M., 'Is television viewing associated with social isolation? Roles of exposure time, viewing context, and violent content', *Archives Pediatric Adolescent Medicine*, 160(4) (2006), pp. 387–92.

13. Vandewater, E. A., Bickham, D. S. and Lee, J. H., 'Time well spent? Relating television use to children's free-time activities', *Pediatrics*, 117(2) (2006), pp. 181–91.

14. Manganello, J. A. and Taylor, C. A., 'Television exposure as a risk factor for aggressive behavior among 3-year-old children', *Archives Pediatric Adolescent Medicine*, 163(11) (2009), pp. 1037–45; Huesmann, L. R., Moise-Titus, J., Podolski, C. L. and Eron, L. D., 'Longitudinal relations between children's exposure to TV violence and their aggressive and violent behavior in young adulthood', *Developmental Psychology*, 39(2) (2003), pp. 201–21; Hancox, R. J., Milne, B. J. and Poulton, R., 'Association of television viewing during childhood with poor educational achievement', *Archives Pediatric Adolescent Medicine*, 159(7) (2005), pp. 614–18; Viner, R. M. and Cole, T. J., 'Television viewing in early childhood predicts adult body mass index', *Journal Pediatrics*, 147(4) (2005), pp. 429–35.

15. Thompson, D. A., Christakis, D. A., 'The association between television viewing and irregular sleep schedules among children less than 3 years of age', *Pediatrics*, 116(4), (2005), pp.851–6; Johnson, J. G., Cohen, P., Kasen, S., First, M. B., Brook, J. S., 'Association between television viewing and sleep problems during adolescence and early adulthood', *Archives Pediatric Adolescent Medicine*, 158(6), (2004), pp.562–8.

16. Birch, L., 'Development of food acceptance patterns in the first years of life', *Proceedings of the Nutrition Society*, 57(4), (1998), pp. 617–24.

17. Ibid.

18. Montgomery, P., et al., 'Fatty acids and sleep in UK children: Subjective and pilot objective sleep results from the DOLAB study – a randomised controlled trial', *Journal of Sleep Research* (2014).

19. Miller, AL., Kaciroti, N., Lebourgeois, MK., Chen, YP., Sturza, J., Lumeng, J. C., 'Dissonance between parent-selected bedtimes and young children's circadian physiology influences nighttime settling difficulties', *Academy Pediatrics*, 14(2) (2014) pp. 207–13.

Chapter 7

1. Forest, M. G., Sizonenko, P. C., Cathiard, A. M. and Bertrand, J., 'Hypophyso-gonadal function in humans during the first year of life. Evidence for testicular activity in early infancy', *Journal Clinical Investigation*, 53(3) (1974), pp. 819–28.

2. Holland, P., 'Take the toys from the boys? An examination of the genesis of policy and the appropriateness of adult perspectives in the area of war, weapon and superhero play', *Citizenship, Social and Economics Education*, 4(2) (2000), pp. 92–108.

3. Rosen, L. D., Lim, A. F., Felt, J., Carrier, L. M., Cheever, N. A., Lara-Ruiz, J. M., Mendoza, J. S., Rokkum, J., 'Media and technology use predicts ill-being among children, preteens and teenagers independent of the negative health impacts of exercise and eating habits', *Computers in Human Behaviour*, 35 (2014), pp. 364–75; Maras, D., Flament, M. F., Murray, M., Buchholz, A., Henderson, K. A., Obeid, N. and Goldfield, G. S., 'Screen time is associated with depression and anxiety in Canadian youth', *Preventative Medicine*, 73 (2015), pp. 133–8; Falbe, J., Davison, K. K., Franckle, R. L., Ganter, C., Gortmaker, S. L., Smith, L., Land T. and Taveras, E. M., 'Sleep duration, restfulness, and screens in the sleep environment', *Pediatrics*, 135(2) (2015), pp. 367–75; Wilson, B. J., 'Media and children's aggression, fear, and altruism', *Future Child*, 18(1) (2008), pp. 87–118.

4. Houghton, S., Hunter, S. C., Rosenberg, M., Wood, L., Zadow, C., Martin, K. and Shilton, T., 'Virtually impossible: limiting Australian children and adolescents daily screen based media use', *BMC Public Health* (2015), p. 15.

5. Bell, J. F. and Daniels, S., 'Are summer-born children disadvantaged? The birthdate effect in education', *Oxford Review of Education*, 16 (1) (1990), pp. 67–80; Armstrong, H. G., 'A

comparison of the performance of summer and autumn-born children at eleven and sixteen', *British Journal of Educational Psychology*, 36(1) (1966), pp. 72–6.

6. Dudley-Marling, C., 'How school troubles come home: the impact of homework on families of struggling learners', *Current Issues in Education*, 6(4) (2003).

7. Michaud, I., Chaput, J. P., O'Loughlin, J., Tremblay, A., Mathieu, M. E., 'Long duration of stressful homework as a potential obesogenic factor in children: A QUALITY study', *Obesity* (2015) [Epub ahead of print].

8. Grossman, J. M., Frye, A., Charmaraman, L. and Erkut, S., 'Family homework and school-based sex education: delaying early adolescents' sexual behavior', *Journal School Health*, 83(11) (2013).

Chapter 8

1. Maraboli, Dr S., *Unapologetically You: Reflections on Life and the Human Experience*, Better Today (2013).

2. Odent, M., 'Between circular and cul-de-sac epidemiology', *Lancet*, 355 (9212) (2000), p. 1371.

Index

Page numbers in *italic type* refer to illustrations

A

adoption/fostering 261–3 (*see also* parenting: gentle, in special circumstances)
resources concerning 280–1
advice on childcare, over past century 5–9
Bowlby 7–8
Ferber 8
Ford 9
Frost 9
Holt 8
Leach 8
Spock 6–7
Truby King 5
Watson 6
Winnicott 7
Ainsworth, Mary 8, 106
Alcott, Louisa May 125
Allende, Isabel 93
alternative schooling (*see also* school):
democratic 199–200
free schools 200
home education 201–4
Montessori 199
Steiner 199
attachment theory 8, 106
authoritarian parenting 11–13
authoritative parenting 12

B

backchat 181–5
behaviour, bad (*see also* tantrums and big feelings):
biting, pushing, shoving, hitting, throwing 146–8
in child at years 1–4 136–7
and distraction 142–3
and gentle discipline 143–6
and naughty step/time out 10, 131, 133, 136–7
behaviour, good:
in child at years 1–4 138–42
and giving praise 140–2
problem with rewarding 138–9
problem with rewarding 138–9
behaviour regressions, coping with 222–3
birth (*see also* pregnancy):
baby-friendly 30–47
and doulas 35
before-and-after-birth comparison, tabulated 52
and birth companions 35–6
and birthing environment 33–5
and BRAIN acronym 33, 38, 44, 49
and cord clamping 43–4

birth – *continued*
  and doulas 35
  and 'golden hour' 41–2
  and infant feeding 44–7
    with formula 44–7
  and labour's onset 31–3
  and pain relief 37
  relaxation strategies for 36
  second and third stages 38–41
  shock of transition caused by
    51–2
  special circumstances 38
biting, pushing, shoving, hitting,
    throwing, in child at years
    1–4 146–8
body autonomy 153–4
boundaries and limits 148–9
Bowlby, John 7–8, 106
BRAIN acronym 33, 38, 44, 49
  and breastfeeding 46
brain development:
  months 0–3 68
  months 3–6 88
  months 6–12 117–18
  years 1–4 172
  years 4–7 213–14
breastfeeding 29, 41, 46
  and baby's sleep 46
  and BRAIN acronym 46
  and co-sleeping 55
  establishing 42
  and newborn calming
    techniques 64
  as norm 44
  and parents' sleep 47
  resources concerning 278–9
  and swaddling 58
  weaning from 101 (*see also*
    feeding)
    and child's age 102–3

C
calming techniques and the
    newborn child 53–68
  carrying 61–2, *61*
  co-sleeping and bed sharing
    55–8, *57*
  movement 53–4
  positioning 67

skin-to-skin contact 54
  swaddling 58–60, *59–60*
caregivers, child's bond with 116
    (*see also* childcare)
Carter, Hodding 191–2
champion, need for, as one of
    seven Cs of parenting:
  introduced and discussed 21–2
  for months 0–3 78
  for months 3–6 91
  for months 6–12 123
  in pregnancy 49
  for years 1–4 178
  for years 4–7 217
child at 3–6 months:
  entertaining 80–4
    environmental stimulation
      83
    everyday objects as
      playthings 82
    play 81, 82–4
    speech and language 82
    and 'treasure basket' 83–4
child at months 0–3 51–78
  baby's development during
    68–9
  before-and-after-birth
    comparison, tabulated 52
  brain development of 68
  and child's sleep 73–4
  and colic and crying 71–2, *72*
  parenting 55–8
    and brain development 68
    and routines vs schedules
      69–71
    and seven Cs of parenting 76–8
      champion, need for 78
      communication 77
      confidence 78
      connection 76
      consistency 78
      containment 77
      control 77
  and sleep 55–8, 73–4
  and unstoppable crying 72–3
child at months 3–6 79–92
  brain development of 88
  entertaining baby 80–4
  introducing solid foods to 86–8
    (*see also* feeding)

and seven Cs of parenting 90–2
  champion, need for 91
  communication 90–1
  confidence 92
  connection 90
  consistency 92
  containment 91
  control 91
and sleep 88
teething 85–6
child at months 6–12 93–124
  and baby's own room/cot
      119–20
  brain development 117–18
  introducing solid foods to
      94–109 (*see also* feeding)
  and maternity leave 107
  and night feeds 120–1
  and returning to work,
      choosing childcare 109–17
      (*see also* childcare;
      returning to work)
  and separation anxiety 105–9
  and seven Cs of parenting
      121–4
  champion, need for 123
  communication 122
  confidence 124
  connection 122
  consistency 124
  containment 123
  control 122–3
  and sleep 118–19
  sleep 118–19
child at years 1–4 125–79
  bad behaviour in 136–7
  biting, pushing, shoving,
      hitting, throwing by 146–8
  and body autonomy 153–4
  and boundaries and limits
      148–9
  brain development of 172
  causing crying in 149–51 (*see
      also* crying)
  good behaviour in 138–42
      and giving praise 140–2
  lying to and by 152–3
  and mind-mindedness
      parenting 134–5
  new sibling for 159–63

and picky eating 164–7
and play, importance of 154–7
and seven Cs of parenting
    176–9
  champion, need for 178
  communication 176–7
  confidence 178–9
  connection 176
  consistency 179
  containment 177
  control 177
and sharing 132–6
  and empathy and theory of
      mind 132–6
sharing mealtimes with 167
    (*see also* eating; feeding)
and sleep 172–5
starting preschool 157–9
  tips for 158–9
and tantrums and big feelings
    126–32
and tantrums and big feelings,
    dealing with 126–32
  SENSE acronym to help with
      130–1
toilet learning for 168–72
  troubles with 170–2
TV viewing by 163–4
child at years 4–7 180–217
  backchat from 181–5
  brain development of 213–14
  and chores and pocket money
      185–6
  and consequences 187–8
  and 'free-range' parenting and
      importance of 'wings'
      190–2
  and gender differences 192–3
  and growing up, talking about
      212–13
  and nature-deficit disorder 196
  sensitivity and shyness in
      188–90
  and seven Cs of parenting
      215–17
    champion, need for 217
    communication 215–16
    confidence 217
    connection 215
    consistency 217

child at years – *continued*
  and seven Cs of parenting –
    continued
    containment 216
    control 216
  and sibling relationships
    210–12
  and sleep 214–15
  starting school 197–208
    alternative schools 198–9
    and behaviour management
      205–6
    delayed entry 197–8
    friendships at 209–10
    and homework 204–5
    part-time start 198
    refusal to attend 206–8
childcare:
  advice on, over past century
    5–9
    Bowlby 7–8
    Ferber 8
    Ford 9
    Frost 9
    Holt 8
    Leach 8
    Spock 6–7
    Truby King 5
    Watson 6
    Winnicott 7
  and child's bond with caregiver
    116
  in day-care nursery 113–15
  in own home 111–12
  in relative's home 112
  on returning to work 109–17
    and flexible
      working/working from
      home 110–11
    postponing 110
  settling child into 115–17
  in someone else's home 112–13
  and transitional objects 116–17
chores 185–7
  making children perform? 186–7
  and pocket money 185–6
cognitive dissonance 226
  using to good effect 228–30
colic and crying 71–2, *72*
The Common Sense Book of

Baby and Childcare (Spock) 6
communication, as one of seven
  Cs of parenting:
  introduced and discussed
    18–19
  for months 0–3 77
  for months 3–6 90–1
  for months 6–12 122
  in pregnancy 48–9
  for years 1–4 176–7
  for years 4–7 215–16
confidence, as one of seven Cs of
  parenting:
  introduced and discussed 22–3
  for months 0–3 78
  for months 3–6 92
  for months 6–12 124
  in pregnancy 50
  for years 1–4 178–9
  for years 4–7 217
connection, as one of seven Cs of
  parenting:
  introduced and discussed 16–18
  for months 0–3 76
  for months 3–6 90
  for months 6–12 122
  in pregnancy 48
  for years 1–4 176
  for years 4–7 215
consistency, as one of seven Cs of
  parenting:
  introduced and discussed 23–4
  for months 0–3 78
  for months 3–6 92
  for months 6–12 124
  in pregnancy 50
  for years 1–4 179
  for years 4–7 217
containment, as one of seven Cs
  of parenting:
  introduced and discussed 20–1
  for months 0–3 77
  for months 3–6 91
  for months 6–12 123
  in pregnancy 49
  for years 1–4 177
  for years 4–7 216
control, as one of seven Cs of
  parenting:
  introduced and discussed 19–20

for months 0–3 77
for months 3–6 91
for months 6–12 122–3
in pregnancy 49
for years 1–4 177
for years 4–7 216
crying:
   and baby yoga 63, *63*
   and carrying 61
   causing 149–51
   and colic 71–2, *72*, 79, 92
   as communication 49, 77, 90
   and sleep 8
'cul-de-sac epidemiology' 228–9

D
day-care nurseries 113–15
democratic schools 199–200 (*see also* school)
distraction 142–3
divorce/separation 267–71
   books to help with 282
   moving forward from 269–71
   telling child about 268–9
doulas 35

E
eating:
   grazing tray for 165–6
   picky 164–7 (*see also* feeding)
   and sharing mealtimes 167
   sharing mealtimes with 167
egocentrism 134–5
empathy:
   as part of SENSE acronym 130 (*see also* SENSE acronym)
   and theory of mind 132–6 (*see also* sharing)
   and mind-mindedness parenting 134–5
entertaining your baby 80–4
   environmental stimulation 83
   everyday objects as playthings 82
   play 81
      and everyday objects 82
      heuristic 82, 83–4
      and 'treasure basket' 83–4

speech and language 82
exchange, as part of SENSE acronym 131 (*see also* SENSE acronym)

F
feeding (*see also* breastfeeding):
   introducing solids 86–8, 94–105
      baby rice 100
      baby's resistance to 97–8
      and baby's teeth 96
      and continued breastfeeding 102
      cow's milk 100
      and day care 101
      equipment for 96
      foods to avoid 99–100
      'on the go' 100
      good first foods 98–9
      honey 99
      method of 96–7
      nuts 99
      processed foods 99
      and weaning from bottles 103–4
      and weaning from breast 101
      and weaning from dummy 104–5
      and weaning style 94–5
   and picky eating 164–7
Feeding and Care of Baby (Truby King) 5
Ferber, Dr Richard 8
fertility treatment or previous loss 263–4 (*see also* parenting: gentle, in special circumstances)
five stages of transition to gentle parenting (*see also* parenting):
   1. feeling of loss of control 220
   2. regression in behaviour 220–1
   3. anger and sadness 221
   4. reconnection, need for 221–2
   5. breakthrough 222

flexible working/working from home 110–11 (*see also* childcare; returning to work)
Ford, Gina 9
Forest Schools 196
formula feeding 44–7
  baby-led 64–7
    ignoring clock 65
    letting baby take bottle 66
    and mindfulness 66–7
    and positioning 67
    respecting baby's pauses 67
    and skin-to-skin contact 66
    slow-flow teat for 67
    watching baby 65
  risks associated with 44–6
fostering/adoption 261–3 (*see also* parenting: gentle, in special circumstances)
  resources concerning 280–1
'fourth trimester', *see* parenting: from birth to three months
free schools 200 (*see also* school)
friendships, in early school 209–10
Frost, Jo 9

G
gender differences 192–3
gentle discipline 143–6 (*see also* behaviour, bad)
gentle parenting, *see under* parenting
'Global Strategy for Infant and Young Child Feeding' (WHO) 46
Goldschmied, Elinor 82
grazing tray 165–6 (*see also* eating; feeding)
growing up, talking about 212–13

H
Henson, Jim 257–71
heuristic play 82, 83–4 (*see also* entertaining your baby)
Holt, John 218
Holt, Dr L. Emmet 8

home education 201–4 (*see also* school)
  frequently asked questions about 203
How Children Fail (Holt) 218

K
Kabat-Zinn, Prof. Jon 15
King, Martin Luther 25

L
Last Child in the Woods (Louv) 196
Leach, Penelope 8
limits and boundaries 148–9
Lorde, Audre 241
Louv, Richard 196
lying, to and by children 152–3

M
magnesium 245–6
mainstream parenting:
  transitioning from 218–30
    and behaviour regressions, coping with 222–3
    and dissonance, using to good effect 228–30
    failure in 225–8
    five stages – 1. feeling of loss of control 220
    five stages – 2. regression in behaviour 220–1
    five stages – 3. anger and sadness 221
    five stages – 4. reconnection, need for 221–2
    five stages – 5. breakthrough 222
    and parenting mistakes, coming to terms with 223–5
Maraboli, Dr Steve 79
'Maternal Care and Mental Health' (Bowlby) 7
Mead, Margaret 1, 272
mind-mindedness parenting 134–5 (*see also* empathy: and theory of mind)

mind, theory of:
  and empathy 132–6 (*see also*
     sharing)
  and mind-mindedness
     parenting 134–5
mindfulness:
  and one's own needs 251
  as relaxation strategy 36, 66–7
Montessori education 199 (*see
  also* school)
Montessori, Maria 199
The Motherhood Constellation
  (Stern) 27

N
name, as part of SENSE acronym
  130 (*see also* SENSE acronym)
National Institute for Health
  and Care Excellence (NICE)
  31
nature-deficit disorder 196
naughty step/time out 9, 10, 131,
  133, 136–7
newborn calming techniques
  53–68
  breastfeeding 64
  carrying 61–2, *61*
  co-sleeping and bed sharing
     55–8, *57*
  feeding 64–7
  movement 53–4
  noise 64
  positioning 63, *63*, 67
  skin-to-skin contact 54
  swaddling 58–60, *59–60*
  and water 68
night feeds 120–1
'Nursery Without Toys'
  ('Spielzeugfreie
  Kindergarten') experiment
  155–6

O
Odent, Dr Michael 228–9
own needs 241–56
  eating well 244–6
     magnesium 245–6
     vitamin B$_{12}$ 245

vitamin D 245
     zinc 246
  mindfulness 251
  moving well 248
  parents' accounts 242–3
  and seven Cs of parenting 252,
     253–5
     champion, need for 254
     communication 253–4
     confidence 255
     connection 253
     consistency 255
     control 254
  sleeping well 246–8
  support network 252
  when you feel like yelling
     248–50

P
parenting (*see also under* child
  at . . .):
  adjusting to, after fertility
     treatment or previous loss
     263–4
  authoritarian 11–13
  authoritative 12
  and boundaries and limits
     148–9
  'free-range', and importance of
     'wings' 190–2
  and gender differences 192–3
  gentle, efficacy of 231–40
     and communication 236–7
     and confidence 237
     and consistency 237–8
     lack of, and what to do
        235–8
     parents' experiences 234–5,
        238–40
     and seven Cs of parenting
        235–6
     THINK acronym concerning
        235
     and tough days, how parents
        cope 238–40
  gentle, introduced and
     discussed 1–13
     and parents' imperfections
        3–4

parenting – *continued*
  gentle, introduced and
      discussed – *continued*
    what it is not 10–11
    why it matters 4–5
  gentle, resources for 277
  gentle, in special circumstances
      257–71
    and divorced/separated
        parents 267–71
    and fertility treatment or
        previous loss 263–4
    and fostering/adoption
        261–3
    and single parents 266–7
    and special-needs children
        264–6
    and twins and multiples
        258–61
  gentle, transitioning to 218–30
    and behaviour regressions,
        coping with 222–3
    and dissonance, using to
        good effect 228–30
    failure in 225–8
    five stages – 1. feeling of loss
        of control 220
    five stages – 2. regression in
        behaviour 220–1
    five stages – 3. anger and
        sadness 221
    five stages – 4. reconnection,
        need for 221–2
    five stages – 5. breakthrough
        222
    and parenting mistakes,
        coming to terms with
        223–5
  and lying 152–3
  mainstream, transitioning
      from 218–30
    and behaviour regressions,
        coping with 222–3
    and dissonance, using to
        good effect 228–30
    failure in 225–8
    five stages – 1. feeling of loss
        of control 220
    five stages – 2. regression in
        behaviour 220–1
  five stages – 3. anger and
      sadness 221
  five stages – 4. reconnection,
      need for 221–2
  five stages – 5. breakthrough
      222
  and parenting mistakes,
      coming to terms with
      223–5
and making child cry 149–51
mind-mindedness 134–5
months 0–3 51–78
  baby's development during
      68–9
  before-and-after-birth
      comparison, tabulated
      52
  and brain development 68
  brain development of 68
  and child's sleep 73–4
  and colic and crying 71–2,
      72
  parenting 55–8
  and routines vs schedules
      69–71
  and seven Cs of parenting
      76–8
  and sleep 55–8, 73–4
  and unstoppable crying 72–3
months 3–6 79–92
  and brain development 88
  brain development of 88
  and child's sleep 88
  entertaining baby 80–4
  introducing solid foods to
      86–8 (*see also* feeding)
  and seven Cs of parenting
      90–2
  and sleep 88
  teething 85–6
months 6–12 93–124
  and baby's own room/cot
      119–20
  and brain development
      117–18
  brain development 117–18
  introducing solid foods to
      94–105, 94–109 (*see also*
      feeding)
  and maternity leave 107

and night feeds 120–1
and returning to work,
    choosing childcare
    109–17 (*see also*
    childcare; returning to
    work)
and separation anxiety
    105–9
and seven Cs of parenting
    121–4
and sleep 118–19
sleep 118–19
and newborn calming
    techniques 53–68
    breastfeeding 64
    carrying 61–2, *61*
    co-sleeping and bed sharing
        55–8, *57*
    feeding 64–7
    movement 53–4
    noise 64
    positioning 63, *63*, 67
    skin-to-skin contact 54
    swaddling 58–60, *59–60*
    and water 68
and one's own needs 241–56
    (*see also* own needs)
    eating well 244–6
    mindfulness 251
    moving well 248
    parents' experiences 242–3
    and seven Cs of parenting
        253–5
    sleeping well 246–8
    support network 252
    when you feel like yelling
        248–50
partner's role in 75–6
    bonding without feeding
        75–6
    protecting the space 75
permissive 13
and pregnancy, *see* pregnancy
and routines vs schedules
    69–71
    spotting hunger and
        tiredness 70–1
strategies for 47–50
    and seven Cs of parenting,
        see seven Cs of parenting

and tantrums and big feelings,
    dealing with 126–32
and safety and empathy 130
and support 130–1
teaching sharing 132–6
years 1–4 125–79
    bad behaviour in 136–7
    biting, pushing, shoving,
        hitting, throwing by
        146–8
    and body autonomy 153–4
    and boundaries and limits
        148–9
    brain development of 172
    causing crying in 149–51 (*see
        also* crying)
    and child's sleep 172–5
    good behaviour in 138–42
    lying to and by 152–3
    and mind-mindedness
        parenting 134–5
    new sibling for 159–63
    and picky eating 164–7
    and play, importance of
        154–7
    and seven Cs of parenting
        176–9
    and sharing 132–6
    sharing mealtimes with 167
        (*see also* eating; feeding)
    and sleep 172–5
    starting preschool 157–9
    and tantrums and big
        feelings 126–32
    and tantrums and big
        feelings, dealing with
        126–32
    toilet learning for 168–72
    TV viewing by 163–4
years 4–7 180–217
    backchat from 181–5
    brain development of
        213–14
    and child's sleep 214–15
    and chores and pocket
        money 185–6
    and consequences 187–8
    and 'free-range' parenting
        and importance of
        'wings' 190–2

parenting – *continued*
  years – *continued*
    and gender differences
      192–3
    and growing up, talking
      about 212–13
    and nature-deficit disorder
      196
    sensitivity and shyness in
      188–90
    and seven Cs of parenting
      215–17
    and sibling relationships
      210–12
    and sleep 214–15
    starting school 197–208
parenting, seven Cs of:
  introduced and discussed
    15–24
  champion, need for 21–2
  communication 18–19
  confidence 22–3
  connection 16–18
  consistency 23–4
  containment 20–1
  control 19–20
  months 0–3 76–8
    champion, need for 78
    communication 77
    confidence 78
    connection 76
    consistency 78
    containment 77
    control 77
  months 3–6 90–2
    champion, need for 91
    communication 90–1
    confidence 92
    connection 90
    consistency 92
    containment 91
    control 91
  months 6–12 121–4
    champion, need for 123
    communication 122
    confidence 124
    connection 122
    consistency 124
    containment 123
    control 122–3

  in pregnancy 48–50
    champion, need for 49
    communication 48–9
    confidence 50
    connection 48
    consistency 50
    containment 49
    control 49
  readers' own notes on, space
    for 274–6
  years 1–4 176–9
    champion, need for 178
    communication 176–7
    confidence 178–9
    connection 176
    consistency 179
    containment 177
    control 177
  years 4–7 215–17
    champion, need for 217
    communication 215–16
    confidence 217
    connection 215
    consistency 217
    containment 216
    control 216
parents' imperfections 3–4
partner's role:
  bonding without feeding
    75–6
  protecting the space 75
permissive parenting 13
Piaget, Jean 134
picky eating 164–7 (*see also*
  feeding)
play 81
  and everyday objects 82
  heuristic 82, 83–4
  importance of 154–7
    and toys, problem with
      155–7
  and 'treasure basket' 83–4
  violence-themed 194
Plunket Society 5
pocket money, and chores
  185–6
praise for good behaviour 140–2
  (*see also* child at years 1–4:
  good behaviour in)
pre-birth planning 260–1

pregnancy 25–50
  and baby-friendly birth 30–47
    and birth companions 35–6
    and birthing environment 33–5
    BRAIN acronym for 33, 38
    and cord clamping 43–4
    and 'golden hour' 41–2
    and infant feeding 44–7
    and labour's onset 31–3
    and pain relief 37
    relaxation strategies for 36
    second and third stages 38–41
    special circumstances 38
  before-and-after-birth comparison, tabulated 52
  and own upbringing 26–7
  and tribes/groups 27–9
  parents' views on 29
Premack, David 134
preschool:
  starting 157–9
  tips for 158–9
previous loss or fertility treatment 263–4 (*see also* parenting: gentle, in special circumstances)
Psychological Care of Infant and Child (Watson) 6

R
resources 277–82
  babies 278
  breastfeeding 278–9
  gentle parenting 277
  LGBT 280
  Ockwell-Smith website 277
  older children 279
  parental separation 280
  pregnancy and birth 278
  recommended reading:
    for children 281
    for parents 281–2
  self-care 281
  SEN 279–80
  single parents 280
  toddlers and preschoolers 279
returning to work:
  and childcare 109–17
  and flexible working/working from home 110–11
  postponing 110
reverse-cycling 121
Roosevelt, Franklin D. 180
routines vs schedules, spotting hunger and tiredness 70 1

S
safety, as part of SENSE acronym 130 (*see also* SENSE acronym)
'Sally Ann' test 134–5
schedules vs routines, spotting hunger and tiredness 70–1
school:
  alternatives:
    democratic 199–200
    free schools 200
    home education 201–4
    Montessori 199
    Steiner 199
  behaviour management at 205–6
  and friendships 209–10
  and homework 204–5
  refusal to attend 206–8
  starting 197–208
    delayed entry 197–8
    part-time start 198
Schubert, Elke 155
screen time, in years 4–7 195 (*see also* TV viewing)
SENSE acronym 130–1
  safety 130
  empathy 130
  name 130
  support 130–1
  exchange 131
sensitivity and shyness 188–90
separation anxiety 105–9
  tips for coping with 106
separation/divorce 267–71
  books to help with 282
  moving forward from 269–71
  resources concerning 280
  telling child about 268–9
Seuss, Dr 51

seven Cs of parenting:
  introduced and discussed 15–24
    champion, need for 21–2
    communication 18–19
    confidence 22–3
    connection 16–18
    consistency 23–4
    containment 20–1
    control 19–20
  months 0–3 76–8
    champion, need for 78
    communication 77
    confidence 78
    connection 76
    consistency 78
    containment 77
    control 77
  months 3–6 90–2
    champion, need for 91
    communication 90–1
    confidence 92
    connection 90
    consistency 92
    containment 91
    control 91
  months 6–12 121–4
    champion, need for 123
    communication 122
    confidence 124
    connection 122
    consistency 124
    containment 123
    control 122–3
  in pregnancy 48–50
    champion, need for 49
    communication 48–9
    confidence 50
    connection 48
    consistency 50
    containment 49
    control 49
  readers' own notes on, space
      for 274–6
  years 1–4 176–9
    champion, need for 178
    communication 176–7
    confidence 178–9
    connection 176
    consistency 179
    containment 177
    control 177
  years 4–7 215–17
    champion, need for 217
    communication 215–16
    confidence 217
    connection 215
    consistency 217
    containment 216
    control 216
sharing:
  by young children 132–6
    and mind-mindedness
        parenting 134–5
siblings:
  new 159–63
  relationships among 210–12
  twins and multiples 258–61
      (see also parenting: gentle,
      in special circumstances)
    and pre-birth planning 260–1
    resources concerning 280
single parents 266–7
sleep:
  and baby's own room/cot
      119–20
  and four-month regression
      89–90
  months 0–3 55–8, 73–4
  months 3–6 88
  months 6–12 118–19
  parents' 47, 246–8
  years 1–4 172–5
  years 4–7 214–15
solid food, introducing (see also
    feeding):
  months 3–6 86–8
  months 6–12 94–105
special circumstances 257–71
  birth during 38
  divorced/separated parents
      267–71
  fertility treatment or previous
      loss 263–4
  fostering/adoption 261–3
  single parents 266–7
  special-needs children 264–6
  twins and multiples 258–61
special-needs children 264–6
'Spielzeugfreie Kindergarten'
    ('Nursery Without Toys')

experiment 155–6
Spitz, René 7–8
Spock, Dr Benjamin 6–7
Steiner, Rudolph 199
Steiner schools 199
Stern, Daniel 27–8
Stevenson, Robert Louis 231
Strick, Rainer 155
sudden-infant-death syndrome
    (SIDS) 45, 46, 55, 58, 63
support, as part of SENSE
    acronym 130–1 (*see also*
    SENSE acronym)
support network 252

T
tantrums and big feelings 126–32
    (*see also* behaviour, bad)
    parenting gently through
        129–32
    SENSE acronym to help with
        130–1
teething 85–6
theory of mind:
    and empathy 132–6 (*see also*
        sharing)
    and mind-mindedness
        parenting 134–5
time out/naughty step 10, 131,
    133, 136–7
toddlers, *see* child at years 1–4
toilet learning 168–72
    troubles with 170–2
Tomasello, M. 138
toys, problem with 155–7 (*see
    also* play)
transitioning from mainstream to
    gentle parenting 218–30 (*see
    also* parenting)
    and behaviour regressions,
        coping with 222–3
    and dissonance, using to good
        effect 228–30
    failure in:
        and attacks by others 227–8
        cognitive dissonance 226
    five stages of:
        1. feeling of loss of control
            220

2. regression in behaviour
    220–1
3. anger and sadness 221
4. reconnection, need for
    221–2
5. breakthrough 222
and parenting mistakes, coming
    to terms with 223–5
'treasure basket' 83–4 (*see also*
    entertaining your baby;
    heuristic play)
Truby King, Sir Frederick 5
TV viewing (*see also* screen time):
    in years 1–4 163–4
    in years 4–7 195
twins and multiples 258–61 (*see
    also* parenting: gentle, in
    special circumstances;
    siblings)
    and pre-birth planning 260–1
    resources concerning 280

V
vitamin B_{12} 245
vitamin D 245

W
Warneken, F. 138
Watson, John B. 6
Wessel Criteria 71
Winnicott, Donald 7
Woodruff, Guy 134
work, returning to:
    and childcare 109–17
    and flexible working/working
        from home 110–11
    postponing 110
working from home/flexible
    working 110–11 (*see also*
    childcare; returning to work)

Y
Your Baby & Child (Leach) 8

Z
zinc 246